GUEST APPEARANCES

AND OTHER TRAVELS IN TIME AND SPACE

Other Books by Peter Rose

AUTHOR

Tempest-Tost (1997)
Mainstream and Margins (1983)
Strangers in Their Midst (1977)
The Subject Is Race (1967)
They and We (1963; 5th edition, 1997)

CO-AUTHOR

Over Vreemdeling en Vluchteling (On strangers and refugees) (1983)
Understanding Society (1978; 3rd edition, 1983)
Sociology (1977; 2nd edition, 1982)

EDITOR

Professorial Passions (1998)
The Challenge of Pluralism: Interminority Affairs in the U.S. (1993)
Working with Refugees (1986)
Socialization and the Life Cycle (1979)
Views from Abroad (1978)
Many Peoples, One Nation (1973)
Seeing Ourselves (1972; 2nd edition, 1975)
Nation of Nations (1972; reissued 1982)
Americans from Africa (1970; rev. edition, 2003)
The Ghetto and Beyond (1969)
The Study of Society (1967, 4th edition 1977)

CO-EDITOR

Through Different Eyes (1973)

GUEST APPEARANCES

AND OTHER TRAVELS IN TIME AND SPACE

Peter I. Rose

Swallow Press
Ohio University Press
Athens, Ohio

Swallow Press/Ohio University Press, Athens, Ohio 45701

Printed in United States
 Published 2003

10 09 08 07 06 05 04 03 5 4 3 2 1

Swallow Press/Ohio University Press books
are printed on acid-free paper ⊗ ™

Chapter 1 first appeared in *Hampshire Life*, January 28, 2000.
A shorter version of chapter 6 first appeared as "Mother's Music" in *Hampshire Life*, December 18, 1998.
Originally published in *Congress Monthly* (November/December 1986), chapter 7 was reprinted in one of the author's earlier books of essays, *Tempest-Tost* (New York: Oxford University Press, 1997).
A version of chapter 8 was published under the title "Good Intentions" in *Hampshire Life*, August 25, 2000.
Chapter 9 originally appeared in the *Chronicle of Higher Education*, September 3, 1986.
Chapter 10 is a slightly emended version of an essay first published in the spring 1999 issue of the *Smith Alumnae Quarterly*.
A shorter version of chapter 13 was published in *Cornell Alumni News*, September 1987.
A slightly different version of chapter 18 was published as "The Good Old Days" in *Congress Monthly*, September/October 1999.
An early version of chapter 19 was published in *Hampshire Life*, December 11, 1987.
Chapter 20 was originally published as "Adventure Tours for Kindred Spirits" in the *New York Times*, Travel Section, July 5, 1987.
Chapter 21 was first published under the title "A Jogger's Guide to World Travel" in the *Christian Science Monitor*, June 10, 1989.
An earlier version of chapter 22 appeared under the title "Not-So-Private Lives" in *Hampshire Life*, July 17, 1998.
Chapter 23 is a slightly expanded version of an essay with the same title published in the *New York Times*, July 31, 1988.
Chapter 24 is an expanded version of an essay first published as "Tracking *Avis Americanus:* A Field Guide to Species Seen in the People's Republic of China" in *Hampshire Life*, January 22, 1988.
Chapter 25 was first published in *Hampshire Life*, June 9, 2000.
An earlier version of chapter 26 appeared in *Salt Magazine*, August 1987.
A shorter version of chapter 28 appeared in *Congress Monthly*, November/December 1998.
An early version of chapter 29 was published in *Hampshire Life*, July 29, 1988.
Chapter 30 was first published in *Hampshire Life*, September 30, 1988.
Parts of chapter 31 appeared as "Profile: Remembering Varian Fry" in *Migration World* 29, no. 1/2 (2001): 35-42. Other parts first appeared, in quite different form, in the author's review, "Debasing Good History with Bad Fiction" that appeared in the *Chronicle of Higher Education*, April 20, 2001.
Chapter 32 first appeared in *Congress Monthly*, January/February 1999.
An earlier version of chapter 33 was first published in *Congress Monthly*, March/April 1999.
Chapter 35 was originally published under the title "The Name Game" in *Hampshire Life*, October 9, 1998.

Library of Congress Cataloging-in-Publication Data

Rose, Peter Isaac, 1933–
Guest appearances and other travels in time and space / Peter I. Rose.
p. cm.
ISBN 0-8040-1052-8 (alk. paper)
1. Rose, Peter Isaac, 1933- 2. Rose, Peter Isaac, 1933—-Journeys. 3. Sociology teachers—United States—Biography. 4. Travelers—Biography. I. Title.

HM479 .R665 2003
301'.092—dc21
[B]

2002030579

“Home is where they have to take you in no matter what.”

—Robert Frost

This book is dedicated to the one who has long provided a warm, safe haven for a restless soul: my wife and partner, Hedy Rose.

Contents

part three
BUSMAN'S HOLIDAYS

part four
CHANCE ENCOUNTERS AND CURIOUS CONNECTIONS

part five
CODA

Acknowledgments

THIS VERY PERSONAL book is the product of many years of growing, studying, teaching, traveling, reminiscing, writing, and rewriting. It is about the people I know and the places I've been. It is about my life course, my family, my work, my hobbies, and my affliction—travel sickness. It could never have been written, or even begun, without the support of key players: parents who instilled in me an avid sense of curiosity and wanderlust, though they hardly traveled themselves; a wife and partner of fifty years who encouraged me to follow my muse and hit the road, even when she couldn't go along; two children, Lies and Dan, who also indulged me in my restlessness and later became good critics and useful editors; the Bogliasco Foundation, which gave me two fellowships to do nothing but write in its fabulous villa on the Italian Riviera; and a host of friends and sounding boards who listened to my stories and read them, even when I'm sure they would have much preferred to be doing something else. In that last group there are several rather special people, editors and fellow writers who offered their professional judgments on my nonacademic storytelling. I am particularly grateful for the advice, sometimes taken, of Margot Cleary, Rebecca Goldstein, Tracy Kidder, Rochelle Mancini, Terry Moratta, Richard Todd, Pam Wood, and my ever-patient, always-helpful editors, Gillian Berchowitz and Sharon Rose.

[prologue]

Marginal Man

> "One day my ship will come in, but with my luck I'll probably be at the airport."
>
> —Charlie Brown

AS I APPROACHED the traditional age of retirement and the bittersweet opportunity to plan what to do with the rest of my life, I began to spend a good deal of time looking backward. I thought about where I came from, what I became, what I accomplished (and what I should have done), and the many places I've been. I realized that it all has to do with travel. Travel in time; travel in space.

Travel, whether longitudinal (as in the life course) or geographic (as in visits to other climes), in addition to often being anticipatory (thinking about what the next stage or place is going to be like), invariably has two other phases. One is existential; the other, postmonitional. The former refers to the fleeting present, the time of being there. Fortunately, today it is possible to record this in real time, either on film or tape. For most of human history such was impossible. Yet, even with innovations in photography, camcorders, and audio devices, it is impossible to capture innermost feelings as they are occurring. Instead, we still do what has always been done; we rely on retrospect to attempt to comprehend and convey to others the visceral, cognitive, and psychic effects of experiences. Thus our realities are invariably reconstructed, reconsidered, and reflected upon—after the fact, sometimes long after. Everyone does it. Everyone has postmonitions. But not everybody writes about them, not even many of my fellow social scientists. Why do I? I think it is because of my background, my interests, my curiosity, and my training as a professional voyeur.

I have always seen myself as a peerer into closed rooms, a guest at the table of life, an informed outsider. I am (to me) the positive side of the often negatively characterized "marginal man." The sociologist Robert E. Park, who coined the expression, defined the marginal man as one "whom fate has condemned to live in two separate and antagonistic worlds." He was thinking particularly of the plight of racial and ethnic minorities, although the concept is applicable to other sorts of dominant-minority situations. As a student of racial and ethnic relations, I understand this orientation, but I also know that there are advantages in being marginal, always a bit on the edge and somewhat apart from the mainstream. My life has been marked by a congeries of experiences in which I have been the odd man out, affording me vantage points that, ironically, have made strange contexts meaningful, even familiar. My travels in time and space have provided an almost endless supply of material for writing about certain aspects of the human condition from one (marginal) man's perspective.

Some would say that I came by my kind of marginality naturally. It was part of my early socialization. Perhaps. But it was also reinforced by any number of serendipitous encounters that led me to take one path rather than another.

Born in Rochester, New York, in 1933, I am the only child of parents who came from families with many children. Although both of my parents were settlement-house workers there and in Syracuse and directors of a series of children's camps steeped in the spirit of "group work," somehow I grew up a loner. While I did have a number of close friends when I was young and participated in various team-based activities, I often felt best when on my own.

When, with my family, I moved from Syracuse to the northern Adirondacks, I left my ski team and scout troop behind and became a solitary skier and a lone—but hardly lonely—scout. I reveled in my independence.

I was one of the only Jews in the gentile world of the rural village where we lived during my last years of high school and one of the few white members of the NAACP when I was in college. Two decades after graduating, I was the only white member of an African

American studies department I had helped to establish. Shortly after returning to full-time participation in the Department of Sociology and Anthropology, I was invited to chair the Advisory Committee on Afro-American Studies. I did so. For twenty years.

My master's thesis was on the "Exemption Mechanism," a fancy term for the "Some-of-my-best-friends-are . . ." phenomenon. My doctoral dissertation, "Strangers in Their Midst," was on isolated minorities.

Although trained—first at Syracuse University, then at Cornell—mainly as an anthropologist, I have always thought of myself as a sociologist. Despite this significant part of my persona and the fact that I have spent more than forty years teaching sociology, whatever good notices I have achieved as a writer have been characterized by a backhanded observation (which I have always taken as a compliment—or a good example of exemption): "He's different. He doesn't write like a sociologist." Or one I like even better (a *Choice* review of a recent book): "He has a sociologist's eye but his essays possess the flavor of personal commentary or journalism at its best: they are readable, moving, and perceptive."

Even more important than eschewing sociologese, that specialized form of academic argot frequently used to complexify rather simple ideas that has given the whole enterprise a bad rep (one wag said that "sociologists have a bad press because they write their own copy)," I have long expressed discomfort with another characteristic of my chosen profession: the claim that we social scientists can be truly value free.

Not a few of my colleagues think my self-description as a "humanistic sociologist" is oxymoronic. It implies too much softness and an unscientific mien. To such a view, I have a simple answer: "Mea culpa." To be sure, I try to be as objective as the next guy in gathering and analyzing my data, but I know that my motivations for doing the research and, equally important, deciding what to do after releasing the findings are, well, my own—influenced and nuanced by personal experiences and political concerns.

Such contradictions are to be found not only in my sociology. Although I have traveled widely in the United States and in more than sixty other countries; served as a visiting professor and resident fellow in many colleges, universities, institutes, and study centers; and lectured, researched, and written about alienation, pluralism, and the dilemmas of diversity, I have spent most of my career teaching at

America's largest, and perhaps best known, women's college: a liberal integrationist in a still-segregated society.

Smith College, my home base for more than four decades, was founded in Northampton, Massachusetts, in the 1870s. Because all-male Amherst College rejected a proposal to admit women along with a proffered gift of money, Sophia Smith of nearby Hatfield bequeathed her estate to establish a college just for women, one that would have a rigorous curriculum modeled not on that of the boys' school over in Amherst but on that of fair Harvard (which, incidentally, wouldn't admit women either).

Despite the fact that Amherst, Dartmouth, Princeton, Yale, Wesleyan, Williams, and every other men's college eventually would go co-ed, and despite a continuing debate among trustees, faculty, and students about what we should be doing, Smith's student body remains "single-sex," except for a small number of graduate programs. Most of my colleagues, male and female, teach only women. Here, again, I have long been an exception.

Part of my job for over thirty years has been directing one of Smith's few co-educational programs, the rather unique one-year international graduate program in American Studies. Over the years the male Diploma candidates, some of whom come to study "minorities," have had ample opportunity to learn the meaning of the term, not only because they, like the women in the program, are literally strangers on foreign soil, but because they are such anomalies on campus. Somehow they manage to survive and benefit from the experience. As have I.

To me, there is something especially challenging and satisfying in being a marginal man. These sentiments go beyond my childhood experiences, school days, and teaching career. The impulse to combine distance and insight (the *sine qua non* for those I once styled "outsiders within") has been a consistent goad, whether I am setting off to do systematic fieldwork, carrying out reconnaissance for future studies, or taking on an assignment to write a travel piece. The settings of my activities and inquiries have been widely varied, including tiny towns in rural America, small college campuses and large universities, immigrant neighborhoods in many American cities and refugee camps in Europe and Southeast Asia, three-day to two-week sailing, rafting, kayaking, bicycling, and mountain-climbing excursions, lengthy stays in England, Japan, Australia, Israel, the

Netherlands, and Italy, and much shorter ones in more than forty other countries. But, whether I am at home or abroad, in a refugee camp or on board a windjammer, my *modus operandi* has been pretty much the same. It's what we sociologists call "participant observation."

The character of the approach and the compulsion that drives it are said to be notable in much of my professional writing. I'm sure they are even more evident in the very personal essays that make up this nonacademic book.

Guest Appearances and Other Travels in Time and Space is a kind of excursion into the luxury of writing about many things, not least those I love and what I love to do, the places I've been, and many of the people I've met *en route.* (In a few of the essays published here I have taken some liberties—changing names, compressing lengthy episodes, and, occasionally, conflating experiences.) There are some commentaries on others' writings, but the takes on works by Jerre Mangione, Andy Marino, Philip Roth, and John Updike are based on or related to my personal experiences.

While many of the stories told here were drafted in reporter's notebooks or on scraps of paper in airplanes, on buses, in hotel rooms, and aboard ocean liners and tall ships, most of them were written, edited, and rewritten in one of three places: my cluttered office on the Smith College campus, just above the exquisite Paradise Pond; the loft of our island retreat, "Nooitgedagt" (Dutch for "Who'da thunk it!"), which overlooks Wellfleet Harbor and some of Cape Cod's most magnificent tidal marshes; and a third-floor aerie in the Villa dei Pini at the Centro Studi Ligure in Bogliasco, Italy, from where I could see the Portofino promontory across the bay and hear the pounding of the water of the Mediterranean's Golfo Paradiso less than one hundred meters below. Each of these aptly named waterside settings is very special to me; each is an exceptionally beautiful place of escape for reflection, recreation, and re-creation. But, like Boris Trigorin, Chekhov's writer-character in *The Sea Gull,* when ensconced in any of these special corners of earthly paradise for more than a few days, I start to feel a bit guilty. "I love this lake here, the trees and the sky, I've a feeling for nature—it inspires me, gives me a violent urge to write. But then I'm more than an artist, aren't I? I'm a citizen too. I love my country and its people. As a writer, I feel I must discuss ordinary people, their sufferings, their future—science, human rights, all that stuff. So I do discuss it . . ."

While I have often said that I have been fortunate to have combined my vocation as a sociologist and teacher and my avocation as a traveler and writer—as Robert Frost said, "as my two eyes make one in sight"—there are times when, like Trigorin, I would like to stay at the water's edge, forget about the world's problems—which are what I usually write about—and concentrate on my love of nature, family, sailing, and sight-seeing.

Yet, again like Trigorin, and like the nameless narrator in Robert Frost's "Stopping by Woods on a Snowy Eve," who is wont to linger but has promises to keep, I have spent my life torn between duty and desire. Usually duty has won out (with a nod to Max Weber, some friends call me a "Protestant Ethnic"), but not always. This book, a marginal man's odyssey through the life course and around the world, is a labor of love. In its pages you will learn something about me, my family, and many of those I have come to know along the way.

p a r t   o n e

How I Became a Man and Other True Stories

[one]

The Great Pathfinder

RECENTLY I CAME across a picture of a very exclusive organization of which I was a founding member. It was called the Robin Club. There were five of us in that charter group; the other four were Michael Weingott, my English foster brother who had been evacuated from London after the blitz; the Holstein brothers, Philip and Jonathan; and my father. Known to the others as "Uncle Aaron," a Pied Piper in a Pendleton shirt, my dad was the organizer. Every Saturday or Sunday he would take us on a hike in the country somewhere in New York's Onondaga or Oneida Counties. Sometimes it would be along an abandoned towpath by a canal; sometimes it would be on a trail in deep woods; occasionally we would drive a long way from our home in Syracuse to go bushwhacking, intending to walk to a pond or abandoned farmhouse my dad knew about. Usually we got to where he'd hoped to get us within fifteen minutes of our planned arrival. But sometimes, especially on those more adventurous hikes, he would get us good and lost. When we realized that he wasn't any surer where he was than we were, Jonathan, the youngest, would pipe up with "Oh boy, Uncle Aaron, the Great Pathfinder." I can still hear him. And I can still see the bemused look on my father's face.

That was sixty years ago.

At the time of our "institutionalization" as a real organization, Jonathan was about six. Michael was eleven, and Philip and I were nine. After about six months of our weekly treks, we decided we should do two things: expand the group and elect a leader. We invited Steffen Wolff, my age, and John Macht, Jonathan's, to join us. Once they were duly initiated (the rite consisted of going to a special place called the "Pig Stand" for hot dogs and ice cream), we discussed who should be our president. Michael thought it should be Philip. But John said he had a better idea: "What's wrong with President Roosevelt?"

In the end my father decided it should be a rotating position—each of us to rule for a month. Philip would be the first president; Michael the second; Steffen would be the third. The presidents would be responsible primarily for calling everyone together, discussing options for where we might go, and specifying what equipment to bring. The last was really unnecessary. Even in those days it was important to have proper gear, the basic necessities for day hikes. No Gore-Tex, of course, but we always took off with canvas backpacks, rubber ponchos, smelly canteens, bulky metal Boy Scout first-aid kits, heavy jackknives, citronella, high-top Keds, and our prized club sweatshirts. (For a reason I cannot remember, and despite the fact that we were "robins," these shirts, which my mother had gotten somewhere, each had a maroon-colored cardinal-looking bird sewn on the front.)

As it turned out, after three months of increasing disagreements about destinations and, more significantly, about who would get to sit in the front seat (Philip said it should be the president), chaos returned, and we decided to let my dad, who was also "The Great Peacemaker," make the decisions about venues as well as the privilege of riding shotgun. He resolved the latter problem by piling the gear next to him on the front seat, taking out the middle seat, and letting the six of us ride lined up like snipers on a mattress in the back of our old wooden station wagon with the tailgate down. (Taking beads on oncoming cars and on people walking along the side of the road, we pretended we were picking off Germans with our toy rifles and our makeshift machine guns.)

Only years later did I realize what a special treat it was to be able to drive out into the country during the war and why we rarely used the old wagon during the week. My father was saving precious fuel for these excursions. Of course, it couldn't last. After about a year, with gas rationing increasing and my dad's work with the USO requiring more and more of his attention (this was a second, wartime, job, alongside his work as head of a large settlement house in downtown Syracuse), the routine began to have a staccato quality. We would go hiking one week, then wait a few more. On those weekends when we couldn't go on a trip, we would go to the Harvard Street Theater for afternoon movies.

It was in that very theater that Michael and I were sitting on December 7, 1941, when, in the middle of one of those *Perils of Pauline*–type serials, the projector was suddenly shut off, the lights were turned up, and the manager came on stage. I can still hear him say, "The Japanese have just bombed Pearl Harbor, an American port. We are closing the theater. You should all go home."

Whether the manager went on to say that the bombing was in far-off Hawaii or not, all we heard was that this country was under attack. Having played soldier every day, despite my mother's desire for us to stop it (unlike my dad, she was a pacifist and an active member of WILPF, the Women's International League for Peace and Freedom), we might have been thrilled at the prospect of a real war. We weren't. We were too upset. As we ran the few blocks to our house, I realized that, whereas I was scared, Michael was truly terrified. Having been under bombardment at home in London, he was convinced that a similar thing was imminent and yelled to me to hurry up. When we got home, he immediately led me down into the cellar where we cowered under a heavy Ping-Pong table. We stayed there for several hours, until my folks came home to comfort us and try to explain what was going on.

Like everybody else, we soon began to shift to a wartime footing, learning to live with rationing, air-raid drills, discussions about the draft, and the progress of the war through *March of Time* newsreels and photo reports in picture magazines, especially *Life*.

The Robin Club remained pretty much intact, but it did change focus slightly. While we continued to take occasional hikes or trips to parks and zoos and museums and to the Harvard Street Theater, we also served "The Cause." We collected string and tin foil, competing to see which of us could make the biggest balls of each of these precious materials. (I can't remember why they were so important.) We also began to collect something else:

military insignia. At this I was the envy of the other Robins and clearly the champion collector. By sometime in 1943, I had several hundred patches, most of them obtained from GIs who stayed at our "open house" on weekends. Our address at 228 Cambridge Street was posted on the bulletin board at the USO, inviting those on leave or liberty to stay with us.

Many a night I would be awakened by the heavy footfalls of men walking, sometimes staggering, upstairs to the third floor, where we had a sort of high-class flophouse. Every Saturday and Sunday morning, Michael and I would come down to breakfast to find six to eight air cadets and young soldiers drinking coffee and waiting for pancakes and, I thought, also waiting to tell us war stories. Only later did I realize that most of our guests had yet to see any action. Later still I found out from my folks, who had stayed in touch with a surprising number of our one-time guests, that many of them were to see too much. Several were severely wounded and several others were killed in combat.

I thought of them all quite recently when I uncovered a substantial portion of my store of their mementos: faux gold wings, two sets of lieutenant's silver bars, a single colonel's eagle, and an assortment of buttons with "U.S."; a caduceus; and—the heart of the collection—private, corporal, sergeant, and petty-officer stripes and embroidered insignia with screaming falcons, parachutes, submarines, and cartoon characters overlaid with division designations. My favorite was from a friend in the Tenth Mountain Division—the one which I, as a skier, had longed to be old enough to join.

While I was collecting my badges, the other members of the club were collecting comic books, begging their fathers for ten cents to buy yet another copy of *The Adventures of Superman* or *Captain Marvel.* I can't help but wonder if they stashed away their treasures as I had mine, then, like me, chanced upon them sixty years later. If they did, theirs would be treasures indeed.

The members of the Robin Club remained my closest friends, but there were strains in the ranks that eventually began to pull us in different directions.

The group finally broke up for good early in the summer of 1944. Many factors contributed to its demise. Different interests.

Different schedules. New friends. D day. (I vividly remember walking down Westcott Street one spring morning and seeing a banner head on the local paper: JUNE 6, 1944: D DAY.)

Once the invasion of Europe was under way, we knew it wouldn't be long before Michael would be repatriated. And sure enough, about a month after the invasion my folks received word that passage had been arranged on a troop ship to take a small number of British refugees home. Michael was in the first group to go back.

When he left, there was a void. Yet, I must confess there was also a bit of relief on my part, for, now that Michael was gone, I thought I would have the undivided attention of my mother and father. But that was not to be.

Riding back from the station where we had delivered Michael to the social workers who were to take the refugees to New York and the point of embarkation, my dad told me they were thinking of adopting one or more victims of Nazi oppression. He explained how important it was to provide solace and security for the dispossessed, like Michael and the other refugees who had lived with us for shorter periods between 1935 and 1940.

Not long ago I found a framed award in an old trunk. The America Jewish Joint Distribution Committee had singled out my father in 1936 for his efforts to save Hitler's victims. The citation he received at the time is now in my office, across from my desk. I look at it every day.

When I found that old picture of the founding members of the Robin Club, I had a kind of epiphany. Aaron Rose wasn't just my father—he was a role model before that phrase ever entered the sociological vernacular.

The Great Pathfinder died in 1975. I still miss him terribly.

[two]

Barney and Tillie

K'TON'TON IS MY cousin. I mean that in a literal, not a literary, sense.

For those who don't appreciate the significance of this disclosure, let me explain. K'ton'ton is the best-known Jewish thumbling in history. This three-inch-high fellow, who has never aged despite the fact that he was born over seventy-five years ago, was the fifth child of my Aunt Sadie Rose Weilerstein. Her others were all quite normal!

Sadie, who died in 1993 at the age of ninety-eight, was a prize-winning writer of children's stories. One of the first women graduates of the University of Rochester, she was eager to augment the meager salary she earned teaching Latin and the even more meager salary of her young husband, Rabbi Reuben Weilerstein of Atlantic City. Her mother encouraged her to try to sell the stories she was always writing. And she did. K'ton'ton was her first imaginative creation. Many other books were to follow. Some were about K'ton'ton's further adventures; others about Jewish heroes and history. Sadie also wrote poems and stories, including many about the family.

She always promised to write a whole book about her parents and their ancestors, especially the family of Isaac Landau, born in Prague in 1690, but she never did. She did retell a story her mother had told her when she was a little girl. *Ten and a Kid* was about children and a baby goat back in the old country.

Sadie's mother, Dena (Tillie) Berger, a diminutive dynamo not an awful lot bigger than K'ton'ton, was a mover and shaker. In addition to raising her own five children—Sadie, Toby, Aaron (my father), Frieda, and Anna—she managed a rather large household and a very active husband. She had two passions: women's rights and Jewish security. She was an outspoken suffragist on Susan B. Anthony's home turf and an active Zionist. Family lore has it that "Hadassah," the name of the well-known Jewish women's organization, was chosen at a meeting at her home at which her friend, Henrietta Szold, presided.

Dena Berger was born in Vishtinetz, Lithuania, in 1874. She came to America with her parents, Isaac and Jennie, when she was ten. She was the oldest of nine children, six of whom were born after they settled in Rochester, New York, their new home. She attended Number 8 School, where, for some reason I could never find out (though many family members have their theories), she decided to change her name and called herself "Tillie." Tillie's schooling ended after the eighth grade. Yet, for an immigrant girl in her day and in her circles, she was considered a well-educated young woman.

The man she seemed almost destined to marry, Bernard Rose, known to most as Barney, had come to America from Russia in 1883. He was the one who proudly traced his ancestry back eight generations, back to Isaac Landau of Prague. (I was named Peter Isaac for that distant ancestor and for Tillie's father.)

Barney was the son of Hirsh and Frieda Bryna Rosuk, who had had a granary in a small town known as Volkovysk. He had been raised in relative luxury, only to have everything fall apart when the family business collapsed. At sixteen years of age he was sent to America, to relatives in Rochester, and there he started life anew. Several years after his arrival, he took a room in the home of Isaac and Jennie Berger. Having had rather little schooling and possessing limited knowledge of English, he, like many Jewish immigrants, sought work as a tailor in the local garment industry. He quickly found he had neither the talent nor the patience for such a precise activity. Instead, he joined his landlord in a new venture: collecting bottles and reselling them. Isaac Berger was no entrepreneur and soon tired of the business, but Barney thrived on the risks of small-scale capitalism. He quickly moved from collecting bottles to making them. Then, with the help of a lens grinder he hired, he moved from grinding, polishing, and selling inexpensive magnifying glasses made from the bottoms of broken bottles to manufacturing cheap telescopes using the smallest lenses. In a short while he hired an engineer, and together they built a business that flourished in a symbiotic way with the growing movie industry, many of whose "nickelodeons" depended on the lenses he made for their projectors.

Barney Rose's Projection Optics Company allowed for a rich lifestyle—a housekeeper, an open touring car, and a summer place of his own—that might have been the envy of less-successful newcomers had he and Tillie not worked tirelessly on their behalf, too.

Barney became a leader in Rochester's growing Jewish community; a founder of the new Conservative temple, Beth El; president of the Hebrew Free School; counselor, arbiter, and go-between in the class, status, and power struggles between German and Russian Jews and between those from Lithuania and those from Galicia; and organizer and backer of various free loan associations. He also made many contacts beyond the confines of the Jewish world, starting with his friend the minister Rev. Herbert Lotie, with whom he shared his interest in nature study and horses—about which Sadie wrote a story called "Dick, the Horse That Kept the Sabbath".

Barney was an Elk, a Moose, a Mason, an Odd Fellow, an ardent Roosevelt supporter (TR not FDR), and a buyer of choice real estate. He was a *macher* in two worlds. Yet, he remained a family man who doted on his children, especially his only son, and his grandchildren. When he had become a grand*paterfamilias*, Sadie wrote a poem about him as if seeing him through the eyes of her own children. It included the line "Bernard, Barney, Beryl, Dov"—names that in English, Yiddish, and Hebrew mean "bear." "He's not the howly, growly kind, he's the nicest grandpa you can find."

While he wasn't howly or growly either, my mother's father, ironically named Wolf, was, in certain ways, the Bear's antithesis. Had Barney not had the reputation of being awfully fair-minded "for a capitalist," he could well have been one of Wolf's many nemeses.

Wolf Feld, a skilled tailor, and his wife, Celia, had come to

America from Russian-controlled Poland around the turn of the century. After several failures at starting their own custom tailoring shop, first in New York City, then in Albany, they, too, moved to Rochester, where Wolf—who came to be known as William—became one of a number of coatmakers at the famed manufacturer of fine men's clothing, Hickey-Freeman. My grandmother did piecework at home. Sometimes he did, too. (I can still picture and smell their third-floor workroom with its sewing machines, tables strewn with scraps of material, small pressing machine, and steaming iron.)

While luckier than many of those who worked in the needle trades (coatmakers being the elite within the hierarchy of tailoring), Wolf Feld was always concerned about worker rights. He was an active member of the Arbeiter Ring, the Workmen's Circle. The Circle was his political anchorage and only social club.

My mother, Lillian, was raised in a secular, socialist home where her father faithfully read the news in the Yiddish-language *Jewish Daily Forward* to himself and often long passages of it, including the advice column, the "Bintel Brief," aloud to his illiterate wife.

One grandfather a capitalist, the other a socialist; one a cosmopolite, the other a local; one very well off, the other quite poor; one dark haired and mustachioed, the other towheaded and clean shaven. "The Bear" and "The Wolf" were as different from one another as are their furry namesakes. But their differences were nothing compared to those of their wives.

While each was, in many ways, tougher than her husband, and both were quite diminutive, Tillie was a feminist; Celia, or "Chippa," as she was called, was anything but. Pretty, kindly, and innately very smart, she felt her place was in the home—and she stayed at home much of her life, caring for her husband and her children and, later, her neighbors. In the Feld family, Wolf was the political activist. In the Rose family, Tillie was.

My mother and her older brothers, Harry and Sam, always claimed they were sent to "Socialist Sunday School" (whatever that meant!). They knew "The Internationale" but almost no Jewish prayers or songs. My mother had rarely entered a synagogue before she married my father in Barney's Temple Beth El in 1931, a place my father knew very well—"Too well," he would say.

At the time they met, my father was a social worker who had no interest in organized religion. (He later explained that, despite his friendships with several religious leaders, early in life he found he was "allergic to the clergic!" His malady was quite contagious. I caught the bug myself—but that is another story.)

Aaron's lack of interest in Beth El was a great disappointment to his father; so, too, was the fact that, after reluctantly working for Projection Optics for three years as a salesman in the 1920s, he reverted to his real love, working with young people. He spent much of his early adulthood running settlement houses and community centers in Rochester and Syracuse and establishing, then directing, "fresh air" camps in the summers.

In the last summer of the war, he and my mother purchased an estate in the northern Adirondacks where they founded Camp Chateaugay, a noncompetitive place that stressed outdoor living, democratic principles, and progressive-school values. Within a few years we left central New York and moved to a little village near our camp.

During the long northern winters by the lake, we were often confined to the house. It was then that my father told me many stories about his parents. One of my favorites was about going with Barney (his daughters called him "Papa," but to my dad he was always "Barney") to buy the family's first automobile. In those days there were few cars. If you were lucky enough to be able to purchase one, you went to the shop, made the deal, and then had the salesman teach you how to drive it.

That is precisely what Barney did. With young Aaron in the back seat, the dealer, who instructed him about using the steering bar, the levers, and the pedals for accelerating and stopping, first drove him around. Headstrong Barney was only half listening. He figured it would be quite easy, and he itched to take over. When he did, he wobbled down the road, shot across an intersection, frightening horses and pedestrians, and plowed right into a millinery shop, coming to an abrupt stop (he finally found the brake) with satin and silk and feathers all over his new car. (N.B. He drove for the next sixty years and, while he never found himself adorned in ladies' hats again, he continued his aggressive, curb-jumping style. When I was very small, I thought it great fun to ride with him. As I grew older, I preferred to walk.)

It may have been because Barney was enthralled with nature, or because he loved uniforms, or because he believed in training his son to be self-reliant, that he encouraged my father to become a Boy Scout in 1912, the inaugural year of the organization in America. His scoutmaster was Barney's friend the Reverend Lotie.

While never much of a marcher, Aaron loved the hiking and camping and the fact that, because he could play the bugle (more or less), he was always the one asked to sound reveille and play taps. Barney, who reveled in pomp and ceremony, was proud of his talented son. He urged him to wear his scout outfit, even when he wasn't going to a meeting or to camp.

The much more pragmatic Tillie liked the uniform, too, but for a different reason. It was related to the fact that her son could make noise on his bugle. She pressed him into service to her causes. On a number of occasions she had someone drive their open touring car down to Rochester's camera works, to Bausch and Lomb, or to another optics company in Rochester (sometimes to their own, Projection Optics) and park it outside, then had my khaki-clad father stand on the back seat and blow his horn to attract attention. Then, depending on the day, Tillie would harangue anyone within earshot about women's suffrage and the need for the vote. Or, targeting the bosses, she would speak out on behalf of religious Jews troubled by the fact that they had to work on their Sabbath and by the signs that said, "If you can't work on Saturday, don't come on Monday."

Barney and Tillie's homes were always gathering places for family, cronies (Barney's friends), and social activists (Tillie's). First they lived in several places in the predominantly Jewish Joseph Avenue section of Rochester. Later they moved to a large house on the other side of town in what was then a sort of *haute bourgeoisie* neighborhood with streets named for prestigious colleges. Their address was 376 Harvard Street.

I remember going to that house as a child and always being awed by the large and dark living room, the dining room with heavy furniture, and the fact that there were two sets of stairs, one going up from the large front hall and the other, for the servants, next to the kitchen. Although somewhat intimidated by "The Bear" and "The Queen Bee," as I saw my paternal grandparents, I was always eager to go to see them if only to race up one stairway and down the other, over and over.

When I was a bit older, their library, actually an alcove in the living room, was my favorite place. There was a treasure trove of books and magazines, including what I think were all the early issues of *National Geographic*. It was while viewing the pictures of exotic places, curious people, and strange animals in the yellow-bordered, slick-covered journals that boobies first intrigued me. No, not the bare breasts of voluptuous females displayed in full color. Birds. While the former doubtlessly aroused budding prurient interests in the red-blooded preteen ethnographer I was then, the odd-looking feathered creatures stimulated a different sort of excitement, the thrill and adventure of discovery by famous explorers and scientists and anthropologists.

My favorite was Charles Darwin, whose book about the voyage of the HMS *Beagle* and his time in the Galapagos Archipelago I also found in that wonderful library. For years afterward I was to dream of going to those magical islands to see what Darwin saw. It would be sixty years before I would manage to do it and to see those boobies in the flesh—blue-footed, red-footed, masked, and unmasked—as well as Darwin's finches and other rare birds, crustaceans, arachnids, reptiles, and Yertle's oversized ancestors.

Thinking about it today, I'm quite sure my grandfather, whose well-worn magazines and books attested to their having been thoroughly read, would never have done anything so adventurous.

Barney Rose was the sort of character E. L. Doctorow is wont to invent. He was interested in travel but he never went anywhere. He firmly believed in higher education although I don't think he ever went to high school. He was rather old-fashioned, patriotic, civic-minded, and, in life as in his faith, Conservative with a capital

C. Put it all together and he was the quintessence of a "High Church Jew."

I heard many stories from my father and his sisters about growing up in Barney and Tillie's various homes. One of the more gruesome ones was about the time the German housekeeper, who, according to my father, "was a bit of a Prussian," threatened to kill his pet lamb if he continued to misbehave. Once, after a series of tiffs with young Aaron, she said she was really going make good on her perverse promise. Two days later, they had roast lamb. She served it saying, *sotto voce*, "See, Aaron, I said I'd do it."

She hadn't. His pet was still alive. But my father never ate meat again. Ever. His vegetarianism, which extended to shunning fish and fowl as well as red meat, was the source of both concern and controversy throughout his life. It also attracted attention from many different quarters. The Vegetarian Party was always after him to join and to work on its behalf. He wasn't interested, nor did he ever try to persuade my mother or me to join him in his abstinence.

I, a natural-born carnivore, was never reluctant to question him about this quirk in his character. Time and again I would ask: "If your life depended on it, would you eat meat?" His invariable response was: "Of course. I'm not a fool; but I doubt it will ever come to that." There is more to tell about this man who, in many ways, remained a Boy Scout all his life, but this is Barney's story, and Tillie's, too.

I remember two large events organized by Barney and Tillie. The first was when I was very young and when, relatively speaking, they were as well; the other was when they were quite elderly. The early one was a Berger family reunion, held in a park on a lake near Rochester. There was a newspaper, the *Berger Gazette*, which kept everyone informed of the family news and the plans for the party, which was a huge success for most everybody, although I sensed that my grandfather wasn't too pleased to be upstaged by Tillie's clan.

The other event was their fiftieth wedding anniversary celebration, held in the back yard of their Harvard Street home in the summer of 1943. Among the guests was a couple, Anna and Alfred

Schwarz, invited by my Aunt Anna and her husband, Warner. Warner, a refugee from Berlin, was a mechanical engineer; Alfred, who had fled from Vienna in 1939, was a physicist and a specialist in shutter designs for cameras. Both had come to Rochester to work in the optics industry. In the small refugee community the two men had become fast friends, and for a time—knowing that neither my father nor my eldest cousin, Herschel, the only scientist in the family, was interested in the business—they thought of seeking financial backing and then making a bid on Barney's company. It never came to pass. But the childless Schwarzes were to enter our family circle a decade later in quite another way.

In 1947 they became the guardians, and a bit later the adoptive parents, of two young girls, Alfred's Dutch nieces Betsy and Hedy Cohen. The Cohen girls and one cousin were the only survivors of a very large family that perished in the war. Along with their mother, Alfred's sister Rosa, they had been hidden in an Amsterdam cellar. (Their Dutch father, Jacques Alfred Theobald Carl Friedrich Cohen, his four brothers, and the rest of the family, including his in-laws, were taken away and perished in Auschwitz.) Rosa died in hiding, and only the children were left.

I met Hedy in 1953, and we were married three years later. When we were first going together, she wanted me to meet her folks. She was startled to learn they already knew me—and my family.

Like so many of his idols, my grandfather died "with his boots on" in 1948. Rumor had it that he fell asleep at his desk at Projection Optics and toppled over, hitting his head.

There was a huge turnout at his funeral, almost as many as the number who came for Tillie's when she died three years later, still involved in her political activities but having added a new role, that of factory manager, to her résumé. At this, truth to tell, she was less than successful.

Projection Optics, which had grown rapidly in the early years of the twentieth century, had survived the Depression and had been refitted to produce bombsights and other needed optical equipment during the war but had not been prepared for the revolution in production techniques afterward and was already struggling when Barney died.

There is little left of the material presence of Barney or Tillie. The house on Harvard Street, which I visited a few years ago, looks much smaller and is much shabbier than I remember it. And all I have of the factory are three magnifying glasses, the barrel of a projection lens, and a few cheap telescopes embossed with "Projection Optics Company, Rochester, New York." But there are memories and a very rich legacy of two who played a special role for so many, including Sadie and Toby and Aaron and Frieda and Anna and their spouses and their real and imaginary grandchildren, K'ton'ton and all the rest of us.

[three]

How I Became a Man

NO FOUNTAIN PEN for this bar mitzvah boy. No chopped liver. No klezmer band either. Not even a cantor. My big present was a horse; we ate fresh-caught speckled trout; there was a choir conducted by my mother made up of friends who sang at the local Presbyterian church; and the occasional music, before and after the service, was strictly Beethoven. (It may even have been "Ode to Joy.")

I was raised in a Jewish home of a decidedly secular, antireligious bent. My mother was a socialist, a World Federalist, and a Quaker-oriented pacifist; my father, though head of a Jewish community center and hardly as political, was an apostate, too. Although he had been given a proper Jewish education and although three of his oldest and closest friends were clergymen—Rev. Herbert Lotie, Father John Geiger, Rabbi Philip Bernstein—he never seemed comfortable with organized religion and often railed against the sanctimony of preachers of all faiths—Mr. Lotie, Father Geiger, and Phil Bernstein excepted! Nevertheless, sometime in the mid-1930s, shortly after we moved from Rochester to Syracuse, my parents did join a Reform congregation, the Temple Society of Concord.

When I was old enough, I, along with the children of other members, was sent to what we called "Saturday-Sunday school." I found it boring and hated going. In my mind I plotted ways to get out of it. Then, just when I thought I was stuck there for good, I was summarily banished from the place for two acts of defiance, the first more innocent than the second.

At thirteen, I was a very junior competitive skier who raced on a local team. One Saturday in the early winter of 1946, a meet was scheduled for 1:00 P.M. Realizing I wouldn't have time to go home to change before going to the slopes, instead of wearing a conventional outfit (shirt, tie, et cetera), I put on my ski clothes—bulky reindeer sweater, baggy pants, and heavily oiled leather boots—and went off to the temple. (It was lucky it was wintertime, for, had it been the following spring, I might have come attired in smelly britches and mud-encrusted riding boots so I could rush to my job as an exercise boy for several show horses owned by a neighbor.)

The "Sunday"-school lessons were always followed by compulsory attendance at the morning service, and I was startled when, at the end of the sermon, the rabbi, who had been scanning the minitudes (only the kids required to be there and a handful of elderly people occupied the sanctuary), stopped and stared down, fixing me in his glare. With his deep, booming voice, he called my name. All eyes shifted in my direction.

"Peter Rose," he repeated, "I want to see you in my study immediately after the service."

Unsure of what I had done this time, but assuming it had to do with whispering and nudging my friends, I went to see him. I knocked on the door. Instead of sitting behind his desk, he stood before it, still in his ministerial robes.

He was a small man, but at that moment he seemed very big. Glaring at me, he asked in his familiar stentorian tone, "Do you think you are properly attired in the house of God?" (Actually, the way he said it, the last word was strung out into three syllables: "Ga-a-d.")

I gathered myself together, then compounded my transgression with the second act of defiance, this time a conscious one. Instead of hanging my head in contrition and making an excuse, I retorted.

"Rabbi, if there is a God, do you honestly think he cares if I wear ski boots to temple?"

I was asked to leave. Trembling a bit but with head held high, I left the premises, stomped down the snow-covered stairs, and vowed never to return. I never did.

I was thirteen, the crucial age when Jewish boys traditionally undergo the ancient *rite de passage* to "manhood," becoming bar mitzvah after lengthy preparation. Not me. Even before my final run-in with the rabbi, I had had enough of religion and had no intention of engaging in such ritual behavior. (Earlier, I had agreed to have a Reform-style "confirmation" if I ever made it through the trials and tribulations of the required number of years in the "Saturday-Sunday school." That, too, was now clearly out of the question.)

The confirmation ploy had been a compromise worked out between my father and me a year earlier. When I was twelve, he said he would let me decide whether or not I wanted to "have" a bar mitzvah. I remember thinking about the few I had attended—most at the Reform temple, two at the Conservative one—and the awful, garish parties that followed. They seemed to be mainly for adults. Somehow none of it sat well with what was then a pint-size, rather puritanical agnostic (today I'm a much bigger one), so it didn't take me long to decide that I wanted no part of this clearly social event. And that was it. Well, almost.

The spring after I had been kicked out of Concord, my father called me into the living room one day and, seemingly out of the blue, asked how I would feel about reconsidering my decision about the bar mitzvah.

My heart sank. Then my spirits brightened as I thought of an easy way to avoid even thinking about any reversal of fortune.

"Too late," I said, "bar mitzvahs happen on your thirteenth birthday."

"They usually do," he explained. He went on to say that his father was very upset and hurt by what "we" (actually I) had decided, especially because I, the apple of his eye, was also the only son of his only son, thus the only one in my generation to carry the family name. (He would be proud to know that the name is now carried not only by my daughter, Lies, and my son, Dan, but also by my grandsons, his great-great grandsons, Jordan and Robert Rose.)

Because the discussion was initiated by the man who had stood by me in my contretemps with the rabbi—and on many other matters of principle—a sort of filial piety and, doubtless, a fair amount of parentally engendered guilt began to weaken my resolve. After much hemming and hawing, I made a deal. I would do it for Grandpa Rose, but only on my terms. I knew no Hebrew, and there was no way I could learn it in the time before the ceremony would be held, so I said I would go along if the service, except for a few prayers, could be in English, including the portion of the Torah I would read.

I wasn't keen on trying to finagle myself back into the graces of my nemesis, Rabbi Friedman, so we could use his sanctuary; nor was I eager to have the ceremony in the synagogue of the very traditional congregation in Rochester founded by my grandfather Barney. Instead, I insisted we have it in the simple nonsectarian chapel at the summer camp my parents ran, a sanctuary in the woods with log rails, wooden benches, a rough-hewn pulpit, and a sign saying, "Let All the Trees of the Forest Rejoice before the Lord." Finally, I said I would go along with this shotgun bar mitzvah if I could have a horse as a consolation prize.

Reluctantly (later I learned just how reluctantly), my grandfather agreed to my cockamamie scheme.

The deal done, my bar mitzvah was scheduled for a Saturday in mid-June.

In April I began to prepare for what, save for the prospect of the horse, I clearly dreaded. I was given some instructions from a student at a nearby university and, in spite of myself, actually began to find what I was learning intriguing. For the first time I began to feel some sense of the history and spirit of "my" people. Unfortunately, neither the lessons nor the mood lasted long enough to stimulate me to really delve into the sorts of things we discussed (that was to come only years later).

Around June 1, 1947, we moved north, to our camp near the Canadian border. It was only a few weeks before the big event. That spring, in addition to getting ready for a summer family of 180 campers and counselors, repairing buildings, moving docks, painting boats, and ordering staples, meat, and produce, much time was also devoted to special preparations to accommodate our extended family—grandparents, aunts and uncles, and cousins I rarely saw.

When the grand day came, it was clear that the hoped-for outdoor venue was being washed out. It was pouring, and, since this wasn't something to be postponed (though it had clearly been "delayed," as my relatives were told), a hasty decision was made to have the ceremony in the living room of the main lodge, once a rich man's summer home. Instead of the sign about the trees of the forest rejoicing before the Lord, we—a somewhat bewildered rabbi, my relatives, and I—stood before a large frieze of Pan and several naked nymphs and other mythical characters cavorting with abandon over a great fireplace. On the edge of a huge mantle were the words "I Cannot Warm You If Your Heart Be Cold." I'm sure it all seemed very bizarre to my grandfather—as well as to the rabbi—but he came through it like a trooper and so, according to my few friends from town (none of whom was Jewish), did I.

I said the prayers and read my portion with more enthusiasm than I had anticipated. I liked what my parents said, too. It was something about learning to be tolerant.

The rain subsided, the sun came out, and we all moved to a reception on the lawn, where I unwrapped my presents. In addition to an elaborately wrapped picture of a magnificent six-month-old black-maned buckskin-colored filly to be given to me by my folks, these included a horse blanket from one aunt, a halter from another, and an elegant bridle from yet another. (They had clearly been briefed.) Needless to say, there was no tack from my grandparents. Though they were animal lovers, there were limits to their tolerance. With hope springing eternal, they gave me a check, a *yarmulke*, and a prayer shawl.

Then there was a two-hour luncheon consisting mainly of local delicacies, including freshly caught trout, potatoes grown on a farm down the road, and all sorts of cheeses from Macadam Cheese in nearby Chateaugay. There was also some "real" bread (as opposed to the *goyish* kind my not-entirely-de-ethnicized dad always said was "filled with embalming fluid"). The bread, like the rabbi, had been imported from Montreal that morning. Lunch was followed by a series of toasts, exchanges of pleasantries with the relatives, and some kidding around with my friends.

The party started to break up. The folks from town thanked my parents and congratulated me, then left. I wanted to go, too.

After another half hour, while various family members dawdled over coffee, I asked my parents whether it would be O.K. for me to leave. They said I could.

I ran up to my room, took off my specially purchased "Sunday-go-to-meeting" (or "Saturday-have-a–bar mitzvah") duds, and put on my tee shirt, jeans, and riding boots. With hangers-on still in the main house or out on the lawn, I walked out, went over to Archie Gadway's stable next door, saddled my favorite horse, Gentleman Jim, and led him out of the paddock. I swung myself into the saddle, gathered the reins, urged him into a canter with my knees, and took off into the woods, smiling to myself and thinking, "I've done it! Now everyone is happy—more or less." Then I laughed, "Today I am a man—more or less."

[four]

School Days

EXCEPT FOR ARMY brats and the children of migrant workers and corporate managers, most of my contemporaries went to three different neighborhood schools—elementary, junior high, and high school—before going to college. Not I. I went to seven: an urban grade school, a junior high in a slightly more affluent area, a one-room school on a mountainside, and four high schools—one in the middle of the city, one on its outskirts, one in a mining town, and one, from which I finally graduated, in a small, rural village on the Canadian border. It was in those very different environs, long before I was trained in the field, that I did my first bits of sociological analysis.

My first school in Syracuse was in an "area in transition," a nice euphemism for one that was still suffering from the effects of the Depression-wracked economy. Even as a small boy I knew it was in flux, which made it exciting to me. Sumner School drew pupils from the poorer parts of the city, from two working-class neighborhoods that were rapidly deteriorating, and from the nearby university section. Almost all my classmates were white, but I remember being struck by the variety of names—Gardner, Greenwald, Kelly, Levy, Montero, Pacelli.

In the first grade there was a lot of banter about comic-book heroes and radio programs. We jumped around the playground saying "the Shadow knows," yelling "Hi ho Silver," and calling each other "Kee-mo-sabe." I thought it great fun. I especially liked doggerel. A favorite was "Eenie, meenie, miney moe / Catch a nigger by the toe."

One day, shortly after learning that couplet, I came home

reciting it out loud. It was then that I received my first lesson in what many decades later would be known as "proscribed speech."

My mother was shocked. She called me into the house and sat me down to tell me why. Sternly she explained that "nigger" was a terrible word. She explained that it was a bad thing to say. It was used to put down "colored people," like the Andersons who lived down the street, and should never, ever, be used.

I must have asked her what the right word was, and she said "Negro."

Long afterward she told me that, to her chagrin, a few days later she heard me say, "Eenie, meenie, miney, moe / Catch a Negro by the toe."

I don't think I was being a wise guy, but then this was my mother's story.

The fact of the matter was that we were all clearly ripe for the propaganda lessons our art teacher gave us several years later in a room dominated by posters of Norman Rockwell's "Four Freedoms" paintings. I remember her urging us to prepare posters of our own. Mine, doubtless copied from something I had seen, showed three graves, each with a headstone adorned with very specific symbols. On one was a swastika, on the second a fasces (a bundle of sticks with an axe head at the top, a Roman symbol of authority adopted by the Italian fascists), and on the third a rising sun. Underneath I had printed in big, bold letters, "Let's Get Together to Bury the Axis."

In the fourth or fifth grade I was a member of the civil defense group. We spent most of our time memorizing the silhouettes of airplanes, "ours" and "theirs." I can still point out differences between Mustangs, Avengers, Wildcats, P-38s, Spitfires, Liberators, and a host of other American and Allied planes and the Messerschmidts, Junkers, and Zeros of the enemy. (To this day, I can't see a car with the name Mitsubishi without remembering that that company used to make the Zero.) I can also still draw ugly caricatures of buck-toothed, slant-eyed Japanese soldiers and goose-stepping Germans, images conveyed to us in the same school's art classes. I vividly remember these caricatures brought to life in exciting movies where clean-cut American guys—with names like Gardner, Greenwald, Kelly, and Levy, and, invariably, a "Negro" named Roosevelt Wilson or something similar pounded the hell out of the pinch-faced "Japs" and monocled "Krauts."

The war was still on when I moved on from Sumner School to Edward Smith Junior High, a school located in a neighborhood that I would know today as "middle-middle class." I recall little about that school, save for the fact that it was from its athletic field that we all watched the first jet fighter streak across the sky. It was flying from Buffalo to somewhere in the east. I, the plane-spotter, was duly impressed.

In the summer after that school year (1945) my parents, both social workers and summer-camp directors, were about to make a life-long dream come true. They bought an old estate and the adjoining property in the tiny upstate village of Merrill, New York, located in the northern Adirondacks. There they built a camp of their own based on the democratic principles of the progressive school movement, a liberal, integrationist ideology, and the outdoor philosophy of rugged activity in a cooperative environment. Unlike camps they had directed for other people for over two decades, one of which they were still running, this new one would be theirs not only in program conception and execution, but in all other respects as well.

The properties they bought consisted of a seven-acre "Lower Camp," on which there was a huge house euphemistically called a "summer cottage," built in the beginning of the 1920s and lost in the crash, and the "Upper Camp," which consisted of about forty acres of land and several old buildings.

In late August 1945 we moved into the main building, soon dubbed "The Big House," and began refurbishing it and other extant structures and planning for the building of six new ones. We all worked like dogs. When the snow started to fly, we packed it in and went back to Syracuse for the winter. I went back to Ed Smith.

We made many trips back and forth in December, January, and February, and then, even before the snow had completely melted, moved back to camp. With four months to go in the eighth grade, I was enrolled in the nearest school. It was in Merrill, on the hard-packed dirt road to Panther Mountain. It had one room, a big bell, a wood stove, one teacher, Molly Gadway, and seventeen boys and girls, ranging in age from six to twelve (me). I was the only kid in the sixth, seventh, or eighth grade. I was also the only one who wore socks and shoes without holes. Some of the children came to school with no shoes at all.

This was my first exposure to rural poverty. It was a bit like going to school on Erskine Caldwell's Tobacco Road, at once intriguing and terribly depressing. I remember having to split wood for the pot-bellied stove in the center of the main room, running outside to the outhouse, and taking my turn ringing the school bell by pulling on the rope in the belfry. I also remember getting good and sick on spruce gum scraped from the trees and chewed. Ugh.

In June I graduated from "Panther Mountain," having passed New York State's eighth-grade Regents Exams. It was the only time I was ever valedictorian, handsomest kid in the class, and most likely to succeed.

That fall I entered the comprehensive school in the village of Lyon Mountain, on the side of the northernmost of the Adirondack peaks. The town itself was owned, lock, stock, and barrel, by Republic Steel, whose deep iron mines were the only reason for its existence. I was the only student in the school whose parents had no connection with the company. I was the only student in the school who hadn't gone through its own elementary and middle grades. And, as at Panther Mountain, I was also the only Jew.

There were two churches in the village of Lyon Mountain. One was Catholic and was attended by those with Irish- and Polish-sounding names; the other was Protestant, and everybody who went there seemed to be of English background.

On Friday afternoons all students were given "released time" for religious education. For some reason I didn't understand (I remembered the "Four Freedoms" and comments at home that, in our country, we had both freedom *of* and freedom *from* religion), it was mandatory. I, who it was grudgingly acknowledged had nowhere to go, was supposed to sit in the classroom until the normal end of the school day (presumably communing with "my" God). Sometimes I would be a good boy and stay there staring out the window, but more often I would play hooky and slip out. No one ever called me—or my parents—on my acts of defiance.

On those days as on the others, I would leave the school, jump on my bike (which my father had put in the back of his old wood-sided station wagon when he brought me to school in the morning), and ride the seven or eight miles down the lower part of the mountain to the lake where our camp was located. I can still smell the balsam and pine forests and see the lake shimmering below as I roared down the hill on my old Schwinn no-speed, only occasionally riding the coaster brakes to slow before a bad patch of gravel.

I attended Lyon Mountain for two months in the fall of 1946, two months in the spring of 1947, and then three months in the spring of 1948.

After my first few months in Lyon Mountain, we moved back to Syracuse, where my father still had a position as the executive director of a social agency. The high school nearest our home was called Central.

There seems to have been such a place in almost every middle-sized city in the 1940s: the old, original high school in a downtown neighborhood that was in transition. At *our* Central High there were very wealthy students from the large homes along James Street; students from the university neighborhood and from a working class area, both near our home; and many from "The Ward," the poorest section, whose residents were European immigrants and southern blacks. The school, as I remember it, was no blackboard jungle but a vibrant place of true multilayered, multiclass, multicultural complexity run by a benevolent principal and a cadre of dedicated teachers. I was particularly fond of several of them, especially a math teacher who made a mathophobe begin to take pleasure in algebra. It was too good to last, for, when spring came, we moved back to the camp and I returned to Lyon Mountain, where, whatever the pleasures might have been, math and Latin, which I had also started at Central, were not among them. I had terrible teachers, something I was to run into in several other places.

In early September of 1947, right after our second summer,

owing to the illness of my grandfather, my mother went to Rochester and I was sent to Syracuse to live with friends. Instead of going back to Central High, which I loved, I was persuaded to seek a transfer to Nottingham High, where my host family's son was starting high school. Reluctantly, I made the switch, leaving the literally colorful Central to enter a homogeneous suburban world of boys and girls from upwardly mobile families. It was a far cry from Central and even farther from Panther Mountain and Lyon Mountain.

A sophomore, I was targeted for recruitment by a variety of clubs and fraternities. I managed to avoid joining any of them. Even the ski club seemed too tame—and *nouveau riche*—for the likes of this maverick. I missed the mix of students and the challenging teachers at Central; I missed the excitement of Lyon Mountain with the constant talk of danger below the ground and of exploitation above it. Strikes there in the mining town were matters of life and death; at Nottingham they had to do with threats to cancel the junior prom.

I never finished the full year at Nottingham, for, once again, we left for the northland sometime in April 1948. I went back to Lyon Mountain. At this point my father resigned from his position at the Jewish Community Center in Syracuse, having decided to move permanently to somewhere near the camp. We settled on Chateaugay, a village only slightly larger than Merrill, and, in September, I enrolled in my fourth high school, Chateaugay High.

We didn't live in the town (a place that was thriving then but was to become a northern equivalent of the one in *The Last Picture Show*). We rented a place ten miles to the south, on the northern end of Chateaugay Lake. I was bused to school every day.

Mine was the last stop on the line. This meant getting up at 6:00 A.M. to be on the road to flag down the big yellow vehicle. There was a time in my senior year when I missed the bus three days in a row and my dad had to drive me. It was during one of the harshest winters in memory, with nighttime temperatures dipping to thirty and even forty below zero and daytime ones not too much higher. It was hard to stand outside with the wind whipping around my legs and the ice devils nibbling on my nose.

Nonetheless, my father, annoyed that I kept missing the

bus, announced that he wouldn't take me to school again. I said, "Yes, Dad," knowing that he, always a softy, would do it if I were really stuck.

Two days later, I missed the bus again and, to my chagrin, was told I'd have to get to school on my own. In a funk, I grabbed my coat, hat, and mittens, stormed out of the house, and started walking and trying to hitchhike. It was to no avail. No one even slowed down on the icy roads.

I must have walked three or four miles in a howling gale when, finally, someone we knew drove by, saw my huddled figure bucking the storm, backed up, and picked me up. He dropped me at the school at around half past nine. It was just in time to get the word that, because of the weather, school was closing at ten. I boarded the bus and rode home to be greeted by a very sheepish father.

In point of fact, I don't think I would have missed much had the school been closed every day. It was a peculiar place with very provincial and conservative teachers, a few exceptions notwithstanding, who clearly saw me as an outsider and sometimes expressed resentment at what they must have thought were my cosmopolitan airs (a relative term I must admit), the only evidence being that we had come from a city (though not *the* city) and that we were Jews (though ones who didn't fit their stereotypes: my folks were neither dealers nor doctors but social workers and social activists).

I did make friends, but I was also seen as a bit odd by some of my peers. I hated *Silas Marner* just like they did. But I didn't hate everything we had to read. I liked *Julius Caesar* and *King Lear* and some of the other required reading. But above all I was drawn to those "Commie writers" (as one of my English teachers called them) whose books I found on my parents' shelves, such as Richard Wright, author of *Black Boy* and *Native Son*, and Howard Fast, author of *Spartacus*, *Freedom Road*, and *Citizen Tom Paine*. That same teacher was pleased that another favorite writer of mine was the historical novelist Kenneth Roberts, who wrote *Northwest Passage*, *Arundel*, and *Lydia Bailey*. (Many years later I was shocked and disappointed to discover that Roberts was a reactionary, a nativist, and a notorious anti-Semite.)

I did enjoy some of my classes at Chateaugay High, but most of the time I yearned to be back in one of the many other places I'd been before, especially good old Central High in Syracuse. If I am honest, I must say that the best times I had in my two years at Chateaugay High were outside the classroom, engaged in such after-school activities as the choral group and the senior play, in which, for some reason, I was given the male lead. (I proceeded to make an utter fool of myself, though my parents and at least two of my friends—no, actually it was one—said I was "Great!") My career as a star-struck thespian ended that very night.

Truly extracurricular endeavors—riding horseback and downhill skiing—were even more rewarding, if a bit lonely. Nobody else in my class was interested in either. The first they thought was for girls or for snobs—or both. The second, in those days when a rope tow as a great luxury, was for fools. Whenever I asked friends to join me on the slopes, they would reply, "Too damn cold" or "It's too hard," then they'd go back to the basketball court. I hated basketball. I didn't care, I said, and so I would ski alone.

There were two activities in which some of them were engaged that intrigued me: beer drinking down in Canada (it was downhill to the border) and cattle smuggling. I participated in the first and envied those who were involved in the second.

Sometimes I would borrow the camp truck, saying I was going to the library or the movies. I would then pick up my friends and cross the border to enjoy the fleshpots of Huntingdon, Quebec. Our biggest excitement was bellying up to a bar in a nondescript café where the French-speaking bartender never seemed to care that we were only sixteen or seventeen. We would pass around a pack of smelly cigarettes, light up, each purchase and drink a single Molson's, and then scoot back to town before our parents got suspicious.

The other activity was considerably more risky.

In my last year of high school, 1949–50, there was an embargo on the importation of cattle from Canada, four miles to the north. That provided the locals with a new way to make a few bucks. It was a case of history repeating itself. Some of their parents had been involved in the extensive movement of liquor across that same border—and along the very same back roads—during the days of Prohibition. That activity had been so widespread that one of the main streets of town, Depot Street, was known by many as "Whiskey Lane."

I learned some things about the old days from talking to many of my parents' new friends while I was in high school, and more from the old-timers several years later when I went back to do more digging for a college course on "folklore fieldwork." My initial "sources" included our closest acquaintances, the elegant Clark Gable–looking Scots-Canadian physician John Emerson McIntosh, and the less commanding but to me more fascinating French-Canadian World War I veteran and storekeeper Maurice (Mike) Lambert.

When I was in high school, Doc Mac often took me trout fishing. He let me ride his saddle horses, Tanna, the palomino mare, and Tony, the buckskin gelding. He also let me ride shotgun when he would hitch the two horses to a sleigh on Christmas Eve and drive his friends to church.

Mike, who had a distinct French Canadian accent, told endless stories about the horrors of trench warfare that always ended with his taking his Springfield rifle off the wall, sighting along its barrel, showing me, with uninhibited delight, how he'd picked off the Huns, and saying, "Some weapon, aye?"

Not only were Doc Mac and Mike Lambert key informants, they were local characters. There were many others, including the proverbial village idiot (who was, in fact, pretty smart), the Stetson-hatted, high-heel-booted drugstore cowboy (who actually had a horse and frequently rode it), and the bigger-than-life priest, Father Hyland, a local boy who made good. The priest became a world-famous chaplain at Clinton Prison in nearby Dannemora where, with prison labor, he built and ran St. Dismas, the Church of the Good Thief. (A book, *Gates of Dannemora,* by Father Bonn of Boston College, told the story of Father Hyland's good works and worldwide recognition.) Father Hyland was later ordered by the bishop to become pastor of St. Patrick's, Chateaugay's Catholic church. Unlike Mike Lambert, he didn't find it easy to come home after he'd seen his "Paree."

Perhaps the most interesting character of them all was a little kid. I'll call him Dickie Goddard. He was tough and sassy and only seven or eight years old when I first knew him. But he was not afraid of anything or anyone.

One day a friend and I were returning to school after lunch. It was in the middle of December, and snow and ice covered everything. We turned a corner and saw Dickie throwing snow-covered ice balls at passing cars. Around the corner came New York State Trooper Stan Zimmons (his real name) in his prowl car. Dickie threw his missile at it. It bounced off the windshield, and Trooper Zimmons skidded to a stop. He got out and stood up, towering over the child. With his coat open and his thumbs in his heavily laden gun belt, he looked down at the boy and said, "Dickie Goddard, you do that one more time and I'll tell Santa Claus on you."

Dickie, defiant as ever, looked up at the six-foot-six hulk, resplendent in his fur cap, greatcoat, jodhpurs, and boots, and said, "You're just the sonofabitch that would!"

Zimmons turned beet red, sputtered something at his pint-size antagonist, got in his car, slammed the door, and roared off.

Stan Zimmons was a friend of my parents. The last time I saw him was at a Thanksgiving dinner during my first year of college. It was one of those occasions I'd prefer to forget. But I can't.

My folks had invited Trooper Stan to join us, which, because his family was back in Albany, was for him a special treat. He came dressed in "civilian" clothes, looking rather strange and out of place without his uniform or the belt weighted down with his huge pistol, handcuffs, and billy club. But my father got him to relax by regaling him with stories of childhood escapades, including Halloween pranks. Stan then told a few of his own. I chimed in, saying what they did was tame compared to what my buddies and I had done the year before. As I enthusiastically told how, as the capstone of my school days, we had lassoed rural mailboxes, tipped over seven outhouses, cut the ropes in the belfries of several one-room schools, and swiped a loaded manure spreader, pulling it down Main Street as it spewed out its contents, I suddenly realized to whom I was telling this. The fuzz!

Trooper Stan looked at me incredulously and said, "It was you. My God. We spent a week trying to figure who was responsible for all that vandalism." He looked very upset.

I didn't know what to say and slunk out of the room, leaving my father—who, I should mention, was a former member of Governor Dewey's Crime Prevention Bureau—to make excuses for his delinquent offspring.

I needn't have worried. I later learned that as soon as I left the room they both started laughing about my errant ways. I had finally made my mark in Chateaugay.

The next day I went back to college.

[five]

Once an Orangeman . . .

I STARTED MY academic career as an Orangeman and am ending it as an Orangeman. I first became one at Syracuse University—a raw, innocent seventeen-year-old freshman in September 1950 who, embarrassment notwithstanding, donned the orange beanie insisted upon by the Sophomore Goon Squad and became a Syracusan. Now, about to retire, I spend more and more time in another House of Orange, the Netherlands, where, among other involvements, I frequently lecture at the University of Amsterdam and chair the International Advisory Board of the very new University College at the very old Utrecht University.

While my latest activities are challenging, they are not as bewildering as those days, more than fifty years ago, when I came to Syracuse.

Although my father was a loyal son of SU, having graduated in the class of 1924, my reason for choosing the university had little to do with family tradition, the fact that I had spent my early childhood in the Salt City, or the promise of a first-class education to be obtained at the school locals referred to as being "on the hill." My thoughts were elsewhere. Indeed, unlike many other teenagers, I knew what I wanted to do with my life. I wanted to ski.

Of course I knew that I had to go to college, but I applied only to those most likely to satisfy my basic need (while I went through the motions of getting a degree). What I liked best about Syracuse was that it had an even bigger ski program than did Middlebury or Dartmouth, the other places in which I was most interested. Shortly after receiving notification of admission, I sent in my acceptance. With the acknowledgment came a questionnaire inquiring about my interests. I remember checking off "Ski Club," "Outing Club," and so on, but nothing more cerebral.

I finished my last year of high school year, thinking of exciting days ahead at Syracuse and of all the things I would be learning—things like how to improve my slalom technique, how to rappel off a cliff, and other useful skills.

I graduated from Chateaugay High School in rural upstate New York on June 26, 1950, the day after the Korean War broke out. For most of my male classmates, the war gave a different meaning to their lives. Some were eager to join, others were simply draft bait. I was neither. Not yet eighteen, I was too young. And so I continued to get ready for college. (This meant running up hills day after day to strengthen my legs for the ski season.)

When I arrived on campus, I learned that I was to live in a place with the romantic name of Skytop. When I asked the person at the orientation where it was, she somewhat hesitantly said, "Well, it's a bit of a way from campus. It's near the ski slope." I thought I'd died and gone to heaven. Then I saw Skytop. It was a village of prefabricated barracks made of tin and cardboard. Mine was M-13.

My roommate, Hank Brown, also from north country, and I settled in and tried to make sense of our new estate.

The time at Skytop was a mixed blessing. While it was very close to the ski lodge and slope where I, a new member of SUSKI and, hopefully, the freshman ski team, spent the fall grooming the hill and running to get in shape, it was indeed pretty far from campus, necessitating a bus ride of twenty minutes or more for meals and classes and meetings. Somehow we all survived, and I began to discover there was more to Syracuse than skiing. In fact, one of the first courses I took was to influence my entire career.

At the time of my entry, Syracuse, like most liberal arts institutions, had "distribution requirements" (you had to take courses in the arts and humanities, sciences and languages). In addition, at SU, all freshmen were required to take a course in the Maxwell School of Citizenship. It was an eye-opener. Among other things, we read about and then discussed three notable challenges to American democracy: the Sacco-Vanzetti case, which resulted in the execution of the two immigrant anarchists; the relocation to internment camps of some 110,000 Japanese Americans in the early days of World War II; and the "Peekskill Riots," the attack by World War II veterans and others on the African American singer, political activist, and recipient of the Lenin Peace Prize Paul Robeson following his return to the United States.

I should confess that, in addition to skiing, I had one other major and clearly unrelated interest: social justice. Not surprisingly, all three cases studied in "Citizenship" fired my imagination and increased my sense of outrage about what I would later learn Gunnar Myrdal described as "the American dilemma," that yawning chasm between our professed creed and our conduct. But, for several reasons, it was the relocation of Japanese Americans that raised the most questions in my mind. We read *The Governing of Men* by the psychiatrist/anthropologist Alexander Leighton, about the camp in Poston, Arizona. I found it fascinating and troubling.

"But these are Americans," I remember saying to the instructor, Michael O. Sawyer. Later to become vice chancellor, Mike was not only a mentor, he was a model—in all ways but one. He was the only Republican in the Maxwell School. I was not about to join his party. In fact, at the time, I found the Democrats a bit too conservative for my radical tastes. (Nearly forty years after I graduated, I was invited back to Syracuse by Chancellor Eggers to give a lecture. I was delighted when I learned that Mike Sawyer had been asked to introduce me. After his warm words of welcome, I walked up to the lectern, thanked him, then asked the audience if they knew that, in 1950, their VC was the only Republican in the Maxwell School. Sitting in a chair next to the podium, Mike whispered, *sotto voce*, "I still am!")

My course on "Problems of Democracy" was not the only one that was important to me.

Because I knew I would have to study something besides citizenship and the latest Arlberg ski technique, I decided to look into the fields of zoology and anthropology, my interest having been piqued by years of reading about—actually looking at—stones, bones, and, especially, the exotic people portrayed in the pages of *National Geographic*, to which my family had subscribed for years.

Thus, in addition to required courses in citizenship and in English, German, and philosophy, in my first year I opted to take "Natural History and Field Zoology." My professor, now long deceased, had great sensitivity to variation among most of the world's fauna, including the lesser primates, but he didn't much care for it in humankind. He was a Darwinist—a social Darwinist and a eugenicist. He was also an anti-Semite. I will never forget his cracks about Jews "who think they're pretty smart" and how he made it amply clear that he would knock them (us) down a peg. I was quite shocked and tried to challenge him by working harder than I ever had. In a perverse way, he, too, had pushed me further along the path I would ultimately travel as a student of and later teacher and writer about race and ethnicity.

I finished the course and took several others in zoology, including one on evolution. I was especially interested in lectures on physical anthropology. (Maybe it was because of the interesting books we read or because of the funny names of some of their authors, such as the pre-Seussian Earnest Hooton!) To do more anthropology I had to go back to Maxwell and to the Department of Sociology and Anthropology. There I met the anthropologist and Japanologist Douglas Haring, author of *Racial Differences and Human Resemblances* (a little volume I still assign my own students) and of *Order and Possibility in Social Life.* Haring was a fine teacher and a wonderful human being.

By my second year, I had run out of courses in physical anthropology and began taking those in social and cultural anthropology. There weren't too many of those, so I registered for some in sociology that seemed most closely related. They were very uneven. By far the best were taught by a then-young theorist fresh from Harvard, Merle Adams, and a middle-aged criminologist, Nathan Goldman. Goldman was actually a psychologist turned sociologist. He had worked as a clinician at the famed Judge Baker Clinic, as well as in the Navy brig in Philadelphia during the war, then studied for a Ph.D. at Chicago. The latter is relevant, for he turned me into a "Chicago sociologist," too.

Nate Goldman was one of the best teachers I ever had. I took every course he offered, even in areas in which I had only marginal interest. These included Deviant Behavior (affectionately called "Nuts and Sluts"), Juvenile Delinquency ("JD"), and

Criminology ("Cops and Robbers"). Late in my sophomore year he would become my advisor and lifelong friend.

I have vivid memories of other courses, even though the names of many of the instructors are hard to recall. For example, in what was I think the second semester of freshman English, I was determined to do well, for I had just learned that my draft board looked at college records before deciding whether to issue students deferments. Thus, particularly anxious about my grades, I used every device to force myself to get a grasp on all the material. One of these was a timely memory crutch I invented to help me conjure the names of all the poets we had to read and know. I can still remember the mnemonic. "*H*ere are [r] *f*orty *s*uckers, *y*oung *e*ager *c*haps *j*ust *w*aiting *f*or *a*rmy *s*ervice." Even more surprisingly, I can also still remember the names of the poets: Hardy, Robinson, Frost, Sandburg, Yeats, Eliot, cummings, Jeffers, Williams, Fearing, Auden, and Spender. More important, many of the poems I read then are fixed in my memory, poems like "The Wasteland," "The Love Song of J. Alfred Prufrock," and many by Robert Frost.

That first year I did many things that were not in the course catalog or in the publicity sent out by College Relations or the admissions office. For example, I learned what it was to hang out, drink beer, and sing the songs of the Tenth Mountain Division with fellow skiers at a place called Tecumseh and to hang out and drink beer—no songs—with my nonskiing buddies at The Orange. I was a "participant observer" (I learned the expression in my first sociology course) at pep rallies, at mixers, and in a memorable water fight that took place on the two blocks between the Deke house and Thornden Park. It turned into quite a fracas, with the city cops embroiled in a shouting match with students while they (actually, we) put sugar in their gas tanks. We were caught and yelled at, but few were arrested.

Somehow I made it through that first year. I learned many things—not least that I wasn't quite the hotshot skier I thought I was (at least in comparison to the real experts on the varsity team). I left campus at the end of the second semester thinking, without any clear idea of what preparation might be involved, that maybe I should become a professor. (At the time, hedging my dreams, I thought it would be especially nice to work at a place like Middlebury, or Dartmouth, or Syracuse, having my cake—I still loved to ski—and . . .)

Knowing that I would never become another Zeno Colò, the great Italian downhiller from Cortina d'Ampezzo who would win gold in the 1952 Winter Olympics at Oslo and who was our hero at the time—or even a credible member of the SU team—in my second year, I attended clinics of the Eastern States Ski Association and the New York State Instructors, got certified to teach skiing, and turned "pro." Thereafter, I devoted my free time to teaching skiing, both at the very fine ski school run by the university and through the city recreation department. I found I liked the teaching almost as much as the skiing. Perhaps it was an omen.

That year I also made the not-too-surprising decision to do a combined major in sociology and anthropology. I took my coursework more seriously and strove to excel in the classroom as I had tried to do on the ski slopes. In the beginning my success rate was about the same, but I was gaining confidence.

And for the first time I got on the dean's list. Unfortunately, it was not the one that parents gloat about.

Sometime in late February of 1952 my father received a letter from Dean Eric Faigle alerting him to the fact that I had taken three cuts in Religion 1b. It went on to say, "We are calling him to the office today and explaining the necessity for him to attend classes regularly. Any student is in difficulty who takes more than three cuts during the term." (N.B. After more than forty years as college professor, I still marvel at the idea that the dean of the faculty knew or cared that I was cutting classes.)

My concerned father did call me and tell me of the letter (which he kept and I still have). In a solemn voice, he told me to shape up. I argued with him, pointing out that the class came in the late afternoon when we skiers had to work out. It was Faigle himself who, at some convocation, had told us "Life is about making choices." And, after all, I was making mine. I can still remember feeling my father squelch a smile while telling me not to be such a wise guy.

My third year was a whirlwind of academic and extracurricular activity. Well ensconced in my major and now working very closely with Doug Haring, Nate Goldman, Merle Adams, and several other Maxwell professors, I also served as a part-time group worker at the Huntington Neighborhood House, spending three afternoons a week with those who in that pre-PC era were variously called "troubled youth," "potential delinquents," or just plain "troublemakers." I also continued to teach skiing, served as president of SUSKI, and chaired the ski events for Winter Carnival. It was a good year, forever marred, however, by the tragic death of my close friend and fellow member of the Winter Carnival Committee, Carrie Lou Andrews. Carrie Lou was killed in a car accident while returning from the Dartmouth Winter Carnival where, we had joked before she left, she would serve as a spy, trying to learn the secrets of their well-known successes.

Shortly after her fatal accident, fellow skiers and I proposed that the ski-jumping events at the upcoming Winter Carnival be named in her honor. I am told that the Carrie Lou Andrews Memorial Jump, the first event of its kind ever named for a woman, continues to this day.

During that third year, while still living in the house on Comstock, Lew Rhodes, my new roommate, Jerry Lish, a skiing buddy, and I decided to tweak the nose of the Interfraternity Council. We started our own little group called Alpha Sigma Sigma, putting the Greek letters on the corner of the windshield of Jerry's convertible and on the door to our room. As part of our sophomoric junior-year prank, we even advertised for pledges. Not long afterward we received a notice from the Interfraternity Council (I seem to remember there was also an article in the university newspaper, the *Daily Orange*) saying that what we were doing wasn't funny, that we were making a mockery of fraternities. I remember feeling like Henry Higgins after Eliza Doolittle begins to speak the King's English: "By George, [they've] got it!"

I was never much of a joiner, but I was always a competitor. Sometimes I won; sometimes I lost. (I had been nominated for election to a senior honors society but hadn't made it.) Arthur Siegel, an editor at the *DO;* several others who had lost out in various campus elections, coveted positions, and memberships in honorary societies; and I organized the "SOBs" (as in "Sorry Old Boy"). It was a losers' society. We talked of having a flag with a purple shaft and lapel pins in the form of golden screws. And, while those remained fantasies, we did write to Adlai Stevenson, the guy we thought was the greatest loser of then-recent times, asking him to be our honorary chairman. He wrote back, agreeing to do it. (I was doubly glad then that I'd worked for his ill-fated campaign.)

Finally, senior year. The 1953–54 school year was made especially memorable by Lanny Okun and Bill D'Angelo's wonderful musical "White Bucks and Tales" (I still listen to the recording); by the Stockingfoot Dance at Drumlins—a sort of public country club—where I, cochair of Winter Carnival, could finally unwind and where I introduced Hedy, my fiancée (and now wife of nearly fifty years), to my friends; and by both the waning of my enthusiasm for living and breathing skiing and the waxing of my commitment to scholarship and activism. Much of my free time was spent trying to learn about, then apply to, various graduate schools. I narrowed the choice to Columbia and Cornell, both of which offered fellowships, and chose the latter, having decided that was the best place for me, for there I could study applied anthropology and work with Alexander Leighton, author of the book on the Japanese Americans' experiences that had so impressed me in my freshman course. As it happened, Leighton was in the field during most of my four years in Ithaca, and I ended up working with other anthropologists and a number of sociologists, too.

That last year I lived in an off-campus apartment with my friend the ski champion Joe DeCarlo, who was in every way much closer in background, looks, manners, and, above all, ability to the wiry Italian racer Zeno Colò than I or any of our friends. In fact, "Zeno" became Joe's nickname. He graduated in January and immediately joined the air force, going to flight school and beginning a career as a second lieutenant, flying fighter planes.

As I sat in Archbold Stadium on graduation day in June, 1954, listening to Harold Stassen tell us to keep the faith (God knows he did—he never seemed to give up his quest for the presidency!), I kept thinking about my four years, the reason I came, and how much more I learned there was to life: wonderful teachers—and some real losers; great friends; memorable lectures, such as those by Senator Wayne Morse and by his nemesis, Senator Joseph McCarthy, and the one at the Phi Beta Kappa initiation, all in Latin, which hardly a single member of our supposedly academically gifted group could understand; special events, conferences, lectures, and concerts; special people like Charlie Noble (the university chaplain), George Earle (the ski coach), Mike Sawyer, and Nate Goldman; and discussions (we called them "bull sessions") about what we all had witnessed together—Nixon's "Checkers" speech, the fall of MacArthur and the rise of McCarthyism, Adlai Stevenson's campaign (I'm still "Looking Forward to Greater Tomorrows," as it said on the placard I carried in political rallies), and the watershed Supreme Court decision Brown v. Board of Education, decided just before we graduated.

Then there were those traditions like Winter Weekends, with races, dances, and ice sculptures, and "Colgate" weekends, too, with games, parties, and great poster contests showing the power of the Orangemen over the puny Red Raiders. (In those days, for some reason, little Colgate—with twenty-five hundred students—was the principal rival of Syracuse, which, at the time, had three times as many undergraduates.) Even today I vividly remember the cleverness of two particular gigantic posters. One of them showed the legendary football coach, square-jawed, close-cropped Ben Schwarzwalder, in a general's uniform pointing to the midline on a map of Korea superimposed on a gridiron. On one end were the words "50 Yard Line"; on the other, "38th Parallel." Schwarzwalder was saying, "No Reds will cross that line."

The second poster was of a huge open book. The left-hand page showed "our" guys in the shower room, wearing nothing but orange towels and big grins. The other page pictured corpses in red Colgate uniforms strewn across the football field of battle. The caption, in giant letters, read, "The Naked and the Dead." The glee on the faces of the Orangemen said it all.

For years on my many trips to the Netherlands, I have been tempted to tell my friends and hosts that there is another House of Orange and that I grew up there. I'm not sure they would understand, but the fact is I, too, am an Orangeman.

Do I have any regrets?

After teaching for many years at Smith, a liberal-arts college with only twenty-eight hundred students, I am often asked if I might not have preferred to have gone to such a place or, say, to Amherst or Swarthmore or Oberlin myself. I am tempted to say, "Well, it would depend on their facilities for skiing and proximity to the slopes." Instead I give them my heartfelt answer. "No, I liked what I had at Syracuse and what it gave me."

I have often described Smith as a miniuniversity. I see Syracuse as the other side of the coin, a college writ large. At least it was in my day. We had a keen sense of community. It was our place.

While I have fond memories and have been generally quite impressed with what I have heard about what has been happening on the hill over the decades, I long harbored a major beef: the fact that some PR person thought the venerable emblem of the university, with laurel leaves and a Latin inscription, was archaic and got rid of it in favor of the stylized "SU" logo, which looks like that of every other school. For me, Syracuse has always meant SUOS CULTORES SCIENTIA CORONAT. I was delighted to see that motto back on the top of a letter recently received from classmate John Beach and to learn that the whole emblem of *our* "House of Orange" has been officially reinstated by the powers that be.

[six]

The Music Lover

MY MOTHER HAD a thing about music. She loved it. Classical, popular, jazz, folk. She went to every concert she could. She went to hear Jascha Heifetz, Artur Rubinstein, the New York Philharmonic, various big bands, Pete Seeger, Josh White, Odetta; she went to operas, ballets, symphonies, oratorios, musical comedies, small ensembles, folk festivals, hootenannies. She bought records, hundreds of them—first 78s, later 33s. There were symphonic performances by the greatest orchestras, concerti with her favorite soloists, arias by opera singers, and "authentic" ballads sung by old crones recorded by Alan Lomax. She loved them all.

It was in 1948, when we moved from Syracuse to a tiny town on the Canadian border in upstate New York, that she really came into her own. Instead of continuing her career as a social worker, she began teaching music appreciation under the auspices of Cornell University School of Agriculture's extension program.

My mother was convinced that, with enough exposure, anyone could come to have her love for music. She often told me that although she came from a family of unschooled tailors from Poland, her parents knew the value of two vital forces: music and education. And if these could be combined, so much the better.

The Felds never could afford a car, but they did buy a secondhand upright piano on which all three kids were given lessons. Harry took to it, and later to the violin, like a duck to water. He won a scholarship to the Eastman School of Music and eventually became a professional violinist. (A classmate, with whom he played quartets in my grandparents' living room, was a young man named Mitch Miller.)

Sam was tone-deaf, or pretended he was. In any case, he was pretty much a musical lost cause. He went to the University of Rochester, then joined the Indian Service, spending his entire professional life in the Dakotas. He retired to his wife's home city of Telaqua, Oklahoma, never, so far as I can determine, having come to appreciate what the rest of the family thought so essential.

My mother took her piano lessons very seriously. She practiced diligently, first with the idea of becoming a professional musician like Harry, then with the thought of at least being his accompanist. She wasn't very successful in either. So she, too, went to the U of R. She majored in German, married my father, who was a social worker, and became one, too. Yet, she would often say that someday she knew that she would return to music, to teach and to study. She began fixating on the cello. She bought recordings of Gregor Piatigorsky, Leonard Rose, and Pablo Casals. She talked about taking cello lessons—for some thirty years.

For her fiftieth birthday, my wife and I, both still graduate students at the time, bought her a rather pricey cello bow. It was all we could afford. We sent it to her accompanied by a note saying my father could buy "the rest of the outfit." He called us the night she opened her present to say that he was sending us a set of piano keys for our anniversary! He also said he had been about to get her the cello but had discovered that it was too late—arthritis had cramped her hands too much to play one. (I never found out why he hadn't done it sooner or why she never bought one herself and started taking lessons.)

Her excursus into teaching predated the business with the birthday bow by some ten years. Music Appreciation turned into three separate courses: two long, one rather short. There was a course on the classics, attended, if I remember correctly, by the leading ladies of Chateaugay, New York—wives of businessmen and wealthy farmers—and by two ministers and a local doctor (the only men in the group.) They would meet in a classroom at the local school, where my father would set up a record player, arrange the chairs, and then head for home to listen to a ball game. Sometimes I would go to the class and watch my mother try to explain something of the history of Western music, starting with Gregorian chants and moving on through the ages and periods. Baroque. Romantic. Modern. Always there were examples to hear, always there were comments about "leitmotivs," "sonata forms," and other esoteric-sounding matters.

I'm not sure how much her students took in, but they did come back, week after week. And some also showed up at the other long-running class, on folk music. For some reason this one was never held at the school, but in our living room. There my mother insisted that everyone sit on the floor. This was no small matter for the ladies, who were a rather prim and proper bunch. Yet somehow she got them to the floor as she would tell them about Leadbelly—"His real name," she would explain, "was Huddy Ledbetter"—and then she would teach them the words to "Goodnight, Irene" one of the folk tunes he made famous; she would tell them that most of what we call folk music wasn't written by an identifiable composer but just grew out of an oral tradition of African slaves and English people who ended up in Appalachia. She always wove a bit of social history into her lectures, relating, for example, stories of the Irish immigrants who came to New York and Boston after the great famine in the mid-nineteenth century, carrying with them old songs like "Danny Boy." Their offspring, she said, would then make up songs about their time and troubles in the New World—songs like "Paddy Works on the Railroad" and "Drill, Ye Tarriers, Drill." She told her students about gospel, blues, even klezmer, at a time when, for most, "Jewish jazz" meant that played by the likes of Benny Goodman or Stan Getz. And she played those god-awful scratchy Lomax records so they could really get the feel of the roots of it all. I remember trying to dissuade her from doing that part of her "listen and learn" exercise, even if the music was, as she always stressed, "authentic." (Years later I would come to appreciate the richness of what the Lomaxes collected and preserved.)

The best—and, to me, funniest—part of each session was the last half hour, when my mother would teach a cowboy song or sea chantey or canon to the rather inhibited women and men and watch them come alive when, on rare occasion, they got it just right. Shyly they would beam, then blush, as if they'd been sinning.

The short course always took place from mid-November to

mid-December. It was focused on Christmas carols and attracted a much greater cross section of locals. Catholics came, as well as the Protestant core. Young people, as well as the older ones. The plan was to create a community chorale to sing to shut-ins at Christmas. It was something my mother thought was a wonderful Chateaugay tradition. Surprised that no one had done it for many years, she, one of the only Jews in town, would meet her group in the Methodist Church one night, the Catholic Church the next, the school auditorium, and then in the basement of the Presbyterian Church to get ready for the big event. For the three nights before Christmas, with me pulling a sled with a portable foot-pumped army-surplus miniature organ, we would go up and down the streets of Chateaugay singing "O Holy Night," "O Little Town of Bethlehem," and some that were not at all familiar until my mother taught them. (The French Canadians especially liked those that were in French; the few Poles also liked one she had learned from a Polish friend and passed on to them.)

On Christmas Eve, many of her choristers—and lots of college kids home for the holidays—would stop by to wish us "Season's Greetings" and to thank my mother for her musical leadership. It was heady stuff, and it could be matched only by her getting me to appreciate it as much as she did.

She tried. She gave me lessons on the piano. I hated it. She let me choose another instrument. I picked the clarinet. I succeeded only in learning a very screechy scale and two songs (one a very primitive rendition of "When the Saints Go Marching In") and in driving both parents to distraction. They let me quit.

The last resort was the osmosis approach. Every day when I got home from school, music would be playing on the Victrola. Sometimes it was one of the folk records in the Lomax collection, but mostly it was classical. I heard it, sort of.

Then, one day, she got what she had longed for, or thought she got it. Her prodigal son called her. She was at a friend's house, and I was at home with a schoolmate, Paul Dupree. "Where," I asked her, "is the Tagliavini record?"

She said, "Look on the second record shelf under the *o*s, for opera." I put down the phone to look. She, I later learned, was beaming at the other end.

I came back to say I couldn't find it. She said I should look under *t*—maybe she'd put it back under the singer's name. I said I'd call her back if I couldn't find it.

She hung up the phone, turned to her friends, and said something to the effect that if you expose people to enough good music, eventually even the most resistant will come to love it.

I called back. "Mom, I can't find that Tagliavini record," and asked her where else I might look. I remember her asking me why I wanted to hear that particular recording. "I mean," she said, "there are other excellent renditions of the same arias."

"Oh," I said, "I want that one. I want Paul to see what happens to the dog's ears when he sings that high note. It's a riot. I mean, Rusty goes nuts, starts howling. You know."

She didn't say anything. In fact, I thought she'd hung up. Then I heard her sigh.

[seven]

On the Slopes of Mt. Allegro

SOME YEARS AGO the editor of *Contemporary Sociology* asked me to review the reissued version of Jerre Mangione's classic memoir, *Mount Allegro.* I did so with pleasure, for it had long been one of my favorite works of "literary ethnography," a wonderful portrait of Italian American life. It is something else, too, as I noted in my review:

> *Mount Allegro* has additional meaning for me, for my mother and her brothers grew up in the very same Italian and Jewish (formerly German and Irish) section of Rochester that Mangione describes. Many of his accounts of Papa, Uncle Nino, Compare Caligero, Mr. Michelangelo, Mr. Bernstein, Mr. Solomon, and *gli americani* have a special ring of verisimilitude, for I had heard the stories—or some like them—long before I first read Mangione's book nearly forty years ago.

The stories I remember best are about the Carbones, Quadrozzis, Tomeis, Regners, Levys, and Felds. But mostly they are about the Felds, my Polish-born maternal grandparents, and the Carbones, their next-door neighbors from southern Italy.

Both families had come to America in the early years of the twentieth century. After several years of struggling in New York and Albany, my grandparents moved to Rochester, drawn by the opportunity to find work as custom tailors in a city that was rapidly becoming the center of the men's clothing industry. Wolf Feld (who became known as William) took a job at Hickey-Freeman's. His wife, Celia, did piecework at home.

The Carbones, John, a shoemaker, and his wife, Jenny, came to Rochester a few years later. Within a short time the two families became next-door neighbors. The families had mortgaged themselves for life, purchasing nearly identical houses on a street that would be known half a century later as the border of the "riot area."

The two men, both quiet and thoughtful, rarely engaged in lengthy discussions. But they were good friends. Their wives, two hardly educated street philosophers with different world views and religious orientations—one was a devout Catholic, the other, like her husband, an active member of the Workmen's Circle and a secular Jew—were close companions and fellow confidants. In accents that were later to be caricatured on such radio programs as *Abie's Irish Rose* and *Life with Luigi*, they shared their hopes and their fears. They gossiped. And they argued about everything.

Together they watched the world around them change. They watched their families grow up. The Carbone children, Roma, Jimmy, and Leah, stayed quite close to the nest, remaining in the immediate neighborhood and raising their own families there. The Felds went farther afield. My Uncle Harry, a violinist, took a teaching job in South Carolina and eventually moved to New York; his younger brother, Sam, joined the Indian Service and spent his entire career in the Dakotas. Both of them and my mother, Lillian (who moved to Syracuse, then to the northern Adirondacks, then to Tucson), kept in touch with the old neighbors. For years they exchanged letters and holiday greetings.

The older women remained close. They attended parties in one another's homes. My grandmother dressed up for Carbone christenings and confirmations and weddings as if they were for members of her own family. On Easter Sunday a troop of Carbone children and nieces and nephews marched through the Felds' parlor showing off their finery. On Christmas those same children delivered delicious pastries to my grandparents' house. And, *quid pro quo,* almost every week plates of gefilte fish and paprika-speckled chicken and pots of soup with homemade noodles were taken next door to be enjoyed by the Carbones.

The families shared hard times as well. One of my most vivid memories is of my grandfather's funeral, when the rabbi called the names of those most carefully chosen to bear his pall. He read from the list my father had prepared: Rose, Berman, Astrachan,

Greenstone, Pelton, and Quadrozzi. Mario Quadrozzi was Leah Carbone's husband.

Funerals inevitably involve reminiscing—and cosmic thoughts. Shortly after my grandfather died, my grandmother and Jenny Carbone, by then both in their late seventies, were sitting on the sun porch of the Feld house, slowly swinging back and forth on an old-fashioned glider. My wife and I were inside. The window was open, and we eavesdropped on a fascinating discussion about life and death and religion. Finally, trying to give some closure to an obviously irreconcilable difference of opinion, we hear my grandmother say: "You know, Mrs. Carbone" (she was always "Mrs. Carbone"), "I figure it this way. We got the father. You got the son. So what?"

Mrs. Carbone thought for a moment, then said to Mrs. Feld (she was always "Mrs. Feld"), "You right."

Neighborhoods change and, as Jerre Mangione relates in an afterword to the Morningside edition of *Mount Allegro*, his did, too. Young people leave. Old people die. New people move in. The rhythms of life are affected. The sounds and smells are different. Often the faces are different, too.

Sometime in the late 1950s, the people next door to us moved out and sold their home to a black family. Mrs. Carbone was very upset; so were many others on the street. My grandmother—perhaps more liberal because of her longtime commitment to socialism or because of the politics of her college-educated children and politically active grandchildren, or because her second son had married a Cherokee woman from Oklahoma in the early 1930s—was deeply disturbed at the attitudes of her neighbors. On the same old glider she admonished Mrs. Carbone, reminding her what it was like forty years earlier when the local residents opposed the intrusion, as they saw it, of Italians and Jews.

"They're different," I heard Jenny Carbone say. "Ma son' Negr'."

My grandmother argued and argued, but to no avail. Mrs. Carbone was not going to be budged. Nor were the others. They were worried about their neighborhood, worried about their property values.

Still, the black family moved in. Mother, father, and five little kids. Most of the people on the street seemed to ignore them, to treat them as if they were invisible. But my grandmother saw them and welcomed them.

Soon the children were in and out of our house, ever eager to enjoy some pint-sized loaves of sweet-tasting twisted bread, *challa*, that "Mimi" made for them.

Not long after they had become part of the local scene, I happened to be in Rochester. I asked my grandmother how things were going. She told me that Mrs. Carbone was still somewhat upset and that, in part, she had a point. I was not surprised that Mrs. Carbone had not yet come around, but was troubled by my grandmother's seeming change of heart. I pressed her a bit for an explanation.

"Well," she said, "they are young people and we are old. We like peace and quiet. They're very noisy. Maybe we've forgotten what it is to have many children running around."

"But," she added with a characteristic shrug, "it will work out."

Two years later, she became very ill and had several lengthy bouts in the hospital. My mother and her brothers made the painful decision that, since she could no longer manage alone, the house would have to be sold. They put it in the hands of a local realtor. They said there were to be no restrictions of race, creed, or color.

The real estate agent found us a buyer almost immediately. He was a young man who was a recent arrival from southern Italy and had come to work at Hickey's. In an age of accelerating change, it seemed that history was repeating itself. The Carbones were delighted.

Another year passed and I was back in Rochester to see my grandmother, now living permanently in the Jewish Home for the Aged. With the family home sold, I stayed with the Carbones. Late one night I returned from the home to find Mrs. Carbone, then eighty-five, still awake, waiting to serve me some of her jet-black coffee and specially prepared *meringhe.*

We chatted for a while and then, still curious about "race relations" in that little corner of the world, I asked her how she felt about the neighbors.

She replied with animated vehemence. Wringing her hands, she exclaimed, "They're terrible. They don't seem to like us. They don't behave nice."

"The Negroes?" I asked her.

"No," she said, "they're O.K. It's those damn *ee-mee-grants.*"

[eight]

Indian Giver

FROM THE START, Camp Chateaugay, established by my parents in 1945 in the northern Adirondacks, bore their progressive-school stamp of "creative camping." There were all the regular activities—water and land sports, arts and crafts, overnight hikes and canoe trips; but there were also a number of program innovations that clearly reflected their liberal attitudes. There were all sorts of projects on folk life and politics and on such subjects as "the dignity of labor" and "comparative religion." There were special days to celebrate the spirit of the United Nations and to appreciate "Mankind" itself. Among the most memorable of our traditions were Indian ceremonies at the beginning and end of each season.

Back in those days, Native Americans and their stereotyped nobility and resourcefulness were an integral part of programs at many summer camps; they were basis for activities like basket weaving and lacrosse and ideas about man and nature. At Chateaugay, as at various camps where my parents had worked before, the season was opened and closed with enactments of dramatic meetings between those representing the indigenous people of the area and the intruders who now occupied their ancient land.

The season opener went like this: With the entire camp community waiting on the beach behind a roaring campfire, the blanketed and feathered representatives of the "Tribe of Panther Mountain" would suddenly appear out of the waning light of dusk, paddling toward them in torchlit canoes. They would land their crafts, then silently walk to the edge of the gathering and one of them, the "chief," would greet my father, to whom he referred as the "Great White Sachem," with a stern-faced "How!"

Sachem would reply, "We are pleased to greet our brothers from across the waters."

Then the chief would continue: "We have waited many moons to hear the voices of children echo from the far side of Shat-O-Gay, the lake that is the source of our strength and sustenance, and from the land of our forefathers where deer run wild and pines grow tall, where the sunshine sparkles on the rocks and icy water reflects the purple mountains and the glories of the Earth Mother.

"And now we come to lend you several of our most important possessions, each to be used with care so your campers can become more conscious of their surroundings, stronger and healthier, and more creative, too.

"In two moons we will return to recover these items."

It was always at this point in the ceremony that some wise-cracking thirteen-year-old would whisper (loud enough for all to hear), "Indian giver!" and all his buddies would start to laugh only to be hushed by a counselor who could hardly suppress his own giggles.

After that almost predictable interlude, the visiting party would present its gifts: a sheaf of wheat symbolizing food and health, a beaded moccasin for arts and crafts, a canoe paddle for aquatics, and a bow and arrow for sports and good sportsmanship.

My father would solemnly accept each item, promising that his campers would use it well and that he would return it at the end of the season for safekeeping over the long winter months. True to his word, each year for two decades he did precisely that.

It never surprised any but the youngest campers that the Panther Mountain Indians were our staff members and that their leader was the head counselor or program director, outfitted in makeshift buckskins and a beaded Sioux headdress of eagle feathers. Yet most went along with the fiction, enjoying the pageantry and understanding the symbolic character of the ritual.

Given my father's plan that I would succeed him as the camp's director, I was destined to work my way up from paddler to torch bearer to chief of the Panther Mountain tribe and, in the future, to take his place on the other side of the beach.

When I became chief, I decided it was time for some innovation. Instead of coming in canoes for the season-ending ceremony, I suggested we hide behind the docks, light kerosene-soaked torches and then, swimming underwater with flames above, rise from the depths and walk onto the beach where the entire camp family of 180 awaited us.

My fellow "tribesmen" reluctantly agreed. Because it was cold, I suggested we coat our nearly naked bodies with grease. It was a big mistake.

Things started smoothly enough. Slathered in Crisco and decorated in war paint, we lit our torches, swam around the docks with only the flames exposed, then rose up and waded ashore. We stood silently. My father and I exchanged greetings, and he gave back each present (with that inevitable snickering Greek chorus murmuring about "Indian givers" in the background). He kept his composure as he solemnly explained to us how each item had been used while we tried to stand still without shaking from the cold or twitching from the swarms of mosquitoes apparently attracted to our tasty torsos. It was a night to remember.

While the anthropologist I became shudders at our repeated violation of a host of Native American traditions and at our creation of rituals based on naïve stereotypes, I must say that the sentiments that underscored the inauthentic pageantry were as genuine as the artifacts that were used—the headdresses and horsehair roaches, the moccasins, and the bow and arrow.

In 1958, illness forced my father to retire, and my wife and I took over the directorship of the camp. But after a few seasons the excitement of being in charge began to wane. After a few more I was ready and eager to move on to other challenges. Eventually I did.

We sold Camp Chateaugay in 1968. I have only been back once. But I understand that those who now stand where we stood still open each season with a visit from representatives of the Tribe of Panther Mountain who bring them four special gifts—a sheaf of wheat, a beaded moccasin, a paddle, and a bow—which they promise to use wisely and return at the end of the summer.

[nine]

Vivat Academia

EACH YEAR THE college with which I am affiliated has an opening convocation. It is a half-serious, half-frivolous convention. Nearly the entire community gathers to hear an invocation by one of the chaplains, a choral piece or two sung by the world-renowned glee club, and a talk by the president. But there is more to it than this.

We on the faculty march in full academic regalia, a parade of robed, hooded, and sweating figures trying to appear solemn as we process into a hall filled floor to balcony with twenty-six hundred whooping, hollering, stomping undergraduates who arrived but minutes before. Waving balloons and holding pennants, they are clothed in every sort of imaginable garb—and some that defies imagination.

Even the singers, already ensconced on risers at the back of the stage, have funny hats that contrast sharply with the austerity of their choirly robes. The absurdity is compounded when they lift their magnificent voices in sounds rarely heard at pep rallies.

With all the craziness, the annual ritual is, as we sociologists say, highly functional. At least this is how I tried to explain the elaborate pomp and curious circumstances to a group of foreign graduate students who had come to spend nine months with us studying American society and culture.

Men and women from very different worlds, from China, Colombia, France, India, Italy, Yugoslavia, and six other places, having been urged to attend all college functions, were astounded at what they observed. They wanted to know what it was all about; they wanted to know its *deeper* meaning, too.

I told them that the convocation is like a rite of renewal.

Homage is paid to the Great Spirit (and to the trustees and other benefactors). Old-timers reassert their fidelity, and novices take their vows to *alma mater*. All are caught up in the fervor of the new beginning, in the excitement of being part of a special community. We reverently salute each other and our spiritual leader. (One year a new bit of campus iconography was a ten-foot-high banner with the words "Hail Mary" hanging from the front and center of the balcony. It was a greeting to a new Smith president, Mary Maples Dunn.)

As I spoke, I realized that I was not being entirely facetious.

American academic rituals are a bit bewildering, even to those who participate in them. And, truth to speak, while I find them all fascinating professionally, certain ones—like our convocation—are a bit much.

Then why do I do it? I don't have to. (The students are expected to attend; we are only encouraged to do so.) The colloquy with the foreign observers made me think about it.

I reflected on my first few convocations at the college. I was a very junior faculty member seated in the back row, catching glimpses of the multitude between the mortarboards of my senior colleagues, shifting uncomfortably on a folding chair, and silently forswearing any future involvement in such ridiculous activity. I remembered that something would invariably happen to turn my annoyance into involvement that would force me to relax and become something more than a reluctant participant.

It wasn't the cheers of the throng or their rhythmic clapping as we marched in, nor was it the words of the speaker, even when I agreed with them. No. Something else got me then. It gets me today.

What then and now still triggers the response that engages me and many of my colleagues, what proves to be the latent function of all this folderol, is the last number on the program, the singing of "Gaudeamus Igitur." The old drinking melody is hoary to some, schmaltzy to many. But we love it. We especially love the third verse, when the tempo picks up, the voices grow louder, and the room resounds with "Vivat academia / Vivant professores." It makes us feel good.

When friends from other universities want me to admit that

our sort of convocation is anachronistic, an attempt to recapture a more innocent past, I am inclined to agree. Yet I confess to giving them a double-barreled response. I say, "Yes, but . . . ," for I know that, at convocation and again at commencement, for a few fleeting moments they're playing *our* song.

part two

Field Notes of a Peripatetic Professor

[ten]

Travel Sickness

MY COLLEAGUES ALWAYS kid me about my peripatetic existence. One never fails to ask if I am making a guest appearance on campus this semester. Another exclaims to all within earshot that I am the only "tenured visiting professor" in the Connecticut Valley.

The fact is that I am on the road (or in the air) much of the time. Almost every break I'm off to somewhere overseas. In between there are regular trips to Boston, New York, Washington, Cape Cod, and Southern Maine.

I don't particularly like to fly or even to drive for long hours. Getting there is not half the fun, not even 10 percent of it. But every time I get a call saying someone would like me to give a lecture, attend a meeting, participate in a conference, or write a travel piece about anywhere from Memphis to Melbourne, I seem to say, "Well, my schedule is awfully tight. You have to give me a few days," and then, not invariably but all too often, I call back to say, "I'll do it."

As soon as I hang up the phone, I call my wife. Depending on the character of the invitation (and the venue), I say, "Guess where I am [or we are] going in March?"

As time for departure on one of my academic, extracurricular, or combined sojourns draws nigh, I begin to get anxious. It never fails.

"Why am I doing this?" I ask myself. "So what if I never get to Timbuktu (or Lahore or St. Petersburg or Boise)!" "Why make yet another trip to Kyoto?" "Can't I live without going to my umpteenth meeting of the Society for the Study of Society?"

Sometimes I say these things aloud, as I lie awake tossing and turning. Quite reasonably, my wife will ask, "Then why did you say yes? Why do you keep aggravating yourself?"

Like my own, Hedy's queries are rhetorical. And she knows it. I do it because I can't say no. I'm a travel junkie.

It's not so much the open road that beckons but the change of scenery, the sights and smells of places near and far, that draws me away from Northampton, Massachusetts, the town local boosters call the "Paradise of America."

Once I am wherever it is I am going, I have a renewed sense of purpose. I revel in the familiarity of strange environs, run and walk the avenues and backstreets, visit new sites, spend hours with hosts and colleagues, and . . . think of *home.* It never fails. Whether I am gone for a week or a month or a semester or a year, there is a time when I ask myself, "What am I doing here?"; when I wonder what is going on back in Northampton; when I wish I hadn't gone away because I suddenly realize that I am missing something I had decided I could do without just to satisfy my need for a travel fix.

My thoughts of home are both general and specific. In my mind's eye I see the town we have lived in for more than forty years and the scenes I take for granted when I am there: the long views of the Holyoke Range above the city, the Saturday market on Center Street, the Mill River and the path where I like to run with my dog, our home on Paradise Road. I even visualize and get nostalgic about the utterly chaotic office I was so eager to escape.

Once I begin to think of such things, I start getting restless. I am torn between obligations yet to fulfill and the desire to wrap things up. Not infrequently I will call the airline to see if I can get on a flight a day or two before my scheduled date of return.

Whether I head back early or according to the original plan, I find that I am just as excited by the announcement that "We will soon be landing at Bradley International Airport" as I was at hearing "We are now approaching Beijing (or Berlin or Bogota)" a few weeks before. I especially enjoy coming into Bradley at dusk, seeing the trees and lights and houses of the New England countryside, then riding up to Northampton the back way, through Suffield, West Springfield, and on home.

The morning after every trip I get up very early. I put on my jogging gear and head down to the river with the dog. There is nothing like it. Nothing in the world.

Back in my office, I enjoy seeing my students, greeting my friends, hearing the same old curmudgeons welcome me home then ask, "How long are you going to stay this time?"

I want to tell them that I'm back for good, but I know it would be a lie.

As I go through the piles of mail on my desk, I feel the adrenaline increasing the second I spot a letter with a foreign stamp. When the phone rings, I can't help but wonder who is calling. I think that maybe it's somebody who wants to invite me to Moscow. I've never been to Moscow. "Now that would be interesting," I say to myself, "I could see Red Square and visit the Kremlin, talk to people about my work . . ."

[eleven]

A Year in the Midlands

SEVERAL YEARS AGO I found a copy of Arthur Koestler's book *The Call-Girls* on the remainder table of a local bookshop. Curious about why he would write about this subject, I started reading it as soon as I got home. It wasn't what I expected, but it had an odd effect on me.

As I turned the pages I was immediately transported back to the early days of my initiation into the rites, rituals, and free rides of academics. You see, Koestler's "call girls" were folks like me. Supported by their institutions or by grants, they would go to conferences in nearby places and those quite far: Gstaad, Copenhagen, Honolulu, and Rio. There they would spend three days complaining about how silly it was to spend so much money to hear people they knew say things they'd already heard over and over at various other places. Then, on the fourth day, they would decide where to meet the next year!

But, of course, academic meetings have other purposes. They serve as job markets and opportunities to meet fellow professors from other places. In fact, I shouldn't bad-mouth the enterprise, because my own international experiences actually began, rather serendipitously, at one of those meetings.

I, a very junior, untenured assistant professor, was sitting in the Sheraton Hotel in Washington, D.C., sometime in the early 1960s. A stout fellow with a heavy Russian accent sat down beside me in the coffee shop. Leaning over and reading my badge, he said, "Hello, Rose, I'm Neustadt. I just read about you in the *New York Times.*"

"Who, me?" I squeaked.

But it was true. An article describing a recent piece of research I had just completed was published that very day as part of a series of articles on the catholicity of papers being delivered at the World Congress of Sociology we were both attending. Neustadt said he would like to know more about my study. I told him, and, to make a long story very short, he ended up inviting me to spend a year at the University of Leicester in England, where he was professor of sociology and, as they say there, head of department.

Within a year I received both a formal invitation and a grant to spend 1964–65 as a Fulbright professor in the English Midlands. I was excited and quickly accepted, but not before asking for and receiving permission to take what is known in my trade as "LWOP" (leave without pay). It turned out that the Leicester stipend, even when augmented by support from the Council on the International Exchange of Scholars, was far less than expected. My wife and I and our two little kids learned to rough it during a year of adventures in merry, cold (it was freezing) England—and on the continent, too.

The first day was especially memorable. After a wonderful Fulbright-funded voyage on the SS *Rotterdam*, we picked up a car and drove from Southampton to Leicestershire, with dreams of Oxonian colleges and other English delights, gleaned mainly from British novels and films, dancing in our heads. Finally, we pulled into the city that was to be our home for the coming academic year, a place that was, well, different from Oxford. I turned to my wife and said, "We've just traveled three thousand miles and ended up in Holyoke." (Holyoke is an industrial city near our Northampton base that had seen better days and is still struggling. Leicester, by contrast, has undergone a remarkable renaissance since we lived there.)

Our initial disappointment was compounded the next day when we learned that we couldn't even speak the language.

Our daughter, Lies, had come down with a bad cold on the ship. She needed cough medicine and Kleenex. I made my first foray into the center of Oadby, the little suburban village where we had settled into a semidetached house sublet from a Leicester faculty member away on leave. (Many years later, when I read David Lodge's inspired satire *Changing Places*, I could not help but visualize, smell, and even feel that "modern" place in Oadby, replete with its coal stove, electric fires, mysterious wiring, multicolored walls, and red carpeting with a skating pattern.) I walked into the village and found a drugstore. Actually it was called a "chemist's shoppe." The proprietress seemed about fifteen years old.

I wandered down the aisles and finally found some syrup and a box of tissues, neither of which had a price on it. I asked the girl how much I owed her and she said, "At'll be three bob' n'thrup'nyluv."

"I'm sorry," I remember saying. "Would you say that again?"

"Threebob'n'thrup'nyluv?"

"Once more," I said, "and slowly, please."

"'At'll be three shillings and thrupence, luv."

It was a rather inauspicious beginning, the first of a number of intriguing encounters with our English cousins.

I was there to teach sociology (which I did) and to learn something about race relations in Britain (which I tried to do). One of my courses was a graduate seminar on research methods. I discussed an array of techniques, indicating that I favored participant observation, defined by some as getting involved while maintaining distance. I started my own research as a nonparticipating observer, but soon became so much involved in what I was studying and in heeding my own admonitions about trying to be neutral that I almost became a nonobserving participant.

Soon after I got to Leicester, I joined CARD, the newly organized Committee Against Racial Discrimination. I helped to organize then got involved in a demonstration against the denial of service to a black woman from the United States in a certain pub in Leicester, got moved out by the police, and was publicly labeled as an "American rabble-rouser." I also gave a number of lectures away from Leicester and engaged in discussions with colleagues and students from Edinburgh to Exeter and many places in between. Some of these began unplanned exercises in "comparative studies": why we Americans do things this way or that in a culture that many seemed to envy and loathe simultaneously.

Like many estranged or disillusioned or highly critical folks who go abroad to breathe others' air and then discover how American they are, I found myself growing more and more chauvinistic as the year wore on. This was doubtlessly influenced by how naïve I thought most Brits were about us. They, at least those I knew, thought we were all materialistic, selfish, superficial, and deeply imbued with what Max Weber called the "Protestant ethic" (regardless of faith or origins). We were seen as a hypocritical people who talked egalitarianism but were, in fact, as class-bound as they; who, though we claimed that our biggest problems were related to race and something called "ethnicity" (a term unfamiliar over there), knew for sure that these were just useful excuses for covering what was class exploitation. I was often accused of being a sentimental liberal. And I suppose I seemed to take on the language of one as, over and over, I heard the term "Yank" used as a four-letter word.

I, of course, had had many stereotypes of my soon-to-be hosts before I arrived in their kingdom by the sea. Living there I found that many of those conceptions, especially the ones relating to social class, odd-tasting food, odder-tasting coffee, peculiar appreciation for arcane things (like cricket), certain academic practices, and language usage, had more than a kernel of truth. I mean it. Moreover, as I learned more about the love/hate relationship my friends there had with my land and compatriots, I came to develop parallel feelings about them—and their Fair Albion. These were nurtured in the homes of colleagues, in Leicester pubs, and in the Senior Common Room of the university.

I visited the great city of London on numerous occasions and, with my family, took trips to various parts of the country and to the continent. I also worked a bit for "Americans for Johnson Abroad." Our principal plea was to support LBJ. "If Barry Goldwater is elected," I would argue, "he will end the War on Poverty and extend the war in Vietnam, starting with bombing the hell out of Hanoi." (In that we were only partially effective. Our man won—then *he* bombed the hell out of Hanoi, while being forced to curtail funding for that other critical war.)

My working base, a room at the University of Leicester, was formerly a padded cell in an old building still labeled LEICESTER LUNATIC ASYLUM. As I came to learn about certain customs, academic and otherwise, the name seemed quite appropriate. First there was the business of who was in charge. I assumed it would be the president or chancellor. I was wrong; the chief academic officer at Leicester and every other English university is the vice chancellor. The title "Chancellor" is saved for the honorary head, like the Duke of Wellington or C. P. Snow. Then there were the rules about registering for courses.

I had a stellar student assigned to me as a "tutee." She was particularly interested in doing research on the legacy of British colonialism to prepare for a paper on current attitudes toward those they called "commonwealth immigrants." I suggested she consider enrolling in a class with a man I had just met, a world-renowned specialist in that very area.

"How can I do that?" she asked. "He is in the history department."

I said I would see what I could do.

I tried. To no avail. When I explained the situation to his secretary, she said, "I'm very sorry, Professor, but he is in the history department and she is a sociology student. It isn't done."

Reluctantly, the student accepted the decision. I did, too. After all, I thought, "When in Rome . . ."

Trying to be a good Roman, I was determined to adapt my palate to the local fare—eggs floating in bacon grease, boiled milk combined with boiled coffee, fish 'n' chips, the aptly-named Wimpy burgers, steak-and-kidney pie, toad-in-the-hole, and more unmentionable delicacies. I never grumbled, but on more than one occasion I must confess to having expressed nostalgia for several "American" specialties—apple pie served with a thick slice of cheddar, decent pizza, and, especially, bagels with lox and cream cheese. One chap, recently returned from a year in New York City and sympathetic to my needs, told me of a place where "baigels," as he called them, were sold every Sunday morning.

The following week we drove off in search of the "baigel" shop, a place that was to become a way station on many a subsequent Sunday excursion. We would arrive there around 11:00 and stand with a dozen English Jews and a few non-Jews (who must also have spent time in New York), waiting for a delivery from a bakery in nearby Nottingham. To the cheers of all, our deliverer came on a shiny motorcycle, his sidecar brimming with large bags of still-warm, fresh-smelling bagels. As we queued up inside to buy our allotments, I would listen to the others talking about what they liked with their "baigels." Cheese. Whitefish. Herring. Marmite.

"Marmite," I said to myself, *"Gevalt!"*

Now I must say that I have a vague recollection that I did come to enjoy some truly indigenous English cuisine—though I can't remember what, in particular, I liked. I do know that, whatever it was, I came to long for it five years later when we were living in Australia, where we often ate bad English food (and that is not a redundancy) in fancy restaurants.

I did come to favor the English tutorial system, English beer, good tweed, the readily available forms of public transport, and much of what we saw on the telly.

Aside from vulgar slapstick comedy that presaged box-office blockbusters like *Mr. Bean* and other recent triumphs of bad taste, Hedy and I were drawn to the in-depth discussion programs and sharp political satire, such as "That Was the Week That Was," that were better than anything back home. We followed the BBC coverage of the British and American election campaigns both taking place that year, enjoyed marvelous plays and concerts, and learned of the death of Winston Churchill and then virtually participated in his funeral, watching—and identifying with—those few surviving Battle of Britain pilots walking sadly but proudly ahead of the caisson bearing his remains. ("At no time in history have so few sacrificed so much for so many," Churchill had said.)

Churchill's death and the subsequent recapping of his life, over and over, led to an important revelation. We learned the extent to which this war hero was held in contempt by those on the left, including many of my younger colleagues and older students. When my wife mentioned to them how, hidden in an Amsterdam cellar during World War II, she remembered the hope that the names Roosevelt, Eisenhower, Montgomery, and, especially, Churchill on a clandestine radio generated, they responded with a "Yes, but . . ." followed by a diatribe about his role in the Boer War and other adventures, and, again, the inevitable reference to class warfare.

While not entirely in sympathy with their views on all matters of politics, I did not hesitate to join them, and others, in a demonstration against blatant discrimination right there in Leicester.

The action was prompted by the denial of service to a colleague and his friend, an African American woman, who had gone in for a pint. When challenged, the publican—not Republican, though he sure sounded like one—had used a simple syllogism to explain why he could act so undemocratically: "One's home is one's castle, and this pub is my home."

Without any such thing as a public accommodation law, unwanted guests had no recourse—unless they could make it costly to the owner or manager to keep undesirables, like blacks and Asians, out.

Various groups at the university decided to do something about it. One faction, Trotskyist in orientation, spoke only half facetiously about burning the place down. Another, far less radical, group suggested boycotting the pub. It seemed a better idea until somebody noted that few people they knew actually went there. And those few who did, including the chap who escorted the unacceptable woman, wouldn't be missed. Then several suggested a sit-in. Get their attention. Get publicity. Embarrass them. Perhaps the proprietor of The Admiral Nelson might be pressed to acquiesce.

I was in the latter group. And that turned out to be more than a turn of phrase. I was the only one around who had actually taken part in a sit-in and was thrust, willy-nilly, into a leadership role, despite the fact that when the landlord saw my short haircut and heard my American accent, I would readily be targeted as a foreign agitator. Still I was persuaded to be among the first to partner with a "coloured person" to try to get served.

An Indian colleague from the English department and I went in with the first wave, sat down and waited. The place was quiet. Regulars looked at us. The landlord glared at us and then sent a waiter over to tell us we were not welcome. We were ushered us out. Half an hour later we went back, this time determined to stay until dragged out.

"Go limp," I told my troops. Still, when the police were called to remove the unwanted patrons (us) from the premises, all it took was a "Move on, chaps" from the guy in charge and the demonstrators all moved out. By then a crowd had gathered, and, while nobody was arrested, lots of pictures were taken. The next day, my role was featured in the local newspaper. The embassy was not very pleased. (I hasten to note that, for a variety of reasons, the landlord did change his policy. We successfully tested the new policy a few weeks after our sit-in.)

I also had a number of less dramatic but equally memorable encounters. One of the most interesting was when the archbishop of Canterbury and I were both scheduled to lecture at the Imperial College of London on the same day.

The rector had invited us both to luncheon. I arrived a bit early, and a few minutes later a white-haired gentleman with bushy eyebrows, a twinkle, and a purple cassock was ushered in. The rector said, "Dr. Rose, this is Dr. Ramsey."

We then had some sherry and started discussing my impressions of British race relations. Then several others entered the room and began "Your Grace"-ing my new friend, Dr. Ramsey. *He* was the archbishop of Canterbury.

The archbishop was intrigued by the character of our civil rights movement and wanted to know more. Perhaps too optimistically I told him how the movement was gaining strength, winning converts, and succeeding in its goal to overcome the barriers of discrimination and increase opportunities for all.

Not long after my visit to the Imperial College, I was asked to participate in a big conference on the racial situation in the United Kingdom. My assignment was to comment on some of the papers written by a group of leading British social scientists. Many of them had been studying the matter for years, and I had little to say other than to summarize the clearly common themes in their papers. In the question-and-answer period someone in the audience asked me for my view. I said something to the effect that I agreed with my colleagues that the United Kingdom, which until 1950 had but fifty thousand "coloured people" and now, fifteen years later, had a million and a half, was rapidly becoming a truly multiracial society. Yet, given what I had heard and seen over the past six months, during a time when the country was gearing up for parliamentary elections and when banners hung across major roads in various hotly contested districts that boldly stated IF YOU WANT A NIGGER NEIGHBOR, VOTE LABOUR, it was doing little to adapt to the new reality. Perhaps, having become annoyed at the widespread ease with which racial epithets were used and the seeming lack of concern for addressing root causes of a growing problem, I became a bit preachy. I talked about the necessity to recognize the strength of diversity. To do what we were trying to do. I quoted John Dewey: "In America, the hyphen connects instead of separates." Then I added, "That doesn't seem to obtain in the United Kingdom."

"Here," I said, "those who are not English are treated as if they are here on sufferance." And then, adding injury to the insult, I said something to the effect that, unless the people of Britain awoke to the blatant racism—they called it "racialism"—in their society and the seething anger of many people of color, I wouldn't be surprised if their cities suffered a fate similar to what had been happening that very year in the United States. I was referring, of course, to the explosions of pent-up frustration, the urban riots, and the rapid mobilization of separatist-sounding organizations calling for recognition, recompense, and even revenge we were witnessing in the United States.

The national conference had attracted the national press. The next day I was in the news again. Different papers reported my remarks in different ways. The slant was usually evident in the title of the article or the lead sentence.

I was also the subject of a short op-ed–like essay by the columnist Peter Simple (aka Michael Wharton) in the *Daily Telegraph*. There he urged me and another American who had just said similar things at the Oxford Union to go back to where we came from. Actually, the head of the piece said "MALCOLM X AND PETER ROSE, YANKEES GO HOME." I'm sure it was the first time either of us had ever been mistaken for a Yankee!

But then, not long after the flap over my remarks had cooled, I was invited to be interviewed on the BBC's *This Day Tonight*. I was asked to discuss what had happened in Selma, Alabama, the day before (this was mid-April 1965). My discussion with the skilled interrogator with the wonderful Icelandic name Magnus

Magnusson took place against a backdrop of pictures of police and police dogs attacking marchers on the bridge during that historic march. Seeing the outrageous behavior of my countrymen, I was brought back to the realization of how far *we* had to go. I wasn't very proud to be an American that day.

[twelve]

Countee Cullen in Kyoto

Once riding in old Baltimore
Heart filled, head filled with glee.
I saw a Baltimorean
Keep looking straight at me.

Now I was eight and very small,
And he was no whit bigger
And so I smiled, but he poked out
His tongue and called me "nigger."

I saw the whole of Baltimore
From May until December:
Of all the things that happened there
That's all that I remember.

COUNTEE CULLEN'S FAMOUS poem "Incident" was the centerpiece of a lesson I was trying to teach to my class of thirty Japanese college professors about some fundamentals of race and ethnicity in America. I was in Kyoto, a member of the visiting faculty of the American Studies Summer Seminar. It was July 1970.

Within the first days of the seminar, I, who had never been in Japan before, became quite aware that even for a group of self-identified budding Americanists, neither "pluralism" nor "intergroup relations" was an easy concept to convey in a society that prided itself on its homogeneity. Almost immediately, I changed my game plan and, if not lowering my standards, lowered my sights. I decided to start from scratch.

As my students were from very different fields—English,

history, and the social sciences—I drew on various sources. Often I would season my commentary by reading passages from the writings of novelists or reciting memorized poems—like Cullen's "Incident"—to illustrate a point or two. Most of what I was saying had to be interpreted by my assistant, a young trained-in-America Doshisha University professor, Akashi Norio. This complicated the process, making it more challenging and also more frustrating.

Even after changing, actually personalizing, my approach, I still found it was hard to get the class to empathize with the little African American child and the three stanzas that were at once literal and symbolic. But they tried.

At the end of the first week and in the middle of one of my very un-Japanese sorts of exercise, we were all startled to hear a deep bass voice singing "I'm comin', I'm comin', though my head is bending low; I hear those gentle voices callin' Ole Black Joe." It turned out to be my American colleague, a historian from Emory University in Georgia, trying to make a point in his course in Southern history just on the other side of the paper screen that divided our temporary classrooms. A few minutes later, I, already startled, cringed as we all heard another line being belted over the screen. "Oh darkies how my heart grows weary, yearnin' for the old folks at home."

My students were fascinated, and one asked, very politely, why I was wincing. I composed myself and used the incident to underscore what I had been trying to convey through the recitation of Cullen's poem the day before. This time I asked if they could think of instances where *they* were subject to such prejudices. None could think of any.

I asked them to think of cases where people like them were disparaged. After a few moments, one of the older members of the class, among the most fluent in English, mentioned caricatures he had seen in a book about American propaganda during the war. He remembered a reprinted poster with a line about the "slant-eyed, buck-toothed, little yellow Nips." (As he spoke I visualized that very poster, which had hung on the wall in my elementary school in 1942 or 1943.) Then a young historian spoke about how Japanese Americans must have felt when, after the attack on Pearl Harbor, they were rounded up and relocated because they were assumed to be disloyal to the United States and potential agents of Japan.

I introduced the concept of scapegoating. The word was hard to translate, its biblical origins quite meaningless in that setting. I groped for a way to explain how people blame others for their own problems and then steered them into a rather stilted conversation about what it might mean to have to live with racism and to face categorical discrimination. Persisting, I broached the more complex matter of coping with the problem of buying into others' views of one's alleged inferiority, of internalizing disgrace. Finally I seemed to strike a chord. Ever so haltingly, one man raised the matter of the widespread humiliation many older Japanese felt during the American occupation. He went on to describe some of the ambivalent feelings he and others growing up in postwar Japan had had about who and what they were.

I remember thinking that we were finally getting somewhere, but also recall sensing a palpable tension in the room. This was clearly a very sensitive topic, and somebody had opened a real can of worms. Feeling we'd done enough for one day, I concluded with "We'll come back to this tomorrow."

We never did.

Still, I pressed on, continuing to try to reach my students, many of whom were much older than I (an especially awkward situation in the Japanese context), by using a variety of ploys to get them to understand what I was talking about.

Unlike the Japanese classroom practice of lecturing from a podium, I paced around, sat on the desk, jumped up and walked around them, then moved to the blackboard. Sometimes I brought in pictures from books, such as Norman Rockwell's portrait of "Ruby," the little black girl being walked to school protected by burly U.S. marshals, and the AP photo of the infamous march across the bridge in Selma, Alabama, in 1965.

As the days turned into weeks, the members of the seminar appeared more tolerant of my quirkiness and my tendency to lead them into discussions on subjects rarely discussed with strangers. I began to have the feeling that more of what I was saying and doing was reaching them. They seemed not only to be grasping the complexities of race relations in American society, but also to be processing them. The discussions certainly became livelier and more relaxed.

A fringe benefit of the long days together was that I got to know many of my students more personally. I began seeing some of them after class. Several from the Kyoto area became the best guides my wife and kids and I had, spending hours taking us to visit imperial properties, shoguns' castles, Shinto shrines, Buddhist temples, tofu factories, and teahouses—and geisha houses, too.

After almost three weeks of talking about dominant and minority relations in my country, and feeling I was on pretty safe ground with folks with whom I had built up considerable rapport, I asked the members of the seminar to tell me something of the situation of minorities in Japan.

Silence.

I asked again, this time specifying my interest in their comments on the Ainu, the Koreans, and the *Eta*, the name I had learned for a large group of people also referred to in the American literature as "Japan's invisible race." Before I could say another thing, Akashi-san tugged my elbow and whispered that I shouldn't use the word *Eta*. He said, "It is like saying 'nigger.' Just like in that poem!" Still speaking in hushed tones, he said the correct term is not *Eta* but *Burakumin.*

Chastened but still curious, I asked the class about the Burakumin.

"Oh," said one English-speaker, "that is an old matter. Since the Meiji Period, all Japanese have equality." The others said nothing.

I let it pass—at least momentarily—and moved on.

"Then what about the Ainu?" I asked.

A history teacher spoke up. "Theirs is a sad story. Like American Indians, they were pretty much, well, exterminated. There are very few Ainu today, so you can't really call them a minority group."

I was to learn that this was a sad truth. The Ainu, a Caucasian-like people who had lived for centuries in the northern part of

Japan, mainly on the island of Hokkaido, had indeed been wiped out in the northward expansion. (Today, in Sapporo, the capital of Hokkaido, there is a fine museum to the lost people. It reminds one of the anthropological museums in Vancouver and Victoria, tributes to the Kwakiutl, Tlingit, Haida, and Salish peoples. The difference is that, in contrast to the Ainu people, the latter groups are still functioning as recognized and viable communities.)

I moved on, asking about the Koreans in Japan. Almost like a Greek chorus, four members of the seminar, all middle-aged English-speakers, said as one, "Oh, they're not Japanese!"

This, it turns out, was not just an ethnic distinction. Koreans constitute a large minority but, despite having been in the country for several generations, are not accepted as Japanese. They are thus not considered to be Japan's problem.

Hesitantly, I maneuvered the discussion back to the subject of the Burakumin. Some members of the group allowed that, despite all the claims to the contrary, the Burakumin were a clearly recognizable, if not officially recognized, Japanese minority, especially noticeable in the cities of the eastern coast of Honshu, including Kyoto. They remained members of a marginal caste still experiencing discrimination owing to their ancestors having been those who did the dirty work of society, serving as slaughterers, tanners, butchers, and gravediggers.

They came to fascinate me the most.

I was actually to get to know some of the leaders of the Kyoto branch of the Buraku Emancipation Movement. I learned about them from a forthright young student of mine—I will call him Sasaki Yoshio here—who at the time was an assistant professor of English in Nagasaki. Sasaki had approached me during a break on the day I first tried to discuss Japan's minorities.

He came over to where I was having a beer. Soon after he sat down and we began to chat, another member of the seminar, a fellow social scientist my age who had become so close a friend that he had taken the unprecedented step of inviting me and my wife and our children to his home for dinner a few nights before, joined us and began listening to our conversation about the Burakumin.

I immediately felt some bad vibes emanating from the younger man. He was not comfortable with the newcomer. Still, I asked Sasaki—who had just asked me whether I would be interested in meeting some of the local members of the Buraku community—to continue. He said he knew some of them very well and would take me to meet them. The other man (I will refer him to as Otani Yasuo), who had been listening, asked whether he might go along. The younger fellow hesitated. It was clear to me that he wanted to say an emphatic, "No," but, after a pregnant pause, he agreed. He left to make another phone call, and while he was gone Otani said this was going to be fascinating. He said he didn't know any Buraku people but assured me that he did know something about them. Now I began to grow uneasy.

Sasaki returned and said everything was arranged. He would pick me up at my hotel at 11:00 A.M. on Saturday and would then swing by for Otani at 11:30.

On Saturday, my escort arrived early. Over a cup of tea, he told me how he had gotten to know the Burakumin.

"I am a Christian," he explained. "I came to Kyoto to study English at Doshisha [a church-related private university], and, while I was here, took part in activities sponsored by a minister of my church. I was very much concerned about continuing discrimination against the people called *Eta*, a sort of untouchable group kept down by traditionalists who said they were dirty."

"In any case," he continued, "I joined with some social workers in their area and got more out of the good work than I expected." He went on to say that he met his wife, a member of the Burakumin there, marrying her despite objections "even from my Christian-but-still-very-Japanese family."

I asked how she was received. Sasaki said it was very hard at first, but when the first child arrived, they welcomed her—and, eventually, his wife—into their home.

Sasaki was about to continue, but, realizing that we were already late, ended the conversation. We got in the car, drove over to pick up Professor Otani, and then went into downtown Kyoto, into a neighborhood by the river. We moved very slowly through the Gion district's narrow but crowded streets, passing a famous theater, many curio shops, and many more camera shops. Every once in a while, we got a glimpse of the hills above the city, every once in a while saw a geisha en route to her club, an acolyte en route to his temple, a bunch of uniformed giggly school girls. It was a visual collage of compressed impressions—old and new, dowdy and bright, sacred and profane. Then we came to a less colorful (and less cacophonous) area. While poor by Japanese standards, it was hardly a slum. It looked to me quite similar to many others I had visited or run through on early morning jogs around the city.

When we arrived at the right house, a man in his midthirties who spoke excellent English warmly greeted us. Several of his friends were there, too.

We were ushered into the "Western room," the kind found in many Japanese homes. It had an overstuffed sofa and matching chair and a low coffee table. The only untoward thing was a large white banner on one wall. It had a bright red crown of thorns, in which was imbedded a red star, and, beneath the crown, some Japanese writing. I asked what it was and was told it was the emblem of the Kyoto branch of the Radical Socialist Buraku Emancipation movement, which had broken with the Christian social workers ("Too much do-gooder in their approach," the leader told me) and also with the Communists ("They want only to use us for their cause"). Before I left I was presented with a smaller version of the banner, used as a headband in demonstrations, and a red armband with the same symbol of political syncretism. (Both are still on display in my office, reminders of an extraordinary meeting.)

For me, it was the first of several meetings. That was not to be the case for Professor Otani.

After being invited to sit down, our host had asked if we would like something to drink, "Beer-u, soft drink?" I asked for a beer. Sasaki said he'd like one, too. Otani hesitated, then asked for Coca-Cola.

The drinks were served and the host raised his glass. "Kompai," he said, and we all took our first sip. Except Otani. He brought the glass near his lips but never touched the rim. He smiled, rather sickly I thought, and put the glass down. The tension in the room was palpable. I had often heard the word "pollution" used to describe the "Eta," but was now an eyewitness to truly insulting behavior. And I was not alone. Everyone glared at Otani. He was clearly embarrassed. But he never did drink from the glass.

After several minutes, acting as if Otani were somewhere else, we began to discuss the plight of the Burakumin. What was especially striking to me, a student of and participant in our own civil rights movement, was that their leader echoed the sentiments of both Martin Luther King Jr. and Malcolm X. This was most apparent when I asked my host what was the most important thing he had to do to help his people. Without hesitation he said, "Get them to hold their heads up." I couldn't help but be reminded of Malcolm's bitter statement that "the worst crime the white man has committed is to teach us to hate ourselves."

After two hours we left, but not before I was asked to come back to see them. "Sayonara," said pointedly to me, was heartfelt. It was very clear that I had been a welcome guest. Such was definitely not the case for Otani, who, as I recall, was given a stiff, cold, but courteous bow, which he reciprocated. Sasaki drove us to our respective homes.

That evening, as planned long before the visit to the Buraku community, I went out to dinner with Otani. We sat cross-legged and shoeless on tatami mats in a favorite neighborhood restaurant and made awkward small talk. As the kimono-clad waitress brought one delicacy after another to our table, bowing, then serving, then pouring more *sake*, I could feel myself forsaking the neutrality of one trained to respect cultural differences and let myself go. I chided Otani about his blatantly discourteous behavior. He hung his head and expressed shame and embarrassment for what he clearly knew was offensive and hurtful.

"We were guests in another man's home . . ." I began. "A home," I wanted to say, "that, while smaller than yours, was just as neat and clean." But I never finished my sentence. Catching my drift, Otani did it, more or less.

"I know that was a very clean place and that the people there were well educated and very respectable, but . . ." Then he added something to the effect that there are things that are not easily overcome. He said, "You know. You're a sociologist. You call it socialization."

I sighed, and we finished dinner in silence. The waitress bowed to us as we left the little room and moved down a narrow hallway toward the curtained entrance. There we took proffered shoehorns from another young woman and put on our shoes. Still we didn't speak. Otani drove me back to the hotel. I got out of the car and nodded to him. He nodded, too. I didn't say goodbye. I didn't even say "Domo arigato" to thank him for dinner.

As I moved across the lobby, Countee Cullen's poignant words kept moving around in my head. A variation on his "Incident" still haunts the memory of an eye-opening first of what would be many trips to Japan.

> I saw the whole of Kyoto,
> That summer long ago,
> Of all the things that happened there,
> That was the cruelest blow.

[thirteen]

Guest Appearances

MAO SAT IN one. So did Deng. I still do. Whenever I am in China or a land of Chinese "compatriots" like Taiwan, Hong Kong, Singapore, or Macao. I am referring to a chair: low, squat, overstuffed. It doesn't have a high back like Kennedy's rocker or a spring-loaded support like the one used to cozy up to computers. It doesn't have wings like the one on the cover of the paperback edition of Anne Tyler's *The Accidental Tourist.* Yet in a way it, too, is symbolic. It is a reminder to me of the Chinese academy and is one of the many touches that leaves impressions on the academic sojourner, impressions as indelible but even more significant than the required walk on the Great Wall, the tour of Beijing's Forbidden City, the visit to Xian's terracotta soldiers, and the stroll along Shanghai's Bund.

The chair, all dressed up in white antimacassars (the sort of doily drapery that adorned Western furniture a hundred years ago), is placed with ten to twenty identical siblings around a tattered carpet behind a small table on which rests a covered teacup, an ashtray, and a large multicolored thermos bottle. It is found in a thousand reception rooms in institutes and universities throughout the Chinese world. Closing my eyes, I recall the chair and how I got to sit in it day after day.

First, there is the pickup at my hotel. An escort arrives in an old Russian- or Chinese-made behemoth, a new Nissan Cedric, or a Toyota taxi. We ride through the crowded streets to arrive at the place where I will deliver a lecture or meet with colleagues. Three persons stand outside to greet us: one is dressed in a Western suit, another in a Mao jacket, and the third, somewhat younger than the others, in blue jeans and a sweater. We exchange warm handshakes, and the senior member of the welcoming committee leads us into the building, up the stairs, down the corridor, and into *the room* where I am invited to sit in *the chair*.

Once settled in, tea is poured from the thermos, there is a pregnant silence, and I am introduced to the others who have joined the squared circle. I tell them how pleased I am to be there. Unless I am speaking at an "American institute" or to members of an English department, my words are interpreted.

If the occasion is a "discussion" I stay put, holding forth for an hour and a half to two hours, with time out for consecutive interpretation. (I talk for three minutes, then my interpreter offers a near-verbatim translation, then I talk for three minutes, etc.)

If I am to lecture to a larger body, I am taken to a classroom or auditorium and reintroduced. Afterwards, usually three hours later, I am returned to the reception room for more tea and some rather formal picture taking. My host sits next to me in the front row, hands on knees, staring straight ahead. Others gather next to and behind our seated figures. I ask them to take a photo for me, and we laugh about all the cameras that suddenly appear. Then I take my leave with the welcoming committee, by now old friends, bidding me a fond farewell and a speedy return. "Xiexie" (thank you), I say to each of them and climb into the back seat of the black sedan.

The "Chair Caper" is but one of the many rituals one grows accustomed to in academic travels to the Middle Kingdom. Comparable things occur on trips to other countries. It is part of being a member of David Lodge's "small world" of mobile dons: visiting professors, research scholars, conference attendees, and what the Chinese call "foreign experts."

As I have vivid memories of genial hosts who lead me into smoky rooms with teacups, brass spittoons, and heavy upholstered chairs—and to sumptuous Chinese banquets where I am treated with the courtesy that I had imagined was only extended to visiting potentates—I have visions of other people and places. For example, in my mind's eye (and stomach) I see and taste the steamed coffee—"D'ya want black or white, luv?"—served to me by a red-faced lady in white in the senior common room of an English redbrick university where I have been invited to speak.

My colleagues and I have repaired there for small talk before the seminar. Balancing the coffee cup and a biscuit on my lap, I sense the adrenaline pulsing through my body in anticipation of what is to come: the thrust and parry of the verbal duel that is the sport of British academicians. The speaker is on one side, another professor and his "seconds" in opposition.

The sharp, sometimes nasty, repartee is followed by sherry, dinner, and, in the end, warm conviviality in a nearby pub. I finally relax.

As *they* say, "It's all a game. Really."

Israelis do similar things—though I remind myself that the verbal jousting has a different spin to it, the sherry is usually grapefruit juice, and the meal that follows rarely meets even English standards. Moreover, if academic one-upmanship is the Englishman's game, in Israel, more perhaps than anywhere I know, the game of choice is "academic geography."

"Do you know Sam Cohen?"

"Which Sam Cohen?"

"The political scientist, used to be at Berkeley, then spent some time in Tel Aviv, a friend of Joe Goldstein, who I think is at Illinois or maybe Indiana."

Japanese academic encounters are also highly predictable. Unlike those in Israel, they are rarely informal, shirtsleeves affairs. One wears a dark suit and tie and, even with those who have eschewed many other traditions, the visit usually begins with the old "double bow."

I accept a proffered name card and present my own. We both bend slightly at the waist, surreptitiously glancing at the other's card, *reading ranks, not names.* What each of us learns determines how much deference to pay in the second bow.

After this exchange, small talk follows, often with an interpreter serving as intermediary. Finding out I am from western Massachusetts, very near to Amherst, I am asked if I know the "Emily Dickinson house" which, it seems, seven out of ten Japanese scholars of American society, culture, or literature have visited, and the other three hope to see on their next trip to America.

In Japan the program begins with the highest-ranking person at the host institution serving me tea from delicate teapots in a well-appointed modern office. We then move to a conference room where I speak and others ask me questions. Unlike in China, in Japan most of my audiences hear me "simultaneously," that is, through headphones. The interpreter is hidden away in a little soundproof both. We all look like representatives at a Security Council meeting. It doesn't make for easy exchanges. Nevertheless, there is some give and take. The seminar or lecture is followed by a reception that begins and ends with toasts and responses, collective activities that bracket a good deal of munching on attractively displayed finger food eaten with lightweight chopsticks and the consumption of lots of beer.

It is very early in my career. I am in Copenhagen with my family, on the first stop of a four-week, four-nation lecture/vacation tour of Scandinavia. Days are spent with colleagues; evenings with family; nights in our very inexpensive mission hotel in a rough neighborhood near the harbor. Our kids, nine and eleven, are excited about everything, but their favorite place is the delightful Tivoli Gardens.

One evening we let the kids persuade us to stay at Tivoli until very late. We finally leave and start walking back toward our modest digs. A woman hands me a flyer; I glance at it and discover it is copy of the *Watchtower*. I read it hurriedly and then toss it in the nearest dustbin. Our daughter asks me what it was.

"A religious tract," I say.

"What d'ya mean?" she asks.

I try to explain.

She says, "Aren't you interested?"

"No, not particularly."

"Why?"

I don't respond.

"'Cause we're Jewish?"

Exasperated, I say, "Yes, 'cause we're Jewish."

We walk on, turn the corner, and enter the red-light district very near our hotel. A lady of the night steps outs and starts to hand her a business card. Before I can react, my daughter says, "No thanks, we're Jewish!"

Ways of sitting, posturing, arguing, playing honored guest, and learning to down (and hold) gallons of tea, beer, sherry, scotch, grapefruit juice, *sake*, and jet-black coffee—and dealing with one's children—are items that are often overlooked in briefing papers prepared for those about to embark on short-term academic tours in foreign climes or a year abroad. There are others. For example, accepting an invitation to give a lecture in Rome or Florence can involve a certain amount of risk taking.

I should have been warned that one can never be certain until the very last minute whether the university building will be open or closed (because of a strike) on the scheduled date and, if it is open, whether the announced classroom will actually be available. (I have distinct memories of senior professors scurrying around to find a place to put a crowd of people gathered in the corridor in front of "our" room, where, in fact, another lecture has already started.) It is worth the gamble, for Italian colleagues are most gracious hosts.

Among many nice Italian academic customs is the practice of taking the visitor out for a fine meal at a favorite restaurant after the lecture. Often junior members of the faculty and assistants are invited to come along.

The most senior of the juniors picks up the professor's briefcase and trails along behind the "principals." They (we), in turn, are followed by the others. At the restaurant the *professore* does the seating and, often, the ordering. During the meal the conversation, covering everything from academic life in Europe and America to politics to the "scourge of persisting elitism," is pretty much dominated by the majordomo—and the guest.

After-lecture excursions are more democratic in Australia. All head for the nearest pub, have a few beers, and exchange banter about the more important issues of the day—like why Australian-rules football is so much more rugged than rugby or soccer. Outsiders sometimes have trouble following the arguments. It is not because they have never heard of Australian-rules football, but because they don't speak "'strine," Aussie slang. It is full of local expressions, some borrowed from the aborigines.

In my particular case, however, the first "Australian" word I heard uttered was far from local. It was "pavlova," as in the sentence "Would you like some more pavlova?"

Pavlova turned out to be a favored dessert in academic households (and others, too, I presume) from Brisbane to Perth. It is a cakelike concoction topped with fruit and heavy cream. It is said to have been named for the genuine article (who, I bet, would have much preferred *blintzes*).

I have other distinct recollections about guest appearances on my half-dozen trips Down Under, such as the times I have taught or spoken at one or another of the newer "plate-glass" universities—Flinders, Griffith, La Trobe, Murdoch, New South Wales—and suddenly had a rush of near recognition, a feeling of being marooned at some way station between Stony Brook and Sussex.

I remember my first trip to Korea in the early 1970s. I was there to lecture in a number of cities. Wherever I went I found my hosts kindly, courteous, and eager to give me a sense of their traditions. The cultural orientation might involve prelecture sightseeing; lengthy discussion of Korean life and politics, ancient and modern; or a wonderful banquet in the middle or at the end of a busy day of academic exchanging. I must confess it is the last activity that comes back to mind most often: the lavish meals that were served by young ladies especially skillful at having patrons, particularly the older men, enjoy their rich repasts—and more. One encounter stands out from all the others.

I am in the provincial capital of Taegu, where I have come to speak at two universities. Between lectures the combined forces of their respective sociology departments escort me to a restaurant where I am both force-fed and fondled. I still recall the awkwardness of eating a strange (to me) looking piece of something and having my mustache fingered by an eighteen-year-old "waitress," while my host, seated on my left, asks me if I don't agree with him that Talcott Parsons is the greatest social theorist since Max Weber.

I pause, think about it, and say, "Pass the *kimchi*."

India has left memories, too. The sights, the sounds, the smells, the colors, the university settings—especially the latter. Sometimes impressions merge.

I am back in a large lecture hall filled with students whose seeming rapt attention to my presence is matched only by their obvious ambivalence about what, regardless of my politics, I represent. In the discussion, which often drifts far from my subject, I am politely but firmly told what is wrong with my society, its values, its foreign policies, its . . . And yet, once the formal part has ended, one after another member of the audience comes up to me to tell me about his or her "sterling record" (to be vouched for, I am assured, "by many friends in very high places") and to enlist help in garnering a scholarship to study in the States.

"But why do you want to go there if you think it is so decadent, so exploitative, so bad?" I ask, thinking *at least a few* will say that they want to get inside the belly of the beast. But that is not the answer.

Déjà vu.

I can hear myself engaged in similar exchanges with young people in a wine bar in Utrecht, in a pub in Bradford, at a café on the Left Bank, at a special dinner in Ljubljana, at a *taverna* in Athens, and in an office in the sociology department at Teheran University only a few months before Khomeini took power. Those to whom I am speaking have different faces and use different words, but often express the same thoughts: the rhetoric of outrage about America's inequities; the petitioner's plea for a way to share in its (presumably tainted) largesse.

There is an interesting variation on this. I remember being in Nairobi in the early 1970s. I am sitting on the veranda of the Stanley Hotel. Three black men with Afros and dashikis walk in and sit down. They don't look African to me (no Africans I knew there wore an Afro, and few wore West African dashikis in that East African place). My suspicions are confirmed when I hear very clear American accents. After a few minutes, they, doubtlessly sizing me up and realizing I am out of place too (despite the bush jacket), start up a conversation.

"Hey, Bro," said one, "where you from?"

"Massachusetts. And you guys?"

"New York City!"

We join forces and talk over our beers for several hours.

They tell me they have come to Africa looking for their roots—and have found out how very American they are.

Ten years later on a whirlwind trip in China I am in an airport in Wuhan. My interpreter, Hu Yafei, and I have been together for three or four weeks. We know each other pretty well by this point and spend much of our travel time teaching each other all sorts of things about our respective societies. One of the things I try to teach her is how to tell Americans from other travelers. She gets pretty good at distinguishing white Americans from other "long-nose types" (meaning Europeans) and at recognizing African Americans as opposed to folks from Africa itself. But Asian Americans baffle her.

As we enter the airport, Yafei spots a group of people in brightly colored clothing—men wearing blazers and chinos and, often, baseball caps; women in skirts, sweaters, and running shoes. "Who are they?" she asks.

"Chinese Americans," I say.

"No."

"Yes," I say, "let's meet them."

We walk over, and I ask the man closest to me where he is from. "Hooston," he says, in an unmistakable Texas drawl.

Yafei asks what they are doing on their trip.

"Looking for our roots."

I ask whether they found them. "Oh yes," they say. Then one says, "Now we can't wait to get home!"

There is an important postscript to this story.

After bidding farewell to my Chinese American compatriots, Yafei and I boarded our flight. As we settled in our seats, she turned to me and made a most astute sociological observation—a commentary on acculturation, American style. "You know," she said, "those people we just met, those Chinese from America, they look like me but they act like you!"

That was a while ago. Since then Yafei has come to America to study with me and with others and to learn about acculturation at first hand. She has settled here and, though she still looks Chinese, she, too, has begun to act like me!

While I don't get to China very often, I practically commute to the Netherlands. Last fall I was back in my wife's hometown of Amsterdam, where my gracious hosts at the university housed me in a modern apartment in a very old building on Gelderskade. Convenience is its virtue. Walk out the door, turn to the left, cross the square, and I'm at the central station; walk out the door, turn to the right, twenty meters, and I'm in the red-light district! There women "of every hue and caste" (as Walt Whitman might have put it) tap the windows of their cribs and display their wares. I'm not buying. As painted smiles turn into vapid scowls, I move along the edge of the canal, toward the university, or, rather, to a part of it.

Like many old city universities this one, started as the Amsterdam Athenaeum in 1632, is really a jumble of old and refurbished structures. Asylums. Orphanages. Churches. Banks. Everywhere there are students, bicycles, and smoke.

My oldest Dutch friend, the sociology professor Johan Goudsblom, has written a masterful book called *Fire and Civilization.* There are times when I think the catalyst for his study was a chain-smoking sycophant. Even if such is not the case, his students smoke like chimneys, as, it seems, do all the rest. They also drink lots of beer and wine and very strong coffee.

A coffee addict, I fit right in, sipping my fourth cup of the afternoon while going over notes for the evening's lecture. Before the presentation I meet with several student organizers and their professors. I join them for a dinner in a nearby restaurant, and then, wined and dined, I have to go to the lecture hall where I am supposed to get serious.

The issue I discuss there, refugees and immigrants in the United States, is of interest to the audience. The Dutch are curious about Americans and, like most Europeans these days, wonder how our growing pluralism will be played out in my country (talk is often of "balkanization") and, with rising inflows of outsiders—especially from "the east"—throughout the area, how it will be played out in their own.

American visitors to former Eastern bloc countries take away many impressions, too. Mainly, until only recently, about things they *couldn't do,* or about a "grayness" that hung—figuratively and literally—like a pall everywhere. That was clearly my experience.

But my personal memories of heaviness, oppression, and sadness—and sameness—are interspersed with moving flash-backs of startling contradiction, some noticeable to all, some highly personal.

It is several years before the fall of Communism. I am in Poland for the first time. During three days in Warsaw, I speak at the University of Warsaw, meet colleagues, and see the sights—including the almost completely rebuilt historical center and the razed area where the ghetto once stood. I also listen to many Polish jokes ("What is the best view of Warsaw?" "The one from the top of the Peace Palace." "Why so?" "Because it is the only place in town you don't have to look at that Stalinist monstrosity!" or "How many Russians does it take to put in a light bulb?"). I eat my meals in special restaurants that cater only to foreigners. Then I travel south on a smoke-filled train to the city of Krakow, where I have been invited to lecture at the Jagiellonian University.

Several Polish scholars I have met in the United States greet me. They are delighted to see me and immediately take me to a nearby café. After lunch they walk me across the square to the university. En route to the auditorium I am led through a magnificent vaulted chamber lined with portraits of important figures in the history of the venerable institution. I am shown a room near where I will speak. Here, I am told, the great Copernicus worked five centuries before.

We finally enter the large hall, and I am introduced. I find that I am shaking. I start to address the audience, but my mind keeps drifting. I am asking myself, "What would my grandparents, who escaped from persecution in this very area at the turn of the century, think of me today? Would they be proud? Would they be angry?"

I compose myself and give my lecture. Its subject is the alienation of the dispossessed.

[fourteen]

A Tale of Two Cities

SOMETIME IN THE spring of 1965, while living in England, I received and accepted an invitation to come to Jerusalem as a guest of colleagues at the Hebrew University. I had never been there before and was eager to visit historic and holy sites and learn something about roots, mine and those of many others with a special interest in that new/old society. On the appointed day, I drove down from Leicester and picked up a Tel Aviv–bound flight at Heathrow. The El Al plane had originated in New York and was filled, so far as I could determine, with tourists of various sorts and some obvious pilgrims, Jewish and Christian.

The plane landed on time, and I followed the crowd to go through the entry procedures. A couple in front of me was overwhelmed with joy. They exchanged "ohs," "ahs," and succinct, telling phrases.

"It's wonderful. Like a dream."

The wife turned to her husband. "Just think," she said, "on the plane already there were Jews running things. The pilot. The stewardesses. And here they are *all* Jews—soldiers, immigration officers, customs officials . . ."

A little old man was sweeping up right next to us. He was also listening to the conversation. Then, when the husband added, "And, Sadie, the cops are Jews, too," the sweeper turned, smiled, and said, "So are the crooks, mister, so are the crooks."

Smugly, I chuckled to myself, then put my wallet in my front pocket, moved through immigration and customs, retrieved my luggage, and caught a cab. It looked amazingly like a 1948 DeSoto, which, of course, it was. It took me "up to Jerusalem."

The next morning I left my one-star hotel and walked over

to the posh King David Hotel then wandered down the hill just below it to the narrow corridor near the famed Mandelbaum Gate. The alleyway was lined with Israeli soldiers facing Jordanian ones on the road into the only accessible part of the post-'48, pre-'67 Old City.

Moving along at a pretty good clip, I came upon a group of Jewish tourists. They were blocking the path. I slowed but couldn't get through without trying to part them, Moses style. Without divine assistance, I gave up fighting the crowd and joined it. It proved well worth it. They had a great guide called Ari (I knew it from his nametag), and from him I learned the first important lesson about an important rule of tour leaders: "Give 'em what they want!"

I followed the entourage and listened to what Ari had to say. When the group reached the top of the hill, I followed them into the remains of an old building, where we were told: "This is where our great King David is buried."

"Ohs" and "ahs" not heard since I'd flown into Tel Aviv. Whispers, too.

"Sam. Did he say King David?"

"Yes, King David. *Our* King David."

We were encouraged to walk around the place for a few minutes, then were led into a nearby building. As we entered, the guide, whose English was excellent, explained, "This is where the Christian people say Mary ascended to Heaven." He paused momentarily, looked at the faces of his audience, and then, with a sort of "if-you-believe-this-you-will-believe-anything" expression, he shrugged. The others smiled knowingly. Then we moved to another place where we were told: "This is where the Christian people say the 'Last Supper' took place."

The last bit of information comment was elaborated upon a bit by one of the men nearest to me. He explained that the Last Supper was, actually, a Seder. As he did, I could hear an elderly woman who had moved ahead quite a way loudly whispering to her husband, "It was a Seder." She knew, too.

When the tourists walked out into the brilliant noonday sunshine, it was very hot. Everyone was sweating. With jackets over shoulders and sweaters over arms, the whole gang tromped down the grade and through the corridor. I followed part way, then stopped at an open-air canteen halfway down the hill, ordered some falafel and a coke, and surveyed the scene.

Hot from the sun, I started to doze. Soon I realized I had been there for more than an hour. I quickly paid the check and got up. As I did, I noticed another group gathering at the bottom of the hill. Even from a distance it was clear it was different from the earlier one. Most notably there were several men in clerical collars and three nuns. They were wearing badges, as were the rest of the group: Christian pilgrims on a trip to the Holy Land.

As they trudged up the hill, I saw that they had two guides: one seemed almost a member of the group (I surmised he was the coordinator of their tour); the other was same guy who had led the Jewish party that morning.

As they passed the canteen, the imp in me made me decide to abandon my plan to go to Mount Herzl. I was going back up Mount Zion. And I did, surreptitiously pursuing the new group, moving in as close as possible to hear the spiel and watch the reaction.

At the top of the hill the Israeli guide told his new charges that: "This is where the Jews say King David is buried," then quickly added, "But, of course, it is hard to know these things for sure."

The listeners nodded and some took notes. Then, as before, he led them to the church next door. This time it was they who did the "oh-ing" and "ah-ing," as he explained that they were standing on the very place from which Mary had ascended to Heaven.

By the time they reached the room of the Last Supper, the voices were hushed. As one, the pilgrims were in awe of where they were and what it meant.

As they slowly began to file out, each one glancing back as if to freeze the savored experience, the guide spotted me. A bit puzzled, he smiled and nodded rather perfunctorily. Then he sort of winked. He let everybody pass and started down behind them. I waited and fell in with him. On impulse I invited him to have a beer with me at a place near where the tour buses were lined up. He agreed.

A few minutes later he and I were sitting at the sidewalk

café. We chatted a while and, after directing the conversation toward the business of tourism, I asked the guide why he had said one thing to the Jewish group and something different to the others. Without batting an eye, he looked at me, smiled, and said, "It's very simple. It's a living."

Ari's remarks that day so long ago got me to thinking about the role of guides, especially on pilgrimages, and about the fact that only rarely had I had the opportunity to hear one speak so ingeniously out of both sides of his mouth. Ari's dishonesty was amusing and, I suppose, harmless. It was very different from that of the bus driver who doubled as my tour guide around Berlin in 1972, about ten years after the wall had divided the city.

Having arrived the day before my first lecture at the Free University, I booked myself onto a city bus tour. I arrived at the appointed time and quickly realized—from their dress and demeanor—that almost everyone lined up to board was a German pensioner from the provinces. I saw no recognizable foreign tourists. I may have been wrong but had the distinct feeling that I was the odd man out.

I climbed to the second floor of the double-decker and moved to the front. Before we started, the driver introduced himself in German, saying his name was Kurt or Klaus or Klemens (I remember only the "K" sound), and welcomed everybody on board. Then he announced, first in English, then in French, that any one who didn't understand German should knock on the inside wall of the bus. "Once for English; twice for French," he said, sharply tapping the wall himself, first once, then two times. I knocked once.

We moved out from the rank, heading down the main street, the Kurfürstendamm, past a number of boutiques and bakeries and the famous broken-towered Kaiser Wilhelm church, which had been left as a war memorial. We turned left and drove through the Tiergarten, then directly toward the Brandenburg Gate and the wall.

The guide must not have heard my rap. From the start he spoke only German, which, I must confess, I can understand reasonably well.

His banter was a combination of straight talk and humor, some of it quite dark and most inappropriate. For example, he would point to a building and say, "There, some of you will remember, they had some great rallies"—ending with a chuckle that made me wonder if he was being sardonic or serious. Then he would offer another little quip about the glory days of World War II. The old folks laughed with him. They seemed to appreciate his openness and his perverse—to me—patriotism.

As we approached Checkpoint Charlie and slowed down to park the tour bus in a long row of similar vehicles, the driver made a number of cracks about the Americans as well as the Russians. This made some of the men poke each other; the women giggled. I was growing increasingly uncomfortable.

Getting off the bus for what had been billed as the highlight of the tour, a glimpse over the wall into East Berlin, I stopped to tell the driver that I was troubled because I had missed so much of his description. I said he must not have heard my knock. He said he hadn't and apologized profusely in heavily accented but perfectly adequate English.

When we reentered the bus, he spoke in two languages, German and English. I was startled by a flashback to my day on Mount Zion. What "K" offered was a most unseemly variation on Ari's "Give-'em-what-they-want-to-hear" theme. I noticed this first when we rode past the place that, he said, had been the headquarters of the Gestapo, and then again as we approached the site of the 1936 Olympics. Twice *I* got a sanitized version. The headquarters, he said (in English), was a place of infamy and shame. He did not say anything like that in German. The stadium was, for my ears, clearly an arena to celebrate Aryan supremacy, a good example of the unfairness of a now-discredited regime. The others were told that it was the site of one of the greatest spectacles ever seen. Describing the staging in terms reminiscent of stills from *Triumph of the Will*, the guide offered a word portrait of a place to remember not for its excesses but for its marvelous pageantry. When he then added something about how much of recent German history had been distorted or treated in a far from "balanced" way, I wanted to bail out. But I stayed to the bitter end.

When I finally got off the bus and started walking away, the driver followed me. He had a rather pained look on his face. I thought he wanted to explain how sorry he was about not hearing me at first and how pleased he was to be able to tell me about his city, at least during the second half of the trip. I then realized he was simply annoyed that I hadn't tipped him.

As I walked away, I called him a Dutch epithet I had learned from my wife.

Two trips. Two cities. Two guides, both beguiling prevaricators. But what a difference.

[fifteen]

The Shop on the Via Dolorosa

JERUSALEM. SACRED CITY. Incubator of faith. Home of Jews and Arabs and Christians. City of miracles. A place so amazing that even Disney couldn't match it. But he came close once. Well, sort of. Let me tell you a story.

Toward the end of a combined working trip and family excursion to Israel in the early 1970s, I remembered the words of an old friend who told us that if we wanted to buy antique jewelry, the best place in all of Jerusalem was the shop of a man named Baduin. The address was 6th Station, Via Dolorosa. Really!

One day I told my wife that I was going back to the university for the day. I lied. I wanted to shop for a present for her.

I found Baduin's place. The door was wide open, and I walked into a magical space. I was struck by how cool it was on that hot, dry day. There was one room behind another; each was filled with treasures: copper pots, terracotta figures, pottery shards, bronze weapons, brass candelabras, and all sorts of jewelry. There were many tourists milling about and several salespeople, old and young and very young.

I introduced myself to the man who seemed to be in charge (and turned out to be Baduin himself) and said I was interested in jewelry—a necklace, perhaps, or a bracelet.

The proprietor nodded and then said, "Roman? Crusader? More modern?"

"Oh," I said, trying to be cool, "Roman would be nice."

He reached into a box and brought out several items. They were stunning. And, I suspected, very expensive.

After hemming and hawing for more than twenty minutes over three different necklaces, I chose one and said, "How much?"

Mr. Baduin stated a figure. "Oh," I said, having absolutely no idea of the actual value but remembering what I had been told ("You have to haggle. It is expected."), "that is too much, much too much."

He came down a bit. But I held firm.

Then he said, "Well, how much would you give me?"

The ball was now in my court, and I was stymied. I thought for a moment and then offered half of his initial price.

He laughed and started to put away the necklace we had been discussing and the other two. He must have sensed my discomfort. After looking at me and hesitating, he brought the box back up to the top of the counter, smiled, and said, "Would you like some tea?"

Almost before I could answer, he sent a young boy to fetch it. While he was gone, we chatted—about who he was (a Christian Arab whose parents' families had lived in Jerusalem "forever"), his family (he had a brother in "L.A."), his kids, and about my family, too.

Twenty minutes after he left the shop, the boy returned with glasses of piping hot mint-flavored tea. He set them on the counter. We sipped the tea while continuing the conversation, still mostly small talk: questions about what I was doing in the country, questions about my reaction to the sticky weather. Nothing too serious. Nothing political. I was getting nervous. I sensed Mr. Baduin was waiting for me to make a new offer on the piece I clearly favored. I didn't crack.

For what seemed like a very long time, neither of us mentioned the necklaces. Finally, the shopkeeper broached the subject.

"Well, perhaps if you bought two pieces . . ."

In the end I did. One, made of many beads, was Roman. "From the time of Christ," he said. The other was even older. It was made of amber.

As we closed the deal, he sent out for more tea. While waiting, I paid Mr. Baduin, and he gave me a receipt and two certificates of authenticity.

Our business finished, I thanked Mr. Baduin and started to leave. He called me back. He said he wondered if I would do him a favor.

"You know," he began, "in America, ladies have gloves to wash their dishes. Here we don't have such things and my wife, well, she has a terrible problem with the harsh soaps and hard water." (I'm thinking to myself: "This is really bizarre and quite wonderful. Here I am in the middle of the Old City, surrounded by the histories, treasures, chants, and shouts—and maledictions, too—of three great cultures; my family members and I have just spent weeks trying to get a sense of the country, visiting ancient synagogues and churches and mosques, going to the Temple Mount and the Wailing Wall, to Masada and Meggido and Bethlehem, to *kibbutzim* and Druze villages and universities. We have met with political leaders and students and discussed timeless issues about turf and tradition and . . . and this guy is telling me about his wife's dishpan hands!") I was snapped out of my reverie by a question.

"When you return to the States, Professor, would you send me several pairs of rubber gloves for which, of course, I will pay you in advance?"

I said I would do it but that it would be my gift to my new friend. That night I wrote to a colleague back home and asked him to airmail a dozen pair of Playtex Gloves and send them to A. Baduin, 6th Station, Via Dolorosa, Jerusalem, with my greetings.

A few days later we flew from Lod Airport in Tel Aviv to Athens. A month later we were back in Northampton. Going through the piles of mail, I spotted a letter with an Israeli stamp. It was a thank-you note from the shopkeeper.

Three months after that I was invited back to Israel. The day before departing I was in a large mall. As I was leaving, I saw a table piled high with leather and woolen gloves and got an idea. I would take Mr. Baduin a Christmas present. I stopped at a nearby store and bought him twelve pairs of Playtex gloves and some fancy wrapping paper.

When I arrived in Jerusalem, one of my first stops was at the shop on Via Dolorosa. I peered into the window. Instead of the bustling activity I had witnessed in the summer, I found the place quite dark and very empty. At first I thought it was closed, then I saw a faint light in the back and walked in. It wasn't pleasantly cool like it had been in the summer. It was freezing. Mr. Baduin was there, sitting very close to a pot-bellied stove, warming his hands with a glass of tea. He looked up, nodded, coughed, and, standing up, said, "May I help you?"

He didn't recognize me. I thought it was because, instead of wearing shorts and sandals and being very tanned, I was now dressed in a coat and tie and was quite pale. Then I laughed to myself, "This is ridiculous—he doesn't know me because I am one of thousands of customers he sees each year."

I was wrong.

After looking at me for a while, he paused, then said, "You're the professor. From Massachusetts. You bought two necklaces last summer. And you got me the gloves. Welcome, sir. And Merry Christmas."

I said he had a great memory and told him that I had come to give him some Christmas presents. I produced a box of candy and the packet of gloves for his wife. He was obviously touched by the gesture, shook my hands warmly, and asked the elderly man sitting in the shadows to bring me some tea.

As his companion scooted out the door, Mr. Baduin said, "Professor, you have two children, a girl and a boy, no?"

"Yes," I said, amazed at his memory of a brief conversation months before.

"I would like to give them some Christmas presents." He then went to a chest, rummaged around a bit and took out several small items. He checked them over, then said: "This is for your daughter," handing me a Roman ring; "This is for your son," giving me an equally old bronze belt buckle.

I was speechless. When I started to say this was far too generous, he made a sign hushing me up.

We drank our tea and I departed, walking along the Via Dolorosa. It was three days before Christmas.

The next spring some close friends were going to Israel for the first time. They asked many people for advice about where to go, what to see, what to buy. They asked us, too. I remember telling them many things, including something to the effect that if they are interested in getting some old jewelry in Jerusalem, they should go to Baduin's shop. And, I added, if you want to do a real *mitzvah*, take him some rubber gloves.

When our friends returned from their trip, they called to tell us all about it. They said they, too, had been moved by seeing people praying at the Wailing Wall, were impressed by the fortress at Masada, excited to have seen Herodion and Caesarea, troubled by the continued tensions between Jews and Arabs that pervaded the atmosphere even in that time of relative tranquility, and delighted to have met our friend Mr. Baduin. They said he was pleased, though a bit puzzled, with the gift they had brought. They told us he had asked them to send a message back to me.

In a quiet, almost embarrassed way, he had said that it was now possible to get rubber gloves almost anywhere in the city and that, if I and my friends kept bringing them to him, he was afraid that he would soon have more than his wife, his sisters, and his daughters could ever use. Then, with a shy grin, he had said, "One day the gloves will take over this place."

When my friend told me this, my very first reaction was an image of the little boy who fetched us tea the summer before with Mickey Mouse ears poking out from under an Arab headscarf, desperately trying to hold back a rising tide of rubber gloves oozing out from a little shop and moving like a gigantic wave down the Via Dolorosa in Old Jerusalem. There was music in the background, too. It sounded strikingly like something composed by Dukas.

[sixteen]

Wrapped in the Flag

I DON'T THINK of myself as a very patriotic person. I tend to recoil at assertions of national chauvinism, especially the kind of jingoism vigorously expressed during run-ups to brush-fire wars (as in Grenada, Panama, and the Persian Gulf), during presidential campaigns, and before and during Olympic Games. I don't even like the idea of putting out Old Glory on Memorial Day, the Fourth of July, or November eleventh (which I still call "Armistice Day").

For my immigrant grandparents, especially on my mother's side, it was a privilege to fly the flag. They had known oppression and escaped to the *guldene medina* to start life anew. It was very difficult in the beginning, but, in time, their dreams of freedom and opportunity were fulfilled. From their earliest days in this country, they never debated whether or not to show the flag. They did so first in gratitude for asylum and later for pride in their new home.

For my parents it was a mixture of involvement and detachment. For my father, one of the original members of the Boy Scouts of America and a member of the Student Army Training Corps in 1917–18, it was simply part of growing up. My mother, a much more political person, was ambivalent and sometimes inconsistent. She echoed her working-class parents' sentiments about why America was different from most other societies, but questioned the terrible inequities she observed wherever she went. For her the flag meant something very special—a totem of an unfulfilled ideal too readily used as an icon for defending indefensible policies and practices.

My view of all this was quite different. I wasn't un-American.

Just the opposite, I thought: a true patriot in the spirit of Tom Paine—or Paul Robeson as he expressed it in John Là Touche and Earl Robinson's powerful "Ballad for Americans." I came to my political awareness in the days of the Southern Compromise engineered by Dixiecrats, a time when the HUAC witch-hunts were just beginning. I graduated from high school the night after the Korean War broke out and from college in the middle of the McCarthy era. Earlier in my life, I had been made aware of the dangers of extreme nationalism and the advantages of alliances to stay the force of fascist dictators and Nazi gauleiters. My mother, a World Federalist, went much further. Doubtless she influenced my own socialization as an open-minded left-leaning young American, as did others who pointed out that, unlike so many other countries, ours was truly what Walt Whitman had called it, "a nation of nations." I came to believe that such a pluralistic view of nationhood was incompatible with the narrow-minded bombast of many America Firsters and many others less expressive in their biases but who still reflected, in their attitudes and actions, deep-rooted ethnocentrism. And, conflating the whole business, I guess my antipathy to intense nationalism was to be found in my "flag-itis."

Given my background and early interests, it was a logical step for me to become a social scientist with particular interest in race, ethnicity, and the nature of our multicultural society. I wanted to try to find ways to reduce prejudice and various forms of discrimination. The vehicles I chose were researching, teaching, writing, and lecturing about these matters in both university settings and outside, sometimes through short stints under contract to several government agencies. Three such experiences—one rather long, the other two very brief—taught me much about myself that I hadn't fully understood, not least the fact that I had some pretty deep-rooted patriotic feelings of my own.

The first incident occurred sometime in the spring of 1957, when I was a graduate student at Cornell. I was asked to take over a course called Public Opinion and Propaganda for two weeks. It was not my field, but I gave it my best shot. The professor left me with an outline of what he had intended to cover.

One of his plans had been to address the idea of investing

inanimate objects with symbolic significance, and to explain how objects so invested then become reified in various ways. Lines and shapes put together to form a crucifix, a Star of David, a swastika, a hammer and sickle, et cetera, et cetera.

I had a great idea. Not only would I discuss the phenomenon, I would illustrate it dramatically, seeking to evoke a visceral response from the students.

The day after I had spoken of the impact of indoctrinating people to respect and sometimes worship certain man-made icons and to hate others, I did the deed. I stepped up on the podium, walked over to the standard holding Old Glory, took the flag, and, holding it by the pole, dragged it across the platform over to the lectern. My ploy had the expected effect—and one that was unexpected, as well.

As I pulled the Stars and Stripes across the stage, there was a hush in the room. Even the most jaded students became very still and very uncomfortable. They got the message. But, as I started to revel in my powers of persuasive demonstration, I realized that I was feeling very queasy. I was sweating. I felt somehow as if I had committed a sin. Which, of course, I had.

"Never, ever let our flag touch the ground," I could hear my third-grade teacher say. "It is a sacred thing."

Sometime in the summer of 1963, I, who had already engaged in protests against sending "advisers" to Vietnam, received a call from the Pentagon. The voice on the other end said he wondered whether I would be willing to come there to serve as a consultant.

"Me? In the Pentagon?" I thought to myself. Surely someone was pulling my leg.

But then, before I made an obscene crack and slammed down the phone, I paused and asked the person to please identify himself. Slowly he said, "I'm Dick Beaumont, undersecretary of the navy for manpower." He went on to explain that he had read my just-published book, *They and We*, and he wanted me to consult with his office and with the "CO"s of various installations in the Fifth Naval District on the "implementation of an affirmative-action program to upgrade the status of Negroes employed by the navy."

I was confused. In my world, "CO" stood for conscientious objector; in his, I quickly realized, it referred to commanding officer! I was also intrigued. It would be challenging to meet with those bull-necked pinheads who were *always* waving the flag. I would teach them a thing or two about America. And so I accepted.

Early on a Monday morning two weeks later I was wandering around the giant maze that is the Pentagon, feeling like the Flying Dutchman. I couldn't locate the room where I was supposed to join the secretary of the navy's team. Finally, with the help of a civilian who must have sensed my despair, I managed to find it. I knocked gently, then quietly entered the room twenty minutes late. I was not prepared for what I confronted. The whole space seemed filled to the scuppers with naval brass. There were, in fact, six admirals, ten captains, a number of aides (mostly lieutenants junior grade and ensigns), a small group of petty officers, and several ordinary seamen acting as gofers. I also noticed about twenty red-faced middle-aged civilians sitting around the perimeter of the room and looking almost as uncomfortable as I felt. At the head of the large conference table, looking rather annoyed, were Paul Nitze, secretary of the navy, Vice Admiral John Hogle, the commandant, and the man to whom I had spoken, Dick Beaumont. Each was identified by a large nameplate.

I was welcomed in a rather perfunctory way and took my seat between two one-star admirals who, like all the others at the table, were dressed in spanking summer whites. Some were also lightly tapping their Annapolis rings on the table.

I asked myself how I ever got myself into this room awash with seaborne warriors and ring knockers and how I would ever get out. The feeling, somewhere between co-optation and panic, was compounded when one of the captains, the head of an air station near Norfolk, Virginia, asked, with a deferential preamble directed to the commandant at the head of the table, why we were even spending time on race relations when we had more important things to do, that is, "Gettin' ready for Veet-Naam." To my chagrin, several nodded in agreement (most of the nods coming from what I now think of as the Greek chorus of rednecks ringing the room). To my surprise, such talk was quickly squelched and the "mission"—to improve the chances for all who worked for the navy—was restated in rather emphatic terms. (Maybe, I thought, some of these guys are O.K.)

Finally, the meeting got started. The commandant asked the COs to give brief status reports on race relations on their bases. Each did. Around 12:30, the last base commander finished his summary, and I was asked to comment. "Briefly, if you please."

Mustering all his strength, this thirty-year-old "professor," as one of the gentlemen at the table called me, said: "Well, it seems to me that there are two general areas of concern in the Fifth Naval District [which extended from Philadelphia to Norfolk and employed thousands of civilians]: a) what the U.S. Navy can do to improve the lot of black employees and enhance their opportunities on the base, and b) what it can do off the base." I went on to suggest several things that might be done in each area.

I mentioned trying to focus networking around job tasks rather than race. I mentioned providing tutorial programs for those blacks whose high-school math and science programs had clearly been inferior to those of white workers, an imbalance that handicapped the African Americans when being tested for better positions, even when tested "blind." I was just getting started when I was interrupted by the commandant, who said it was time for lunch.

"Thank you," he said, "I appreciate your ideas. Now, Gentlemen, I call a recess until fourteen hundred hours."

Breathing heavily, I sat down.

Nobody invited me to go with him, so I wandered out into the maze once again. I found a hot-dog stand and had a stand-up lunch. Finished in four minutes, I decided that, since we weren't expected to resume our session until two o'clock (I'd figured it out!), I might as well look around. I shouldn't have tried. After walking for about fifteen minutes, I turned around and started back again and got lost for the second time that day. It took a while, but, with the help of a friendly air force lieutenant, I found my way back and reentered the meeting room at exactly fourteen hundred hours. It was already filled with the straight-backed senior officers clearly miffed at my lackadaisical, civilian, academic, liberal-left style. (Those were the adjectives I imagined were racing around in their heads.)

The commandant welcomed me back and pointed to the board, where he had written what he thought I had said at the end. It was a rather jumbled version. He asked me to comment. I said it was close, but he had missed several points.

"Why don't you come up and show us?"

I walked up, took the eraser, and wiped the board clean. As I wrote down what I had actually said, a kind of collective gasp was heard. (Sometime later I learned that one doesn't remove what the chief honcho writes unless he gives permission.) The damage was done. My *faux pas* was duly noted by all those familiar with military etiquette. To add insult to my embarrassment, the commandant then suggested, "Since you are so skilled at organizing things, why don't you stay up here and be our recorder."

I didn't like where this was leading. I declined the offer and retorted, "What about one of those young men [pointing to the junior officers]? Surely one of them can do it." And I went back to my original seat.

My first challenge paid off almost immediately. Instead of buckling under, I had asserted my independence. I felt better and, despite the knots in my belly, began to actually enjoy the charged atmosphere.

Finally, we got to work. It took us five more days to reach some accord and hammer out a reasonable "affirmative action" program, modest by today's standards but quite radical then.

I should note that things improved on the luncheon front, too. The second day one of the captains, a medical doctor who headed a hospital, took me with him to a little sandwich place in the building. The third and fourth days I went with two rear admirals. On Friday, just before "recessing for lunch," Admiral Hogle invited me to join him in the Flag Officers' Dining Room. Of course I accepted, and we went to a top floor room where almost everyone was in uniform.

The hats on top of the coat rack were laden with gold braid

and scrambled eggs. When we entered the room, I understood what the words "top brass" really meant. There were high-ranking officers in marine and army as well as navy uniforms, all with at least two stars on their epaulets. There was also a small party of civilians. At the head of the table sat a man of about forty-five with a ruddy face, rimless glasses, and slicked-down black hair. My excitement about having arrived in the *sanctum sanctorum* of the Pentagon soured considerably when I realized that it was Robert McNamara, the man my friend Aron Krich called the "Secretary of Death." I wanted to get up and leave. But I didn't.

I had my meal, and Admiral Hogle and I talked not about the war but about *our* mission. I remember suggesting to him a strategy that might prove useful, if rather unprecedented: urge the COs to consider skipping the normal chain of command and calling the greenest NROTC ensigns in to recruit their cooperation as tutors. "After all, they are just out of college, know the latest stuff, and, being 'officers and gentlemen,' might well be flattered being asked by their commanding officer to take on such a task." I didn't say it would also look good on their records. It was implied. I was learning and using the ways of the military in spite of myself.

By the end of the week together, we had figured out a number of ways to provide release time for further schooling, find tutors (the commandant did use my idea and, as I had suggested to him, presented it as his own), and redefine jobs so that they would no longer be implicitly race specific (e.g., "aircraft cleaner" had meant scut work for blacks). I found, however, that the toughest job was to persuade the all-white civilian supervisory group, many of whose representatives were in the chorus of silent resisters seated around the naval officers, to accept the inevitability of a truly integrated work force. That, I discovered, could best be accomplished by, well, waving the flag.

"It was the president's order that established the meeting and the mission; it is your patriotic responsibility to carry it out."

I didn't actually say it, but Admiral Hogle did. I was impressed by the sincerity with which he and the once-skeptical cadre of commanders—save for the one guy who still grumbled about "our mission in Veet-Naam"—now forcefully argued for fairness. One, a captain with an Italian-sounding name, later wrote the introduction to a brochure ("A Career in Shipbuilding") designed to attract a cross section of new workers. He spoke of how his parents had come from Naples; of how, like him, there were people in the navy and working for the navy from every corner of the world—Europe and Asia and Africa. That, he said, was the *American* way.

I came away from Washington with a somewhat different perspective on the military—and on patriotism. I did not suddenly start saluting the flag at every street corner, but I did gain some new respect for some of those who did.

Shortly thereafter, "McNamara's War" began to escalate, and I went back to the picket lines and to the vigils. But I cringed at the thought of burning the flag and found myself in awkward conflict when I witnessed such acts committed by my fellow protesters.

Some ten years later I was in Taiwan, the fifth stop on an eight-country lecture tour sponsored, in part, by the U.S. Information Agency's Speaker's Bureau. I had flown from Taipei to Kaohsiung in the south to speak at a university and then at the American Cultural Center. The subject of my evening lecture had something to do with higher education in the United States.

The BPAO (Branch Public Affairs Officer), a young man named Larry Daks, ushered me into the small auditorium where I was to speak. The room was filled with young people and a few older ones. (I guessed they had come as much to practice their English as to hear me talk about the aftermath of the Berkeley crisis and about flower power and curriculum reform.)

My host introduced me, and I gave my talk.

Immediately afterward, a middle-aged man stood up and said, in very proper schoolboy English, that he had a question for me. Before I could even acknowledge him, he said, "I want to know the professor's position on the war in Vietnam."

I said I'd be happy to tell him, but suggested I wait until others had a chance to ask me direct questions about my talk. He wasn't pleased but nodded and sat down.

There was about half an hour of Q & A on some of the things I'd said (with considerable interest in the idea of an open, unstructured curriculum). Then Larry Daks started to thank me.

The earlier questioner stood up again. "Professor," he said, this time quite emphatically, "you said you would tell us your view of the war in Vietnam. I still want to hear it."

I went back to the lectern and said, "I'm pleased to tell you. [I paused.] I have been opposed to our involvement in Vietnam since John Kennedy sent advisers to Saigon in the early 1960s. I . . ."

I couldn't finish my sentence, for he interrupted, shouting, "You're a Communist. A Communist!" Then, turning to Daks, he said, "How can you have such a person speak for the U.S. government? This is outrageous."

I said, "Let me answer that."

"First of all," I said, "I am not speaking for my government. They knew I would be in East Asia and that I would, as I have done on many occasions, give lectures at American cultural centers." (The cultural attachés arranged the venues and advertised the lectures, and I would speak—on my topics, in my own words, offering my own opinions, some of which were quite critical of official government policies.) Then, rising to the bait, I said, "If I am to believe the supporters of the war in Vietnam, we are there to help bring democracy to that beleaguered society. Democracy means, and will mean if it is true, that one can speak one's piece without fear or favor. That's what America is all about."

I sat down.

The interrogator stared at me briefly, packed up his belongings (which, I then noted, included a tape recorder), and walked out.

As we left the hall, I asked Daks if he knew who the man was and what had prompted his desire to have me make a statement about the war. Daks explained that he was a "KMT [Kuomintang] agent" who always came to meetings at the center and always tried to go on record showing that he was concerned about communism. Then, turning to me, Daks said, "You know, I've rarely seen anyone wrap himself in the flag the way you did in your response to that guy. It was masterful."

I was both proud and troubled. I still am.

[seventeen]

New Americans

IT IS 1981. I am in Thailand. In a place called Phanat Nikhom, a refugee camp not far from Bangkok. It's stifling hot, and I am sweating—and swearing under my breath. I am wondering when I will see the American immigration officer who was supposed to meet me two hours ago. He said he would be here at 8:15, "right next to the first building you see as you enter the camp."

I am not alone. There are many men and women around me. Some are holding the hands of children. Most are arrayed in three queues that snake back around the building. I think to myself, "These people must be feeling the heat, too. But they are stoic, patient, resigned. They seem used to waiting."

We are all assembled outside the gray concrete building. It has a thatched roof, large windows without panes or screens, and a wide-open doorway. I take off my sunglasses and try to peer into the dark interior of the room. Inside, three uniformed officers of the U.S. Immigration and Naturalization Service are sitting with interpreters beside them behind long tables. Opposite each pair are lines of refugees from Vietnam and Laos and Cambodia.

I am there hoping to get permission to speak to some of the American officials; the others, all Indochinese refugees whose final approval for admission to the United States now depends only on the results of the INS interrogation, are waiting to be interviewed by them. As they get close to the doorway, I note their stoicism is turning into trepidation.

Finally, I get to see my man. He too is sweating. And swearing. "Christ, it's hot here," Charles Bailey says to no one in particular. (I know his name from a tag over his right shirt pocket.)

"Sorry I'm late," he says, not sounding like he means it. "Now what was it you wanted to talk to me about?"

I explain that I am writing a book about how American refugee policy is being carried out from the perspectives of those who make it and those who implement it. I want to talk to him as I already have talked to many others—foreign service officers, UNHCR officials, interpreters, representatives of nongovernmental agencies, refugee workers, and refugees themselves. I want him to help me tell the INS side of the story accurately. He gives me a sardonic smile and says, "You want to know what I do?"

"Yes," I say. "And I want to watch you do it, to sit in as you interview some of these folks in the queue [all petitioners for asylum and resettlement in the United States]. I want to see you in the process of making decisions."

"Well," he says, "I don't know about that. I have to check with my supervisor."

He disappears into the building, and I watch him lean over to the officer at the first desk. There is animated discussion. I can't hear anything. After a few minutes he comes back and asks, "Do you have a diplomatic passport?"

"No," I say.

"A special one?"

"No. I'm strictly unofficial. But I do have letters of introduction . . ."

The officer interrupts and asks me to wait again. I am growing increasingly embarrassed, as the real petitioners are now bunching up behind me.

Although clearly not pleased, for whatever reason he relents. (Maybe his boss thinks I'll write something nice about him and his fellow agents.) Grudgingly, Charles Bailey leads me into the room and invites me to sit down next to him at a table just to the rear of those I could see from outside. On his other side are his interpreter and another American.

An elderly man is motioned to come in. Hesitantly, he approaches us and places his documents on the table, keeping his hand on them as if to say, "You know, they're mine."

Bailey, having reverted to his official role and rap, whispers something to me about the "regs." Then he asks the refugee a battery of questions. "What is your name? Where were you born? How far did you go in school? Were you in the army?" Every query could have been answered by scanning the paper in front of him that I was reading over his shoulder. But the dutiful interpreter asks the refugee each question. The answers are repeated in English. "Pho is his name. Pho Trang. He was born in Saigon in 1921 and had six years of schooling. He served in the French army. He was a soldier in the South Vietnam army."

"Ask him if he is a Communist." (A routine but obviously crucial question.)

The interpreter complies and asks the question.

"'No,' he says," says the interpreter.

"Ask him why he wants to go to America."

This time the response seems canned.

"He says, 'I want to be free.'"

Bailey looks at me, at the interpreter, at the petitioner. He shrugs. He picks up a stamp and bangs it on the top of the document. ACCEPT.

Another man approaches. He is followed by his wife and four children. They are all invited to sit down. On the sheet, which the man turns over and the officer hands to me to peruse, there is a notation: "Ethnic Chinese."

There is a change of interpreters, and the process begins again.

"What is your name?" "Your wife's name?" "Children?" "How old are you?" " How old is she?" "And the children?" "Where are you all from?"

I am getting a pretty clear picture of what my friend in the refugee field calls "INS-ing." Still, I sit through a number of other nearly identical interviews.

There is a break after the first hour. Bailey goes out back. I follow him.

"Mind if I join you?"

He shrugs. Then he walks over to a shaded area, lights a cigarette, and leans against the building.

We make small talk. He still seems very suspicious. He appears relieved when it is time to get back to work.

For another hour I am a bystander at what seems to be a

bureaucratic ballet—petitioner enters, nods, officer acknowledges with a head gesture and words to the interpreter "Ask him to sit down," then looks at the sheet given to him and then at the refugee. "What is your name?" "How old are you?" "Where are you from?" By one in the afternoon I can do the interrogation myself.

Quite abruptly, Bailey looks at his watch and waves his hand to a family standing in the doorway, indicating they will have to wait.

"Lunchtime," he says to me, getting up rather abruptly and walking out into the sunlight. Again I tag along. This time I ask Mr. Bailey to join me for a beer.

"It's Charlie," he says, and then agrees. Together we go to a makeshift bar set up against the fence at the camp's outer perimeter.

I urge him to give me his take on what is going on, but he says very little more than a reprise of what I had been witnessing all morning.

"They come up. They give me their papers. I ask them questions, mostly to be sure they're not commies because we don't take them—or bigamists or people with a 'social disease.' I approve most of them. I mean," he is tapping his fingers, "you do what you can for the poor bastards."

He stares into space while wiping his forehead with a soaked handkerchief. I look at his face, then glance down at his hand. He is wearing what looks like a high-school ring. I ask him about it.

He tells me it's from his high school in Canton, Ohio, a place he left ten years ago after he joined the army. He was an MP, and, yes, he did fight in Vietnam. After eleven months there he was rotated stateside, spent four more months in the army, and then left it for good. He went back home and tried to get into the police academy. For some reason he didn't make it. He joined the Border Patrol and, after some training, was sent to "work the border" not far from San Diego. When the call went out for volunteers to do the INS-ing in Thailand and other "first asylum" countries in Southeast Asia, he signed on. Once back in the area, he says, he had serious second thoughts. "But," he shrugs, "I'm doing my job. Three more months left."

And that is it. I can't get anything more out of him, especially when I try to get his view of the process of which he is a crucial part, actually the linchpin, and of the refugees he interviews. He has said his piece. I thank him for his time and insights.

In the afternoon I manage to sit with one of Bailey's colleagues. Then I catch a ride back to town in a UNHCR van.

Five days later I am at another camp. This one is a rather seedy complex of buildings situated right in the middle of Bangkok, on Wireless Road (also known as Embassy Row.) The camp is called Lumpini. It is across from a huge park with the same name.

The camp is a transit center where those who have been approved for admission to the United States are gathered up from various other places all over Thailand, including Phanat Nikhom, the place where I watched Charlie Bailey and his fellow officers interviewing some of these very people. There are no Charlie Baileys here—only Thai and UN officials and a dozen or so refugee workers.

For people about to make the big journey to America, the refugees seem amazingly quiet, even apathetic. (On reflection I realize they are not apathetic but terribly anxious. But they are not showing anyone, including family members, how they really feel: scared.)

It is one of my last days in the area. Within the week I will be returning to the States, where I plan to witness the admission process and see how officials and refugee workers operate as agents of assimilation.

I move about Lumpini, observing, talking to the UN officials, to refugee workers, and, through my interpreter, to some of the refugees.

Perhaps not surprisingly, though I am startled, I spot a few familiar faces, including the Chinese family from Laos I had seen being "processed" in Phanat Nikhom. I even remember the name, Chang, and the fact that they are Chinese from Laos. There were six of them together, two adults and four children. I recall their interrogation. I remember that the man said he was a tailor and that they had fled from the Pathet Lao, crossed the Mekong, and then spent nearly two years in a camp called Ubon in northern Thailand. They had been brought to Phanat Nikhom a few months before. Now they are waiting to fly to the United States.

Although Mr. Chang doesn't seem to recognize me, I feel an odd bond with him. Suddenly I have the urge to go with him and his family, to share the experience of the next stage of their odyssey. My fantasy becomes plausible when I learn that they are to be resettled in San Francisco.

Later in the day I speak to friends at the office in the city that coordinates resettlement, the Joint Voluntary Agency/Thailand. I tell them that, instead of taking the flight on which I am booked, I'd like ride on the World Airways charter heading for the Bay Area and wondered if they would pave the way. (They had been most helpful in opening many doors and gates to closed camps for me over the previous two years.) It won't work. I am told that I cannot fly with them, that, indeed, nobody, not even *bona fide* refugee workers, can go on the fully packed charters except for nurses from the Geneva-based Intergovernmental Committee for Migration, the agency that is involved in moving people from one country to another.

I have another idea. I will play leapfrog and beat the Changs to America.

Two days later I am on my way back to the States, having managed to change my original return ticket and leave for San Francisco three days earlier than planned in order to arrive just before the charter from Bangkok lands in Oakland.

My plan works.

It is a Monday morning, and I catch a ride to the Oakland airport. I enter the building and spend nearly an hour arguing with the immigration authorities, trying to get them to allow me to go into the arrival zone, a place that is clearly off limits to unauthorized folks, including immigration lawyers, family members and sponsors, and reporters. Fortunately, the letter of introduction from a high-ranking official that had helped me so much in various countries in Southeast Asia finally does the trick. I am permitted to enter the area.

Once inside I seek out my contact, Nguyen T. Nguyen, known by everyone, I am told, as "NTN." NTN is an energetic young Vietnamese American who works for the International

Rescue Committee out of its San Francisco office. As he walks with me into the restricted zone, the 505 refugees—men, women, teenagers, little kids—who had just arrived from Bangkok are being led into the large hall.

Once they are all in the auditorium, they seat themselves on plastic chairs or on the floor. Suitcases are piled up next to numerous oddly shaped bundles. In many ways it reminds me of the many black-and-white photos I have seen of Ellis Island. Only the faces beside the piles and the costumes are different. In the old pictures, people were almost invariably white, sallow faced, and dressed in unmistakable European clothing. The Indochinese sitting in the room have Asian countenances, but they are not dressed in stereotypical "Oriental garb." Instead, all but a few are wearing very modern, very Western clothing—bright shirts, jeans, running shoes.

More striking than the contradictory sense of déjà vu and the awareness of the clear differences between the old immigrants and these newer ones is the fact that the place, filled wall to wall with humanity, is surprisingly quiet. It is like Lumpini.

When the people do speak, it is in hushed whispers. The loudest sounds in the room come from crying babies. And clacking typewriters.

I spot a nurse who, I am just told, was on the flight from Bangkok. I ask her what it was like on board the plane.

She tells me that the refugees, most of whom had never flown before, were clearly confused about where they were going and must have been wondering if they ever should have applied for resettlement. "They clutched the armrests and closed their eyes. And, except for the babies," she says, "they didn't sleep."

She adds that most were reluctant to leave their seats, that they had difficulty eating the strange food, that quite a few felt—or got—sick, and that they were frightened by the odd toilets, despite the fact that instructions about how to use them were posted in Vietnamese, Khmer, Lao, and Chinese, as well as English.

I walk around the perimeter of the room. It is filled wall to wall—and row after row—with hundreds of exhausted people. I look for the Changs. I cannot spot them in the sea of people almost indistinguishable from one another. (I chide myself for thinking such seemingly racist thoughts. But then I assuage my own guilt. After all, those who filled the receiving halls at Ellis Island a century before all looked a good deal alike, too.)

I notice that almost all of the refugees are carrying large plastic bags (about twenty inches square) marked "ICM" (the acronym standing for the Intergovernmental Committee for Migration). The bags have words or symbols written on each corner. NTN teaches me how to "read" them.

He explains that the graffiti immediately tells him names, how many people are in the family group, their final destination, the agency that is handling the case. Inside each bag—one to a family, NTN says—are all their critical documents: visas, tickets, and papers relating to their new status as legal refugees about to enter the United States.

I ask him whether he can help me find a family I met in Thailand and know was on the flight. "No problem," he says. And he looks up the name and finds the number. Then he asks someone to call out both in Chinese over the loudspeaker. Hesitantly, a man dressed in clearly brand-new but very wrinkled clothes rises in the back of the auditorium and comes forward. Looking astonished, he recognizes me. As he approaches, I read his bag. In the upper left corner it says CHANG; in the upper right SFO (San Francisco area). At the bottom it says IRC, and the number six is circled (six people in the group).

I bow to Mr. Chang and try to communicate. There is no interpreter at hand. He smiles at me rather shyly. I smile back and nod to his exhausted-looking wife and sleepy kids.

Suddenly, the room, which had been rather dimly lit, brightens. As the lights come on, the number of uniformed officers quadruples. The processing is about to begin.

NTN has a list and a microphone. He starts calling out IRC "clients'" names. When the refugees hear theirs, individuals or family groups get up and move to a desk where an ICM worker reads the information scrawled on the outside of their plastic bags and checks the color of the stickers affixed to them.

After it has been determined that the papers are in order, the refugees go to the quarantine officer to have their medical records checked. Once released, they go through "immigration." An INS officer reviews each set of documents and, if all is in order, stamps the precious I-94 form. The most important piece of paper, it serves in lieu of a visa and, for a time, will be the family's main source of official identification.

The last stop is "customs." The check there is not entirely perfunctory, for some inspection of luggage and packages is made; but it is not a very long or thorough search.

The refugees then pass through heavy glass doors and officially enter the United States.

As I watch, I am emotionally caught up in the significance of the moment. Yet, I have the feeling that, for them, it isn't so definitive.

Whatever the case, two minutes later they are back in a "waiting mode" once again, in a room like the one they have just left.

They made it. Yet, they are still waiting, and they must be wondering, "What's next?"

At last, it is time to move again. Some names are called. There is confusion. In the room there are many Nguyens; many Phos and Hongs and Lees. And several Changs. They strain to hear their names and their still-useful numbers. Finally, things sort themselves out, and several individuals and three families gather their belongings and follow an official who takes them to meet relatives there to welcome them to California.

One after another, those culled from the crowd eagerly scan the faces of those just beyond the plate glass window, then brighten when a loved one is sighted. The reunions are simultaneously joyful and painful to watch. I observe a pat on the back from an older brother; a stare of disbelief from a teary daughter seeing her parents after a long separation, then an awkward embrace; a solemn handshake from old grandfather whose face is nearly expressionless but whose body seems wracked with emotion.

Most of those who have come to Oakland on Flight 50 are not met by anyone. Those still in the transit lounge are informed in four languages that they will be boarding buses that will take them and their belongings to Fort Hamilton, an old military post in Marin County now used as an ICM transit facility, for the night.

Finally the buses arrive. The refugees walk out of the stuffy airport into the brilliant California summer sunshine and get on one of the buses. This time I am allowed to go along.

The trip to Fort Hamilton, up Route 80, past Berkeley,

across the San Raphael Bridge, past San Quentin, and into Marin, one of the wealthiest counties in America, must be, for most, a blur. They are dazed and confused and near exhaustion.

Arriving at Hamilton, the refugees are greeted by representatives of various agencies, who, using interpreters, explain where they are, what is going to happen next, and when they will move again. They are given bedding and toilet articles and shown to rooms in the barracks. Leaving most of their luggage—two cheap suitcases and three bundles—in a storage area, they pick up hand baggage, along with the ICM bag, and start trudging across a big yard. I watch as they slowly walk up two flights of stairs into a small room and shut the door. It is time for me to return to the city. I will see them tomorrow.

The tomorrow that is the Changs' first full day in America comes very early. Their migration to America is about to take a new turn—and I am there to share it with them.

I meet the bus that brings them back to San Francisco and accompany them to the regional office of the International Rescue Committee (IRC), located on busy Van Ness Avenue.

Once there the Changs are introduced to Li, their caseworker, who speaks to them in Mandarin. She seems to be most efficient—both hard and firm. From the local IRC director, Don Clement, I learn that those in his office believe that refugees must learn to stand on their own two feet as soon as possible, to become independent, not dependent.

Li follows what I later learn is a standard procedure. Documents are checked. Several are kept, and the I-94 forms are returned to the head of the household. Mr. Chang puts them in his pocket, a minor but significant *rite de passage.* There is no further need for the ICM bag, although it is not discarded. Mr. Chang is then given a promissory note for money that will be advanced to him from the IRC. He is told that an apartment has been rented for his family, that the first month's rent and the key money have already been paid, and that he will be given ninety dollars for groceries for the first week and eighty dollars for the second and so on until welfare payments began or he had employment. He is handed the first check for ninety dollars and sent off with a refugee worker to cash it in a nearby bank using his precious I-94 as an ID. I tag along. Mr. Chang follows the instructions. He approaches a bank officer, has the check approved, stands in line at the teller window, gets his money, counts it (though I have the feeling he really has no idea of its value), and we go back to the IRC office to wait for a ride to the new apartment.

While we wait, with Li serving as interpreter, I learn a bit more about his background, his life in Laos, his attitude toward the Communist regime ("a government of liars"), his escape by paying a fisherman to row his family across the Mekong River, and his stay in the UNHCR-administered refugee camp at Ubon.

Prior to his flight from Laos, Chang says he had had no thought of going to America or anyplace else in particular. He says he just wanted to get away from Communist persecution and ethnic discrimination—"to live free." While he had few ideas about the United States, he was positive about what Americans had done in Laos. "Good things," he says. "They are kind people."

Once in Ubon, he tells me, he heard more about America from others in the camp and soon decided to apply for resettlement because, he says, "Of all the places I thought America best." The UN authorities put him in touch with American resettlement workers from the refugee office in Bangkok. Eventually the family was moved to Phanat Nikhom.

In that camp things were different. He studied—or tried to study—English with American teachers and had some cultural orientation. ("Very practical things," he says, "like how to shake hands.") His wife also took the same courses.

He went for two hours each morning; she in the afternoon. (My impression was that they learned very little English). After three months, the course of study was ended, and the Changs were told to watch the board for their number. Finally, he saw it there.

"How did you feel?" I ask through Li.

"Good," he says, "we were going to America. But we still were anxious—not sure when we would go or how. Finally, after several days, we were told to pack up again. We boarded buses and were taken to Bangkok. Then I knew it was going to happen."

"And the flight?" I ask. "What about that?"

"It was long, very long."

"Were people excited?"

Li, the caseworker-interpreter, explains to me that he doesn't know what I mean.

I try again. It doesn't work.

Finally, I ask Mr. Chang what he wants to do. He tells me that is a hard question. He has virtually no English skills. Still, he hopes to find work, any work, but especially in a factory. Perhaps he will be a tailor, for that is what he did before he fled from Laos with his family.

"And the children?"

"School. Then they will decide. But as much education as they can get. That is very important."

At long last a Vietnamese paraprofessional worker, who, like the family, is of Chinese background, comes back to the office, and the eight of us and all of the Changs' possessions—including bedding and kitchen utensils supplied by the IRC—are piled into his big old car for a short trip to the apartment on Jones Street in the depressed and depressing Tenderloin area, a place long inhabited by poor and dispossessed people, now including a number of Indochinese refugees.

We carry the baggage into the building through a door which Mr. Chang unlocks with the key he has just been given, his *own* key, and take the elevator the sixth floor. We walk down the hall and wait while, again, the head of the family opens the door. Everyone is eager to see the place.

It is a large, bright, somewhat shabby unfurnished two-room place with two closets, a bathroom, and a small kitchen. Not much for six people. But it is theirs. The furniture—beds and tables and chairs ordered by the IRC office—is due in an hour, but Chang can't wait. He moves several suitcases and bigger bundles into a big closet, unpacks a large, square Laotian mat, spreads it out, and tosses four of the new pillows on it. As if on cue, the children all kick off their shoes, crawl over the mat, and promptly fall asleep. Mrs. Chang smiles shyly. Her husband looks at me and at the interpreter and at the neighbors, a Chinese-Vietnamese family from downstairs, who have come in to help. He smiles, too.

The Changs are settled in, and it is almost time for me to leave. But Mr. Chang says he wants to buy some food, and I decide to go with him. As we leave the building, his new neighbor tells him not to bother, that he and his wife will give the family supper. Chang is obviously touched by the gesture, but still seems eager to go out and bring something back. So we go.

We walk up to a neighborhood grocery store. It is not a supermarket, but to Mr. Chang it is unbelievable. "So much food," he says through the IRC volunteer who has accompanied us.

I am struck by another common chord. My Dutch wife, a refugee from an earlier war, has often told of how, leaving Ellis Island and being taken into the city in 1947, one of the first things that caught her eye was a fruit stand. "I hadn't seen bananas or oranges or tangerines since before the war," she has told me many times. Chang buys rice, noodles, soup, and eggs—and some bananas, too.

I walk him back to his new home. We get there just as the furniture truck pulls up to deliver the beds and dining-room set ordered by the IRC. Everyone helps to move things in.

It has been but ten days since I observed the Chang family's interview at Phanat Nikhom, a few days since I saw them in Lumpini and a mere thirty-six hours since I was at the Oakland Airport when they arrived in America. They are no longer strangers to me.

The bag on which their number, 152902, was scrawled is gone. In fact, as I look around, I don't see it anywhere in the apartment. It is already part of the distant past. Part of yesterday.

But their journey is hardly over.

Regardless of their new status, they are still refugees. Perhaps, like so many others, they will always be refugees.

Whether those forced to flee arrive in America by sea or by air, as did nearly one million Indochinese people, all seem to undergo a similar experience. Like passengers on aircraft that are flown into hurricanes, they are whipped around and buffeted, first by home-grown cadres or foreign occupiers and then by international bureaucrats and resettlement officers; shunted around the countryside, moved first hundreds then thousands of miles; and then, finally, find their place of refuge—a flat in the Rainer Valley of Seattle, a tiny apartment in Boston's Chinatown, or a few rooms on Jones Street in San Francisco. It often proves to be but a temporary haven in the eye of the storm. They have to go through much more turbulence to get to the other side.

For the Changs, and all who came with them, the third stage—call it "Becoming American"—is only just beginning.

[eighteen]

An Unnecessary Excursion

HIGH ABOVE THE Bavarian resort town of Berchtesgaden, in a sylvan area called Obersalzberg, is Adolf Hitler's *Berghof*—or what is left of it. There in the midst of the alpine wilderness one can see an intricate maze of underground bunkers, the foundations of his once-palatial retreat, and a huge souvenir shop. It is a noxious place. Quite literally; it made me sick.

I was attending a meeting in Salzburg. Despite an uneasy prescience and considerable ambivalence, I decided to join some of my fellow conferees in accepting an invitation from Timothy Ryback, director of the Salzburg Seminar and author of a powerful new book on Dachau, *The Last Survivor*, to have a look at "where it all began." The *Berghof* is only forty minutes from Salzburg, just across the border in Germany.

As we set out from our base, we were told that we would be traveling on the route of the Anschluss, the road down which German troops had moved to occupy their generally sympathetic "victims," the Austrians. The road leading out of the suburbs of Salzburg goes past handsome houses on well-appointed grounds. We left the town and drove through a bower of trees which spanned the completely open border, then took a turnoff and started climbing the mountain. Halfway up, we pulled into a large parking lot. (Had we gone on up the Kehlstein Road, eventually we would have reached Hitler's still-extant aerie, "The Eagle's Nest." But our objective was not to see the views but to get a sense of history.)

As we got out of the van, we saw a number of people milling around a large area dominated by a small hotel and a huge souvenir shop. Amongst the piles of tee shirts and racks of *lederhosen*, hunting style jackets, and peasant skirts and blouses were pointy alpine hats, assorted badges of silver and enamel (some with the word BERGHOF baked in), many postcards, and all sorts of literature. No swastikas or deathheads or armbands, but there was Nazi memorabilia nonetheless. Especially prominent were photos of the place in the good old days, picture books, and volumes about Adolf Hitler's life and Eva Braun's, too. There were several books about the *Berghof* itself. They told how it was built; who lived there; who came to visit. The only thing that suggested the evil that had been hatched was a commentary in one of them on the two hundred Germans who were killed when the redoubt was hit with the bombs of the Allies. No mention anywhere about the incalculable numbers murdered in the name of the inhabitants of the *Berghof*.

Standing before a large pair of before-and-after photographs and a map of the area, an English-speaking guide matter-of-factly addressed a large group of tourists. He briefly described the history of the place, then indicated where Martin Bormann, Hitler's deputy chief of staff, had lived; where Reichsmarschall Hermann Goering had had a house; and where the barracks for the SS security forces were located. After a brief pause he swept his hand over a greatly enlarged picture of the biggest structure.

"There," he said, pointing to one part, "was where Eva Braun and her friends talked shopping." Then, indicating another section of the now-destroyed building, he added, "And that is where Adolf Hitler and the men talked business."

The visitors nodded. Then the guide repeated the whole thing in German. Nobody asked what the business was. Nor did he volunteer to explain why that locale was, in Tim Ryback's words, "one of the most important historic sites in Germany": the place where *Mein Kampf* was finished, where the plot to find *Lebensraum* was incubated, where the "Final Solution" began. On these details the guide was silent.

It was time for us to move on. Our small group crossed the parking lot to the Berghof Hotel. We put our tokens in the heavy revolving gate, which admitted us to a tiny room with more books in English and German about Hitler and his mate. We started down the stairway into the bunker. I was last in line. Ahead of me was Brenda Gourley, vice chancellor of the University of Natal in Durban, South Africa. Two steps down the steep staircase I froze. I felt I couldn't breathe. Brenda, I soon learned, was feeling the same constriction and nausea. Without consulting one another, we turned on our heels and climbed back up into the light and fresh air.

We took a walk.

First we were silent. Then we started sharing thoughts about persecution, suffering, and the problems of dealing with the past for both the perpetrators and the victims, something that is a subject of everyday discourse in Brenda's homeland.

Eventually the rest of our group surfaced, and together we all walked a bit higher up the mountain to the ruins of the retreat itself.

The house had been located on the edge of the mountain on a flat area in what is now a large clearing surrounded by tall trees. The place glistened in the damp morning air. It had a Wagnerian aura. A kind of dissonance between the mythic and the real was palpable as we looked at places already quite familiar. Through the wisps of fog we could envision exactly where Eva gossiped with the girls; where Adolf and the boys discussed "business."

Perhaps to avoid the place becoming a shrine or sanctuary for unreconstructed pensioners and neo-Nazis, there are no official markers, no signs, and no explanations. If this is the reason, it is not entirely successful. On the day we were there I noticed several neatly carved runes on some of the trees, including the double lightning bolts of the SS. Clearly, they had been there for some time. When I commented, Tim said that, on other visits, he had also seen little shrines ringed with rocks and adorned with flowers and small flags. They were, presumably, memorials to the martyred heroes now lying in their own special Valhalla.

I found it all terribly disconcerting. Certainly, I thought, there ought to be some way of conveying the horrors that had been concocted in this mystical glade. I thought of those who were forced to flee their native land. I thought of the millions who could not escape. I thought of my wife at home in the States and of her sister in Canada, once two little girls hidden in an Amsterdam cellar, the only survivors of a very large family rounded up, deported, and killed in the death camps because they had been deemed *Untermenschen* by the creator of the *Berghof.*

I felt the bile returning to my throat and turned to leave the site. Brenda joined me.

We got back in the van and waited for the others. When they came, we drove straight back across the border to our Salzburg base. No one said a word.

That evening, sitting in the grandeur of Schloss Leopoldskron (the place once owned by the exiled German Jewish impresario Max Reinhardt), Ed Berger, dean of the faculty of arts and sciences at Dartmouth College, the sponsor of the meeting we were attending (and one of those who stayed behind), asked me how I felt about the excursion. I told him. He nodded and said, "I didn't want to go. I didn't need to go."

"Neither did I," I thought.

I was very sorry I went, for I saw there both what Hannah Arendt called the "banality of evil" (which I suppose I had expected) and its perverse perpetuation, right there at the very tranquil place where much of what was wrought by the Third Reich had been planned, ordered, and celebrated.

I can't get the place out of my mind. I keep thinking that, since it is unlikely that anyone will be willing to finish the job begun by the Allied aircraft at the end of the war, then at the least the authorities there should seal up the bunkers, put a small plaque in memory of the victims at the entrance to the site, and close the damn souvenir shop.

Tillie and Barney Rose, paternal grandparents.

Celia and Wolf Feld, maternal grandparents.

Aaron Rose, "The Great Pathfinder," 1920.

Lillian Rose, "The Music Lover," 1948.

Mother (Lillian) and son (Peter), Rochester, New York, 1933.

The Robin Club, Syracuse, New York, 1941. Left to right: Jon Holstein, Philip Holstein, Peter Rose, Aaron Rose, and Michael Weingott from London.

Aaron and Lillian Rose, Camp Chateaugay, Merrill, New York, 1946.

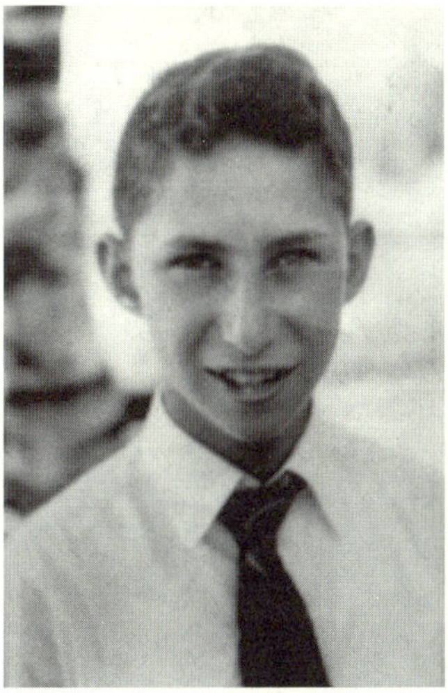

The day Peter became a man.

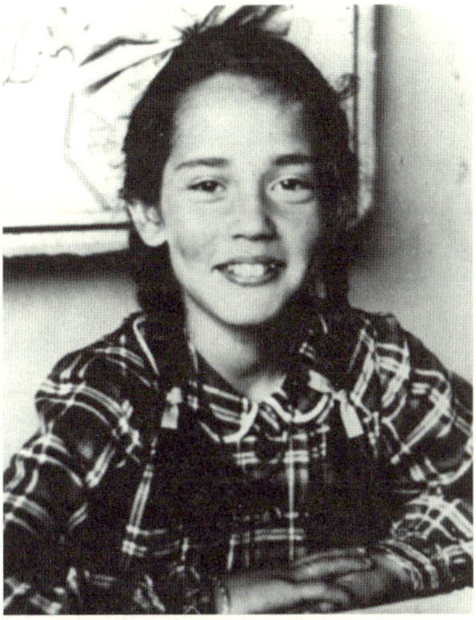

Hedy in school in Amsterdam, 1947.

Peter, 19, and Hedy, 17, summer, 1953.

Hedy with Lies and Dan, London, 1964.

At the shoebox on Cape Cod, 1970.

At the Damascus Gate, Jerusalem, 1975. Photo by Peter Rose.

On the Jungfrau in Switzerland, 1978.

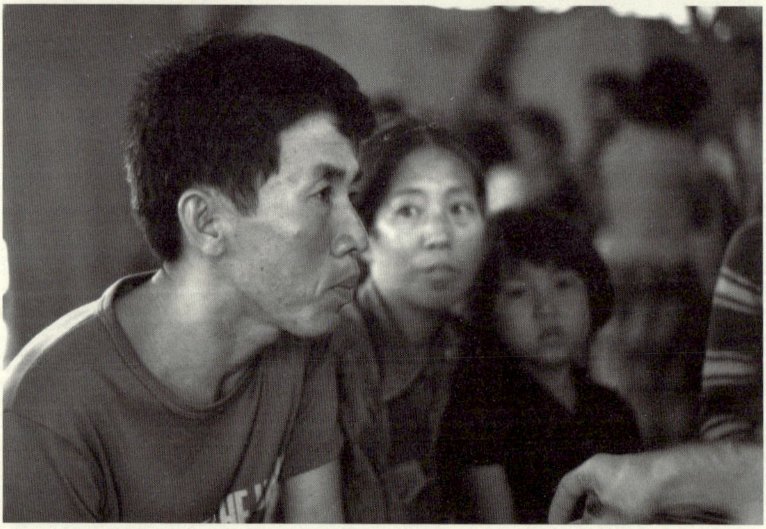

The odyssey of the Indochinese refugees. Photos taken in Thailand, the Philippines, and San Francisco by Peter Rose, 1980–81.

New Americans (from Laos) in San Francisco, 1983. Photo by Peter Rose.

Tokyo conference, 1985.

With members of the Social Science Department, Jiaotung University, Shanghai, China, 1986.

Conference in Kyoto, Japan, 1990.

Peter and Hedy on the occasion of Hedy's M.A. at Smith College, 1974 (she received her doctorate from the University of Massachusetts in 1987).

Peter surrounded by the ordered chaos of his Smith College office, 2002.

Dan, Hedy, and Lies with Peter on his fiftieth birthday, Wellfleet, Massachusetts, September 1983.

Peter and Hedy at the helm of the 100-foot ketch *Angelique*, Penobscott Bay, Maine, 1988.

With longtime friend Barbara Honeyman Roll on the occasion of her honorary degree, Smith College, early 1990s.

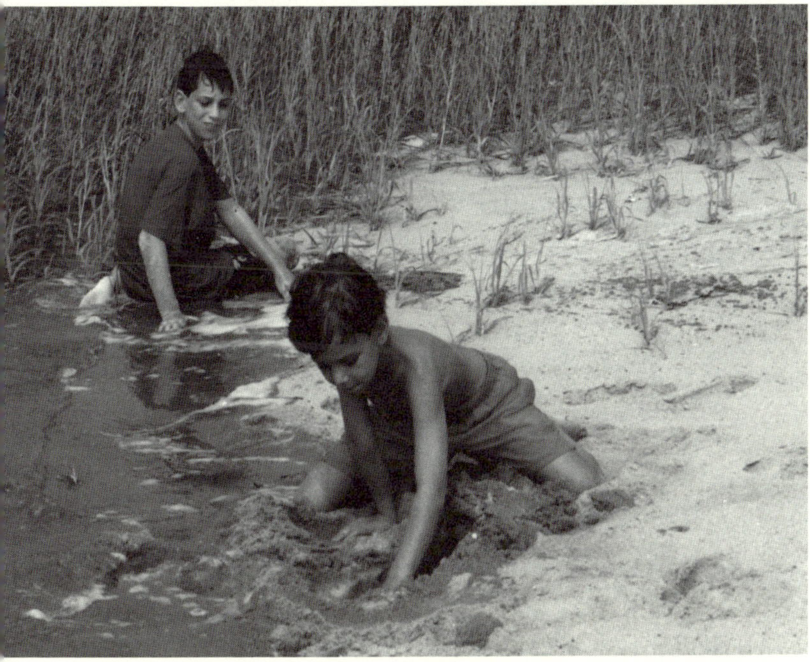

Grandsons Jordy and Robert Rose, Lieutenant Island, Wellfleet, Massachusetts, summer, 2001.

Peter and Hedy at the Centro Studi Ligure per le Arte e Lettere, Bogliasco, Italy, 2001.

part three

Busman's Holidays

[nineteen]

Being Prepared

"OH, OH," I tell myself each time I sort through my mail. "Here's another one. I should just throw it out."

I don't. I take it back to my desk, set it aside, and go back to work. But not for long. I can't resist a quick look, even though I already know what I'll find when I flip through the pages.

Catalogs. The objects of my obsession are colorful catalogs of sporting gear, outdoor equipment, and travel goods produced by those who are making fortunes from the fantasies of would-be Hillarys, Cousteaus, Chouinards, and, of late, Krakauers.

Like millions of others, I am inundated with information about 60/40 jackets and those made of cotton, polyester, microfiber, and old-fashioned wool. There are pages of intriguing photos and personal testimonials to the merits of all sorts of life jackets, compasses, diving gear, kayak paddles, mountaineering equipment, mountain bikes, hybrid bikes, and road bikes, including one that is just the same as Lance Armstrong's. I am caught up in competing appeals to buy a real Swiss army knife: one claimed by Victorinox to be the "original," the other made by Wegner, whose promotional copy says only *it* is the genuine article. To the amateur, there is actually no difference between them. But to a careful observer, it is possible to discern that the manufacturers are right. It is all revealed in shape of the Swiss-cross logo favored by each company.

The fact is that there are differences in seemingly similar items all around us. For example, there are differences between the standard-looking oxford button-down shirt I have been wearing since 1946 and the ones touted by the "specialists" in Dodgeville, Wisconsin; Manchester, Vermont; and Freeport, Maine. While some may have difficulty distinguishing between shirts that feature "single-needle tailoring, with seven-button placket front, left breast pocket, back box pleat and locker loop, classic button-down collar, and sleeve placket button" and those that feature "a full, comfortable cut, 3⅛-inch button-down collar, seven-button top center placket, sturdy cross-stitched buttons, single open pocket, and long sleeves with finish placket," I can. After all, one has a locker loop but no cross-stitched buttons.

You see, it takes an expert.

Want to know the difference between Gore-Tex and H2No, Synchilla and Navylon, polyprop and neoprene, Polartec and EBTek, canvas and Cordura, and the sorts of soles you can get on rock-climbing boots? I'll tell you. But before I do, I have to note that my expertise isn't purely academic. I don't rely simply on reading the texts that accompany the pictures of wares displayed by perfect human specimens rarely more than twenty years old. No sir. As my wife—and the various mail-order departments—can attest, I am an unpaid equipment tester *par excellence.*

I am also a sucker for whatever is being plied: multilensed cameras, ice axes, pitons, carabiners, altimeters, and super backpacks to use on my next trek up Everest; spelunking and scuba-diving gear; pocket survival tools and machetes for the jungle; sleeping bags of varying materials; and safari jackets so I can look like a big game hunter or foreign correspondent. I see them, learn how useful they are, and decide I have to have them. And I do.

My closets are filled with mountain parkas and ponchos; running shoes for hard surfaces, cinders, and woodland paths; belts that stretch, belts that hold money in secret compartments, belts that support an arsenal of weapons (just in case). My dresser has shirts of denim, gingham, chamois, and corduroy, and, of course, oxford cloth. My desk has an array of miniature radios for working hours and for play. (I have one that weighs fourteen pounds and another that is only three ounces.) And, for my wrist, I have a variety of digital and analog watches (and one that is both) for running, swimming, traveling (with twelve time zones), reading the temperature, assessing the altitude, even for telling time.

I am so familiar with the publications of the mail-order businesses that I feel a keen sense of personal kinship with Eddie Bauer, Moss Brown, the Gleason Brothers, Royal Robbins, Norm Thompson, and L. L. Bean; with J. Crew, J. Peterman, and J. Press; and with Mr. Orvis and Lands' End. I also have a special relationship with the folks who live by the James River, across Coldwater Creek, beneath the North Face, down in the Banana Republic, and those who are ever getting set for the Territory Ahead. I am at one with those whose monograms are EMS and REI, people I hear from far more frequently than I hear from my children or grandchildren! I know them all.

So, if you want a testimonial . . .

By the way, I don't let the stuff I accumulate go to waste. I use it.

Ever see the layered look? All the specialty outfitters swear by it. Me, too.

Picture this: Lifa underwear covered with Hind tights and a pair of Patagonia climbing pants held up by suspenders from Palo Alto Bicycles. My tee shirt is from Holiday River Tours (and says "Go With The Flow" in bold letters across the back). Over that I am wearing an L. L. Bean red-and-black-checked shirt with tan sleeves (just like the kind old L. L. wore when he got dressed for action), and, in case it gets cold, a Sherpa sweater and a Marmot Mountain Works vest. On my feet I wear Blister Resister socks under my Wigwam raggs and Raichle boots, over which I have pulled on my IME gaiters. On my head I have an Outdoor Research cap with earflaps and logo, topped off with an MSR climbing helmet. Around my waist is a Lowe fanny pack, in which I've put my Helly Hansen rain gear, my Sharper Image short-wave radio, my Silva compass, my 9 mm x 27 mm x 50 mm Tasco zoom binoculars, my Nikon, and my lunch. I'm prepared for anything.

There is only one problem.

I can't move. I can't breathe.

I'm catalogged.

[twenty]

Challenging Days, Star-Studded Nights

"ENJOY UNSPOILED WILDERNESS." "Sail away from it all." "Rock and roll through a sandstone chasm." "Go with the flow." "Have the adventure of a lifetime."

Such phrases advertise carefree vacations on foot, afloat, and on a bicycle. Further copy promises that outfitters with such intriguing names as Backroads, High Desert Tours, Arabella Adventures, Tailwinds, and Yankee Packet Company will supply everything from board and bedding to a cohort of kindred spirits. They also promise to provide skilled crews to serve as guides and gofers, plus high adventure and breathtaking scenery.

Ever a skeptic, even I have found that there can be truth in advertising.

Over the past three decades I have taken part in a number of three-day to two-week packaged expeditions. With members of my family, I have cruised Penobscot Bay aboard the 125-year-old schooner *Stephen Taber* and the Caribbean on the brigantine *Belle Blonde.* We have also sailed "Downeast" from New York City to Camden, Maine, on the ketch *Angelique,* and from Rockland, Maine to Boston and back on the pinky schooner *Summertime,* rafted the Grand Canyon from Lees Ferry to Lake Mead, paddled Oregon's "Wild and Scenic Rogue River" (we called it "wild and woolly"), and been inn-to-inn bicycle wanderers in Vermont.

On my own I have gone windjamming through the Hawaiian islands and the San Juans, floated and bounced through Cataract Canyon in Utah, kayaked the Klamath River in California, done some social climbing with the Ryder/Walker hiking company in

Switzerland, and taken numerous bike tours, including those that looped through the wine country in Napa and Mendocino Counties, up and over the Continental Divide in Colorado, from Santa Fe to Taos and then around the Sangre de Cristo Mountains in New Mexico, down the coast of Oregon, and around the Big Island in Hawaii.

There was sameness about these excursions. I mean this in an analytical (not a pejorative) sense. They were all appealingly advertised, well planned, and well orchestrated.

To all outward appearances, the organizers of such expeditions and their crews seem quite sensitive to the problem of bringing strangers together to travel and live in close quarters. The clients have varied motives for joining such adventures. Some are energetic but lonely singles looking for companionship, and some are retirees who like to do interesting and different things each year.

Others are people like me, who, though they prefer to do things on their own, also like many activities that take considerable planning and organization for which they have little time.

For those in each of these categories—and others—the full-service guided tours fill several needs at once. They promise their clients (or "guests," as the outfitters prefer to describe them) packaged experiences with challenging days, star-studded nights, and ample conveniences for their care and feeding. And they assure them that the groups will be small and congenial.

Many years ago a favorite student put a "Peanuts" poster in my office. On it Linus proclaims, "I love mankind; it's people I can't stand." It seemed an appropriate joke-shibboleth for a sociologist.

The fact is that though this social scientist really does like people, I admit to having thought of that epigram the first time my wife and I signed on for one of these trips. I wondered if we would be herded and regimented and expected to sing old college songs around a beachside campfire, play charades, and be sociable even when we wanted to be left alone. My fears were hardly eased the first night when, together with fellow shipmates on the squared fantail of the sixty-eight-foot schooner the *Stephen Taber*, Mike Anderson, the skipper, tried to get us all to know each other. It was a bit unsettling, and I wondered how we would survive the voyage.

In fact we managed very well. And we later learned that many of those with whom we sailed had had the same apprehensions.

Weatherwise the trip was a disaster, with rain and fog for six days. We were grouped together in the tiny galley and smaller day-cabin much more than even the most gregarious of our group would have wanted or dreamed possible. But we got along, and it turned out to be a great vacation. In fact, the next season we took a second weeklong trip on the *Taber*, and that time the weather was perfect!

The skipper's briefing on the *Taber* proved to be standard procedure. There is always that first awkward encounter on such trips. Names are called out, hands are shaken, and everyone is told something about rules, routes, and daily routines. Afterward the entire group has dinner together.

The meal is a kind of rite of passage. Conversations tend to center on the fleshing out of cryptic words of identification made at the earlier meeting. "Sam Jones. I'm a teacher from Indiana and this is my wife, Sally. We grew up on the Connecticut shore and miss the salt air. We try to do something by the sea—Atlantic, Pacific, you name it—every summer." "George and I are retired. We just love to hike; in fact, we've just come back from the Italian Dolomites. Rugged but fantastic." Personal anecdotes get related, especially about other vacations, and reputations get established.

Regardless of the type of trip, the next morning is always a time of high excitement and, for many, trepidation. What will it be like if the wind really picks up? How will I deal with the rapids and holes in the river? What does it mean to do fifty miles over "fairly hilly" terrain? How will I look to the others?

For some, the last question becomes especially crucial now that everyone knows who's who—and might remember how, the night before, during the nervous banter of that first supper, they had boasted of talents and experiences they now wished they'd kept quite about.

It is a time of testing, and of stoking up.

Finally, pushing away from a table stacked with plates that had held three-egg omelets, bacon, pancakes, sweet rolls, and toast, the time of reckoning is upon the group. Gear is stowed and sails are hoisted; camp is struck and rafts are loaded; boots are tightened and packs are shouldered; tires are checked and helmets are buckled on. What all have been waiting for is now reality. There is no turning back.

The first full day—getting one's sea legs, sensing the power of white water, climbing the first long hills—is exhilarating and fatiguing. There is so much to take in; so much to sort out.

After several hours of sailing or rafting or paddling or riding, there is a break for lunch. Tour organizers do not skimp on meals. My amazement at the amount of food available—sandwich makings, homemade breads, salads of all sorts, cookies, and fruit—is topped only by my amazement at the amount consumed.

After a leisurely rest, the entourage is off again. Aboard ship one can continue to relax and enjoy the sun; on the river or the road there is still work to be done for there are, quite literally, "miles to go . . ."

Once the mooring or campsite or lodge is reached, the guests' "workday" is pretty much done. They may help to lower and furl sails, unload rafts, gather firewood, set up tents, or move bikes under cover, but, by and large, it is a quiet time for reflecting on the day's accomplishments—and waiting for the next meal.

Whether on a water or land trip, by the second evening the sociologist in me notes how we move into the next stage of group dynamics: establishing a quasicommunity. By the end of the first full day, the guests, more secure in what they are about, already begin to sort each other out, gravitating more to one person or couple or group and avoiding others in a polite but noticeable way. This pattern becomes clearer the next morning, when individuals and couples gather for breakfast. They hesitate, waiting for a seat next to somebody or away from somebody else.

The eggheads always seem to find each other; so do the jokesters, the oldsters, the drinkers, the yuppies, and the diehards. The last bunch often includes the sort of people who own their own boats, hike, kayak, and bike a good deal, and come on these trips not because of the uniqueness of the activity but for the convenience of the provisioning. Ever talking about equipment, weather conditions, distances covered and energy expended, they are often seen by the others as "purists." Those who view them as such seem to have little idea that real purists would define them as phonies for taking part in such ersatz expeditions.

By the third day things have shaken down, and a kind of rhythm has been worked out. It is the same on board as on the river or road. Those with similar backgrounds and interests stick together; so do the skilled and the not-so-skilled.

In addition to the formation of cliques, another sort of bonding invariably takes place. It is most noticeable on sailing trips, where the working passengers (they do help to raise and lower sails, weigh the anchor, and, sometimes, stand watch) quickly come to identify themselves with the boats they are on. This becomes especially apparent on "shore leave," when all are given a chance to wander the main streets of little coastal villages. There they exchange greetings and compare notes with those from other boats (who, like they, already feel they are a cut above the regular tourists they see). They then hurry back to the harbor for the yawl boat that will ferry them back to their mother ship.

On biking and hiking and kayaking tours, without the floating base of a windjammer on which all are literally living together for long stretches, such a feeling of identification is more symbolic than real, but the vessel-loyalty of the participants upon meeting those in other groups is very much the same. (Doubtlessly, the tee shirts and caps with company logos that everybody buys and wears enhance the sense of solidarity.)

The social systems established early on any given trip generally remain intact. Not only do people tend to maintain the attachments they form the first two days, but the intensity of their relationships grows—up to a point. Whether the trip is four, five, or six days or two weeks long, it seems to reach its zenith sometime toward the end of the last full day.

On the final evening, *gemütlichkeit* fills the air as the members of the subgroups begin to set aside their differences and join together.

Often there is a party to which everyone contributes something—beer and wine, talent (guitar playing is still very much in), contributions for a collective tip, or tales of misadventures with other groups that were "never, ever, as congenial as this one."

The last morning is usually much like the others; the routine still holds. But when the long trip back to base gets under way, an interesting thing happens. People who have just spent as much as a week or two together begin to draw back into their own worlds.

As the gangplank is lowered for the last time, as the rafts are deflated and stored in the outfitter's trucks, as the kayaks or bikes are racked on the trailers, as the vans are loaded for the bus station or airport, hands are shaken, hugs are exchanged, and promises to "keep in touch" are given, but too often the gestures are perfunctory. The guests are going their different ways. Suddenly it all seems quite ephemeral.

What is forgotten first, and there are some exceptions, are the people with whom one shared a most intense experience. What lingers are memories of long days at sea under full sail, of the high excitement and potential danger of rafting through huge rapids that the boatmen called "the best in the river." Remembered too are such rare moments of Walter Mitty-ish transcendence as when, after a week of pedaling nearly 350 miles in high country, it seemed possible to climb any mountain.

[twenty-one]

Running around the World

FOR ME THERE is nothing better than getting up at the crack of dawn, slipping out of a hotel in the middle of a strange city, making a turn left or right, and then jogging off on a new adventure. I do it all the time, in the United States and abroad.

Over the past ten years I have run around the Charles River Basin in Boston, San Francisco's Embarcadero, Chicago's Loop, Vancouver's Stanley Park, Sydney Harbor, and the Ringstrasse in Vienna. I have run down broad dusty roads in suburban Nairobi, through narrow, crowded alleys in Hong Kong, in and out of little villages above Lake Como, down bustling avenues in Beijing, by the canals of Venice and the Klongs of Bangkok, and along the banks of the Liffey, the Thames, the Seine, the Amstel, and the Rhine.

Such running around the world has a special quality to it. It is a kind of inversion of the oxymoron "same difference" we used to use when we were cool teenagers. The *different sameness* of what I do to keep in shape and to see new places before starting a day's work is a most satisfying fringe benefit of my itinerant lifestyle. Research projects, meetings, and lectures keep me on the move.

While I have occasion to meet many people and to visit many interesting places on my trips, it is on early-morning jogs and weekend wanderings that I can especially feel the wondrous unity and amazing diversity of the human family. Time and again I am struck by continuities and connections with those whose habitats provide me with "field sites" for comparative study.

It is when I am quite literally on the road that much of what

I study, write, and teach about, namely, culture and character, becomes most personally meaningful.

Most of the people I've encountered in my off-the-tourist-route excursions are warm and friendly. In places unused to the likes of me, they are sometimes confused by my half-dressed presence as I suddenly appear from around a cobble-stoned corner or over the brow of a brick-laid hill. I have often seen the proverbial "double take" as early risers look at me, stop, and look again in cities as diverse as Madrid, Melbourne, Mexico City, New Delhi, Dubrovnik, Suva in the Fijian Islands, and Sendai in Japan.

Sometimes they do more.

I was once stopped by an elderly street cleaner on a corner in the center of Graz, Austria. Shaking her finger, she lectured me in German for at least five minutes, explaining that "one must not cross the road against the light," even though it was 5:30 A.M. and there was no traffic anywhere in sight.

"Rules," she said, "are rules. And here, in Austria, they are obeyed."

Not, apparently, in Italy. There, by contrast, taking morning jogs on various trips to Rome as well as Florence, I have been laughed at by passersby as I *waited* for a light to change in the first rush of traffic of the day. Some have even asked me what I am waiting for!

Like a Pied Piper, I've been followed by groups of Chinese children along Shanghai's Bund and by Malay kids down by the beach at Penang, Malaysia. I've been cheered by Swedes who called, "Hup, hup, hup" as I ran along Stockholm's quay and by New Zealanders as I headed into the sheep-covered hills above Christchurch.

My obsession has rarely gotten me into serious trouble. On the contrary, it has often opened doors. I've found that occasional stops to talk or to try to communicate with the local people can pay off in a variety of ways.

I remember a morning in Xian in the People's Republic of China. I ran from the grounds of my big Soviet-style hotel, off to the right, toward the center of town. There, in a giant plaza, were hundreds of people in groups ranging from six or eight to forty or fifty, all doing their exercises.

Few paid much attention to me as I jogged by, but I was most curious about them.

I ran for another mile or so, then retraced my route. As I returned to the area of all the activity, I stopped nearby and watched. At one point a young man came up to me and, in schoolbook English, said, "You jog, sir."

"Yes," I said.

"I do not jog. I exercise with this," he said, showing me his wooden sword.

I asked him to tell me what he did with it. He bade me to follow him. We walked past several clusters of older people doing a kind of stylized shadowboxing to a waiting group of young men. My new friend nodded to me, then joined the others. They started an elaborate routine of thrusts and parries, all accompanied by carefully choreographed foot movements.

While participating in the swordplay, the young Chinese who brought me there did not look at me—but I did notice him turn slightly and smile shyly when, after ten minutes or so, I waved to him and took my leave.

Then there was the time I was running in the woods near the famed Holmenkollen Ski Jump high above the city of Oslo. It was a fantastic fall morning. Everything was in tones of yellow, green, and blue.

Quite unexpectedly, I heard footsteps behind me. Someone was gaining on me. I suppressed the urge to speed up and decided to let him or her pass. He, who turned out to be a man about my age, didn't. He merely caught up, fell in with my pace and started to chat, first in Norwegian, then, sensing my incomprehension, in English.

We ran along together for another two or three kilometers, getting to know each other and learning not only that we were both university professors and in the same field, but that he would be attending my lecture that very afternoon.

The next morning I ran with my new friend in another part of the city, and, in the afternoon, he took me to a fishing village

I would never have seen. That was twenty-five years ago. We are still in touch.

What advice can I give to fellow runners who are traveling?

First, if you want to take the tried-and-true routes, ask a concierge where you can run. It's pleasant to discover that, even in those places where the natives think joggers are a bit crazy, the activity has become sufficiently commonplace that they can usually tell you where to go.

Second, don't let the desire to get in the miles distract you from the fringe benefits. Watch where you put your feet, as you always must in strange places. But also slow down so you have time to look around, sniff the air, drink in the atmosphere.

Third, keep your shirt on! I have learned that even in warm-weather ports, where runners are not uncommon, local customs often demand a certain decorum, even in the wee hours when most of those who set the standards are still fast asleep.

[twenty-two]

Italian Promenade

THERE IS A promenade hard by the sea that goes for several miles along the Italian Riviera. It is in the upscale town of Nervi, a suburb of Genoa. It starts at the Marina di Capolunga, just west of the village of Bogliasco, winds along a great sea wall past the famed late-sixteenth-century Gropallo Tower, and ends in a tiny harbor, the Porticciolo di Nervi, at the Via Giovanni Caboto. (It was from this very place that Caboto, otherwise known as "John Cabot," set sail on his adventures.)

From almost any point along what the locals called the *passeggiata a mare* (the walkway by the sea), you can see across the bay to the massive Portofino promontory. And on the water itself you can see cargo ships, tankers, passenger liners, small fishing boats, sailing vessels of all sizes and shapes, and, closer to shore, sea kayakers furiously paddling in the surf and rubber-suited divers adjusting gear aboard their zodiacs, getting ready to slide into the roiling sea. It is all quite spectacular. But the real action is on the *passeggiata.*

Winter and summer, spring and fall, from late morning to well into the evening, hundreds of well-dressed locals—mostly middle-aged and older—take the air along the brick-laid path. A select few do their ambling much earlier in the day.

A two-month stay in the area, during which I took early-morning jogs and almost daily afternoon walks on the *passeggiata*, gave me ample time to observe the scene and get to know a number of the regulars. I was especially struck by their manners of dress, the ways they interacted with one another, and their various speeds of locomotion. The majority may be classified as strollers—they move at a slow but steady pace. Others range along a continuum: from runners to fast walkers to path-blocking lumberers. Although I didn't know their names, I often gave them ones I thought were fitting.

I remember some of them very well. In my mind they are divided into two rather distinct groups: those to whom I say "Buon giorno" and those to whom I say "'Sera." Morning people and afternoon (or evening) people.

First, some of the early risers.

"Bruno" is one of those I see every morning at about 7:15. A bear of a man wearing a brown suede jacket and heavy shoes, he walks purposefully, ignoring the cleaning crews and the runners, intent on his daily exercise. He stops only to call and admonish his fuzzy-faced dog, which likes to dawdle. Sometimes, exasperated, he takes out a leash and hooks it into the collar of his four-legged companion. Then they march on together. "Bruno" with head held high; "Pisola," the pup, with his drooping.

Then there is "Big Red," a striking carrot-topped giant who stands out from all the others not only because of his extraordinary height, but also for the color of his hair. Everyone else on the promenade—save for bleach-blond women of a certain age—is dark-haired or graying. "Big Red," always dressed in tee shirt, shorts, and Nikes, looks like a runner, but is, in fact, a loper. He bounds along, an Italian gazelle, oblivious to the world, nodding to his acquaintances (I became one after three weeks of seeing him), but never saying a word. Not even "Buon giorno."

"Big Red" often overtakes me. But then I always pass "Mutt" and "Jeff" (or maybe "Mutto e Geffo"), two walking/talking machines—one tall and skinny, the other short and squat—who stride along from one end of the *passeggiata* to the other in constant conversation. I have no idea what they are talking about, but from the way they lean toward each other—Mutt listing downward, Jeff stretching to catch Mutt's ear—I convince myself that it is conspiratorial. (They are probably plotting the way to bring down Italy's forty-seventh government since the war. Or is it the forty-eighth?)

On many a morning I see, believe it or not, Princess Di's double coming toward me. She is a strikingly beautiful fair-skinned young woman, wearing the latest in jogging togs and always escorted by her Dodi. He is about ten years older than she, has a dark complexion, wears jeans with a V-necked cashmere sweater (a different colored one each day) and a jacket draped like a cape over his shoulders. She talks. He nods. Neither moves very fast. Even the runners hesitate as they approach. Except for "Rocco."

"Rocco" is roughly my age (sixty-five), roughly my size (five-ten), and roughly my speed (about nine minutes to the mile), but is always trying to prove that he's faster. Regardless of the temperature, he is always dressed in running tights and a sweatshirt. He wears a white towel around his neck with the ends stuffed into the neck of the shirt. He also wears a headband over his ears and a pair of gloves. He looks like he is ready to ski the Engadine Marathon instead of to go for jog in the very temperate clime of the Golfo Paradiso.

It seems he is there waiting for me each morning near the western end of the *passeggiata*. As I approach, he is doing deep-knee bends or stretching against the railing, pushing so hard that I'm sure those who are not cognoscenti think he is trying to push it into the sea. Then, as I go by, he starts off. And the pursuit begins.

I feel his presence behind me and step up the pace just a notch. He matches it. I speed up. "Rocco" does, too. Then, tiring of the game, I ease back and let him pass. With stoicism born of being a real amateur, he won't even acknowledge his victory but smugly runs by. I, on the other hand, look over and note that he is flushed, breathing hard, and dripping with perspiration. It is probably the unnecessary layers of clothing, but I, who have hardly broken a sweat, like to think I am actually giving him a run for his money.

In addition to that short list of regulars, there are a number of others. Two are real runners, Gianni and Francesco (no quote marks here; I heard them calling each other many times). They are the only ones who seem to be in training for something other than maintaining fitness in order to down the next Ligurian five-course meal. They, too, do the end-to-end turn-around-and-go-back routine, but they do it at least three times each morning. I know because on several occasions I sat down on one of the benches for an hour or so and watched them do their multiple circuits.

There is a woman—small and dark and Spanish looking (I think of her as "Margherita")—who is also a serious runner, and there are two middle-aged race-walkers ("Gina" and "Gilberto"), who do their peculiar hip-swiveling thing in precise synchronization, not side-by-side but one behind the other. They move to the rhythm of the waves beating on the shore.

Last among the most memorable of the "Buon Giorno Brigade" are "the Three Stooges." Perhaps that is an unfair sobriquet for a trio of rather heavyset fifty-year-olds who each morning walk arm in arm along the pathway, but I can't think of any other label for them. One has frizzled wiry hair, one is bald, and the other, whose hair is slicked down, is always poking the others.

In the afternoon and into the early evening there are so many people (perhaps one hundred times as many as in the morning) that it is much more difficult to single them out. Indeed, many look strikingly alike. This is doubtlessly compounded by the fact that they are not only similarly dressed but also similarly *over*-dressed for both the setting and the season. (I was there from late February through April, when the temperature seldom dropped below fifty degrees Fahrenheit). Still, instead of running gear, sweats, or even informal sauntering attire, many if not all of the female regulars along the *passeggiata* take their daily strolls bundled in furs or, by mid-March, in fine cloth coats usually worn over designer sweaters or suits. The men wear shirts and ties, and sweaters, too, beneath their own suit jackets. And these are often topped by coats of loden or tweed.

Weekends are different. Everyone is more informal, and the old *borghesia*, while still there, share their turf with groups of less colorful, less stylish, less self-conscious, and louder lessers. And many more children.

Whatever the day, the afternoon crowds move along, usually quite slowly, taking the air, talking, and seeing friends. Being seen, too. Sometimes they stop to chat with those coming from the other direction, sometimes they pat a dog (there are many along the walkway—and many reminders of their presence even when they are not), or they sit for a while to soak up the sun, read the paper, or fuss with their cell phones. Rarely do they stop to look at the brand-name handbags, watches, sunglasses, assorted trinkets, carved animals, scarves, and costume jewelry displayed on ground mats every few hundred meters by African vendors, the only nonwhites ever seen in the area. (No, that is wrong, there are two East Asian–looking street merchants who have their own displays. Neither deals in knockoff Louis Vuitton bags, Rolex watches, or Bolle sunglasses, etc.—their knockoffs are all electronic: battery-run toys, tiny phones, and little calculators.)

In the lengthy period I ran the run and walked the walk, only once did I ever see anyone buy anything. That exception was my wife. She purchased two carefully carved letter trains spelling out the names of our grandsons. (Most of the displays were euphonious choo-choos—G-I-U-S-E-P-P-E, A-N-T-O-N-I-O, and A-L-E-S-S-A-N-D-R-A—chugging along with a locomotive in front and a caboose at the end.)

While most of the weekday passersby are a furry blur, a few of those in what I still think of as "The Matinee" stand out from the others. For example, there is a couple, "Marcello" and "Sofia" (as in Mastroianni and Loren). He is handsome, with silvery hair and a fine mustache (not too thin, not too bushy), and always dressed with a kind of elegant casualness. She is tall, trim, striking, dressed in stylish black pants and long black coat, with a colorful silk scarf. They walk arm in arm. I am not the only one who notices them. As I slow my pace to fall in behind them (something I must have done a dozen times), I listen as person after person bids them "Buona sera." They acknowledge each supplicant with a collective nod, then turn back to their conversation.

As I move along or stop to sit on a bench to watch the passing parade, I keep trying to conjure the lives of those before me. The handsome couple are not really movie stars or actors at all but tintypes for the real Marcello and Sofia who play *them*, members of once-wealthy and still-prominent families, the sort who built and lived in the great villas of Nervi and Bogliasco before they were turned into apartment houses, offices, or foundations or were sold off as weekend retreats for the *nuovi ricchi* from Milano and Torino.

"Natalia," "Anna," and "Erica" also stand out from the crowd—not because they look like somebody others would try to emulate, but just the opposite. They are anti-Christs in the parade of believers. Like "Sofia," they, too, wear black. But their stylishness (to be generous) is more in sync with Piccadilly than the *passeggiata.* To match their black jeans and long wrinkled and shabby-looking black coats, they have black fingernails and black lipstick. Each is wired to a radio or Walkman. One of the three—it is "Anna," I think—often breaks ranks with her sisters in a perverse concession to those who gape then turn away. She, too, has a fur coat over her shoulders, but hers is rather ratty and, instead of being sable or seal or mink, seems to be possum or raccoon, circa 1925.

"Who are these three outsiders?" I ask myself. Then I answer my own question: they are not really outsiders at all but local rebels, the children of "Marcello" and "Sofia" and their friends.

There are three other significant groups to be seen each day: mothers in their twenties and thirties, grandparents, and the charges of both (or either): little children, from those in carriages to those about ten, most of them looking uncomfortably overdressed—and overfed, as well. What is missing is the teenage set—save for the triad of "Natalia," "Anna," and "Erica."

There is a brief time each day, immediately after school, when thirteen- and fourteen-year-old boys and girls in down jackets, American Timberland sailing shoes, and colorful bookbags crowd the *passeggiata,* but I rarely see high schoolers or slightly older youngsters along the promenade, not then, not early in the morning, not late in the afternoon. Not even on Sunday. Maybe they had enough when they were smaller and have forsworn ever going there again. My guess is that twenty, thirty, and more years from now, they will be there, wheeling prams, minding toddlers, jogging, walking, and talking. Some will become fishermen, too. Like my favorite character of them all, "Giacomo, il Pescatore."

"Giacomo" is but one of a small number of men, most of them in their sixties or seventies, some older, perched on ledges on the rocky coast below the promenade anytime from early morning to dusk. Some are there all day, every day. What makes

"Giacomo" stand out from the others is not his garb—like most of the others he is wearing rubber boots, a dark jacket, and either a Cousteauian toque or what I always think of as a Greek fisherman's cap—but his beet-red, expressive face and his wonderful smile.

His special place is about as close to the *passeggiata* as one can be and still reach the pools beneath the swells with hook, line, and sinker. Each time I pass nearby to where he is standing, pole extended, looking intently at the water, he turns, looks right at me, laughs, and tosses his head a bit. He never speaks a word, but I have the feeling that he, a retired physician or banker or police commissioner, is having the time of his life, doing exactly what he had always dreamed of doing, especially in the days and years when, every afternoon, he would walk along the Passeggiata Anita Garibaldi (its official name), taking his constitutional with his fur-bearing wife, nodding politely to the others, and wishing he could be down below, just fishing.

[twenty-three]

The Second Time Around

THEY SAY THAT love is sweeter the second time around. I wouldn't know. I'm still enjoying the first tour. But I do know that when it comes to foreign, as opposed to domestic, affairs, attempts to maintain sentimental relationships born of impetuousness are not always easy. They are fraught with unanticipated frustrations that play havoc with the emotions.

Infatuation often begins with a sudden rush of passion, a sense of excitement, an idea, however silly seeming, that "this is what I've been waiting for!" Travelers describe their first encounters with particular places using language that is just as visceral and often as sensual. Words like "heart-stopping," "thrilling," and "overwhelming" commonly appear in notes on postcards picturing the Jungfrau and her well-recognized peaks, the Dome of the Rock bathed in the warm glow of a Jerusalem sunset, or the Taj Mahal reflected in the pool before it.

It isn't just special sights that give off such affective charges. While many places are interesting, even captivating, some seem to have a personal appeal. Sometimes a city turns people on in unexpected ways ("I love Paris in the springtime"); sometimes it is a neighborhood or a little village.

The first symptoms of ardor, at least as far as I can determine from my own reactions, are inchoate, but they soon resolve into a feeling— "This is it. This is where I belong" —and a decision to return as soon as possible.

Of course, not all or even most travelers who make such heartfelt resolutions carry them out. But those of us who do often learn that the second time around is very different from what we expected. I think of my encounters with Wengen in the Swiss Alps.

On my first visit, I arrived at twilight. It was still light enough to see the mighty massif of the Jungfrau looming high above the little town. From the balcony of my one-star hotel, I drank in the scene—the neat little houses and the barns and the newly mown fields against the backdrop of snow-covered mountains. It was . . . breathtaking.

That night I wandered the few streets, peering into shop windows and even into those of the homes of the residents. I nodded to passersby. I was excited. I couldn't get enough of the atmosphere, and, incredible though it seems today, I began musing about what it would be like when, someday soon, I would return to settle down right there. I even speculated on whether I would live in the village proper or on the slope behind it.

I spent the next week hiking, eating, shopping, trying to communicate with the proprietors of the local establishments and some of their regular customers, and just sitting over a cup of coffee at a café near the station watching the local people and the Swiss hikers, especially the old ones with their craggy faces, well-worn leather rucksacks, and hobnailed boots and the little apple-cheeked kids. I was totally enthralled by Wengen.

When it was time to leave, I was terribly sad, but this was tempered somewhat by the knowledge that I would be back. It turned out to be a long while before I actually managed to return.

Going back for that second visit, I found myself in a steadily mounting state of anxiety. As I boarded the cog-railway train at the junction town of Zweilutschinen for the last lap of my return journey, I had all sorts of pangs. They increased as we chugged up the wooded slope.

I began to worry that what I had longed for might have changed, that my personified Swiss nirvana might not be so pretty, so stimulating, so *gemütlich* after all.

As I stepped off the train, I immediately took heart and began to relax. The village was exactly as I remembered it. I was back on familiar ground, back where I belonged.

Although I tried to keep it in check, my proprietary attitude may have been palpable to those around me. I couldn't help displaying some resentment when the damned tourists crowded the little park, the restaurants, and the historic sites, intruding on the serenity of *my* little town.

Undoubtedly wishing to believe that, somehow, it really was my turf, I also felt a sense of union with the native population. Of course, whatever was going on in my inner fantasy world, my rational self kept warning me that even the hoteliers, restaurateurs, lift operators, and shopkeepers with whom I had had contact before, and whom I recognized immediately, could hardly be expected to remember me. Yet I was troubled when they didn't. It gave me pause.

The disconcerting lack of recognition was compounded by other signs that contributed to a growing feeling of estrangement, even exclusion, from my paradise. I began to think I wasn't wanted. I noticed that certain others with whom I had begun to identify appeared to be accorded different, more favored, treatment. It didn't seem fair.

Had I probed, I would have quickly learned that those others were expatriates who *had* made the move, who lived there on a more-or-less-permanent basis. Had I pressed further, I would have found that even such settlers were themselves seen as outsiders, as, at best, constituents of the foreign colony who were to be treated with a sort of benign indulgence. And for good reason.

Like first-time visitors and returnees, they helped to fill the coffers of the business people, and they provided plenty of material for the local equivalent of cracker-barrel colloquies.

After ten days back in Wengen, much of the time spent walking by myself, I packed up again and left with a heavy if not completely broken heart. As I descended into the Lauterbrunnen Valley, I remember laughing to (or maybe at) myself and thinking how true it is that unrequited love is difficult to sustain.

What I learned in Wengen explains why some second-timers never go back again. Others, and I am one of them, slightly battered and doubtlessly wiser, will not give up. We will return. But when we do, it will never be the same. I know. I spent a third, most satisfying but hardly thrilling, holiday in Wengen this summer. This time I wasn't sad at leaving. It wasn't the least bit heart-wrenching.

For all of us who have fallen in love en route, it can be said that second visits can be most educational and most sobering. They teach us a good deal about who we are and who we are not, dreams of foreign affairs with other *Jungfrauen* notwithstanding. Or they should.

Let me tell you something I hate to admit. After learning my lesson, I left Wengen behind. But soon after I really fell in love with an Italian hill town I visited before going home. This is different. I mean the place is incredible. It is luscious, with a special aura, a rich fragrance, and a unique appeal. I could stay only two days, but I can't wait to get back.

[twenty-four]

Birds of a Feather

ON A SIX-WEEK lecture tour in China in the 1980s, I was accompanied from city to city by a research fellow from the Institute of American Studies in the Chinese Academy of Social Sciences in Beijing. A specialist in contemporary American literature, she had read all of Bellow, Cheever, Mailer, Malamud, Roth, and Updike; she knew her Oates and her Heller, her Baldwin and her Ellison, and she was in the process of writing a long essay on E. L. Doctorow. Hu Yafei knew American writing, but she did not know America—or Americans. She was to be my guide, but it soon became clear that I might teach her something, too.

As we flew from the capital to Xian, Hu Yafei asked me to tell her what Americans were really like. I said, half-facetiously, "Just watch them" and pointed to a group of tourists sitting in the back of the plane.

For the next few days, I tried to teach Ms. Hu how to spot Americans in airports, restaurants, and museums and along the streets of the cities we visited. It wasn't long before she learned to pick up on certain cues like manners of dress, body movements, ways of walking, and ways of greeting one another.

As Hu Yafei became skilled at distinguishing the light-colored *Avis Americani* from other long-beaked types, all referred to as "Europeans," I refined the game, separating tourists from businessmen and visiting scholars, then subdividing the first category into four or five more-or-less-discrete "subspecies" and one other type.

By far the most numerous of the odd birds we saw were the "Packaged Tourers." The males, mostly middle-aged or older and predominantly white (or, as Yafei noted, red or "red faced"), were usually dressed in zippered golf jackets or sport coats with badges denoting their tour companies pinned on their chests, tennis shirts, slacks, and, doubtlessly following the advice of travel agents, "sensible shoes." (I told Hu Yafei to take a careful look at the men's shoes, especially the brogans with thick double-leather soles that came close to being the "clodhoppers" she said she had once read about.)

The men also wore baseball caps advertising the names of favorite teams, sports clubs, industrial concerns, or car manufacturers. Many said "Nissan"; only a few said "Ford"—a fact that confused Ms. Hu.

Female members of the company, by contrast, tended to go bareheaded, except in the rain or when they wore cheap green Chinese souvenir caps with red stars. It was obvious they thought the caps were stylish and very Chinese. My Chinese escort and her friends found this all a bit odd. The green caps and matching Mao-style jackets, which some still also wore, were reminders of the terrible days of the Cultural Revolution not so long before.

Aside from their plumage, we noted something else about the flocks of Packaged Tourers when we moved alongside them in places like Beijing's Forbidden City or at the site of the one-thousand-man terracotta army at Xian. They chattered a lot.

Second were the "Tough Old Birds." Rugged, robust, ruddy (but somehow healthier looking than the "PT"s though they were seldom under sixty-five), they were often members of study tours. They looked like Sierra Clubbers and, in many cases, probably were. In addition to being well attired for travel—in a subtle camouflage of subdued greens and khaki—they all carried small daypacks for their sweaters and cameras and the notebooks in which they recorded what they were learning. Unlike their compatriots in the first group, we noted that these Old Birds listened a lot.

Third in my taxonomy of tourists were the "Variegated Trekkers," usually seen in small bands. Dressed in red, green, or blue mountaineering anoraks, tee shirts, worn jeans, and running shoes, they often carried heavy backpacks stuffed with everything needed for an Asian—or 'round-the-world—odyssey, including newly purchased down vests or jackets from the government operated Friendship Store. Not only did they look alike, they smelled similar. Musty, sweaty, and sweet—like smoky grass! They clutched well-worn guidebooks that told how to get away from the tourists (meaning presumably the Packaged Tourers) and meet the people.

Then there were those I came to think of as the "Regal Rovers": first-class, worldly-wise excursioners who usually traveled in pairs or small parties. They were invariably well coiffed, well heeled, and well dressed in the latest travel fashion—from understated tweeds and cashmeres for the cooler weather and summer suits for the heat, to bush clothes for that studied world-traveler look.

I explained to Ms. Hu that the Regal Rovers were recognizable in another way. They not only looked different from the Packaged Tourers and the Tough Old Birds (though many were the same age), but, more often than not, were accompanied by private guides and drivers who rarely left their sides. Sometimes they were also accompanied by teenage or grown children who looked—and occasionally smelled—just like the Variegated Trekkers and gave the distinct impression that they wished they could join that other group.

Two subgroups among the general run of American tourists were of special interest to Hu Yafei. One was rare in China but recognizable to the Chinese, for many of them had seen movies with black characters. Hu was not surprised that their behavior was so similar to that of the mainly European American ("long-nosed") tourists. But the others confused her. They seemed, at a distance, strikingly similar to *local* birds. Up close they appeared to have hopped off the screen of Peter Wang's wonderful movie *A Great Wall.*

While sharing the physical features of their Chinese hosts, this group, Chinese Americans (I came to call them "CAs" or "Sojourning Seeays"), were readily distinguishable by their speech, body language, and trappings: the latest in U.S. fashions—sweat suits, jewelry, and spanking-new running shoes. They were easy for Hu Yafei to pick out of a crowd and easy, she said, to distinguish from their "louder and more aggressive" cousins from Hong Kong. She was amused to hear them speak English, particularly those with Southern or New York accents.

After all those tourist types, the second-largest band of American birds we saw were the "Red-White-and-Blue-Breasted Boosters," the businessmen (not business people, it should be noted, for there seemed to be as few females on the Silk Route in those days as there were in olden times). Hu Yafei had little trouble spotting them in hotel lobbies, in restaurants, or on the street. Once she got the knack, she could tell me what to look for, as one might in a real bird-watchers guide. "Blue suits, briefcases, short haircuts, and a kind of 'all-American' look, like we see in the movies." "And," she would add, "big shoes."

I spotted a few international-lawyer types ("Double-Breasted Grackles") and high-ranking American diplomats ("Balding Eagles") and started to explain who they were and what they did but then hesitated. Enough is enough. Enough, that is, except for the fellow members of my own flock, the "Foreign Experts."

That is what we are called there. It is a catchall label for visiting professors, research scholars, specialists in medicine, industrial design, engineering, art, architecture, filmmaking—just about every field imaginable.

Foreign experts, who come for anywhere from several weeks to several years, are generally assigned to a unit. (Mine was the Foreign Affairs Bureau of the Chinese Academy of Social Science.) Many are affiliated with particular universities, scientific institutes, or provincial academies of science or social science. Some are attached to government ministries.

I discovered that, just as I can often pick a foreign academic out of a crowded American airport, I could easily tell who were FEs (or "Effees") in different Chinese settings. In addition to horn-rimmed or large-lensed plastic spectacles (which give many a wise-owl appearance), they wear the same garb in the field as at home: on working days, ties, light blue button-down oxford shirts, sport coats, and chinos, or skirts and blazers. On weekends and holidays, they (we) look, if not smell, like aging Variegated Trekkers.

I soon found myself batting around .750 when I used this

mirror index to find birds of my own feather. It was then that I told Yafei to look for people who looked like me. Within two days she began to get it right more than half the time. Her average improved considerably when she realized that, like me, other Effees had interpreters, like her, with them much of the time. And that, like the two of us—and like the Regal Rovers—they sometimes had their own drivers and cars and special escorts who shepherded them from place to place.

The lessons I learned were not one-sided. Hu Yafei also tried to help me begin to understand the taxonomy of those in her own vast aviary. At the time of my visit, the plumage was pretty uniform. But my good guide was able to help this neophyte observer of Avis Sinica to begin to be able to distinguish the subtypes that abound in the Middle Kingdom. Which she did.

[twenty-five]

Destinations Unknown, Inc.

YEARS AGO I was in Aruba at a weeklong anthropology meeting. With most of the other conferees, I stayed in an old oil-rigger's camp far from Oranjestad, the main city. On the last evening a member of our group who had decided to forgo the joys of roughing it in the boonies for the comfort of the Holiday Inn near downtown, invited me to be his guest at dinner. It was quite a contrast to our camplike digs.

Unlike our *lager*, the hotel seemed familiar. Almost too familiar. The decor, the menu, the people all dressed in resort togs circa 1965 were little different from what I had seen in St. Thomas, St. Maartens, and Nassau on other trips to the area.

As I sipped my scotch and water and played with the swizzle stick, I noted that it was embossed with the words HOLIDAY INN SAN JUAN. I wondered whether anybody else noticed it and, if they did, whether they thought it in any sense odd. I did, but only for a moment. Then I changed my mind. It didn't seem so strange after all.

From the look of the clientele, most had spent their vacations basking on the beach, drinking, eating, relaxing, and paying rather little attention to the external environment, meaning the local scene. What they wanted was Caribbean sun, sea, and sand and the amenities of American-style care and feeding. Aruba or Puerto Rico, Barbados or Anguilla—it really didn't seem to matter.

Once back in the States I thought of writing a story based on the swizzle-stick switch, but I never seemed able to sketch out a worthwhile plot. After several false starts I gave up. I didn't think about my trip to Aruba more than a few times over the next thirty years. Then, several months ago, I read about an incident in the Caribbean in which tourists, having just arrived on one of the islands, ended up in the middle of a civil war. It wasn't much fun, they reported, but, boy, did they have stories to tell.

The news item jarred my memory. Suddenly I was back in the Holiday Inn in Oranjestad. I ran to my laptop. At last I knew what to do about the swizzle sticks! I could even get rich—if only I could find the right backer.

My plan was simple. With the support of some very adventurous capitalists with scads of money to invest, I would start a travel company called "Destinations Unknown, Inc." My partners and I would sponsor "Mystery Tours" to the Caribbean, guaranteeing five days on one of the many tropical islands, first-class accommodations, and loads of local color.

To meet these needs, we would buy and refurbish some old beachfront hotel on an American island like Vieques off Puerto Rico (after the navy stopped using it for target practice, of course), rent and refit an old Boeing 707 and a big bus with wire-mesh windows and shades, and adorn them all with our "DU" logo. And we would also order a number of huge signs saying WELCOME TO NEVIS, BIENVENUE A MARTINQUE, BIENVENIDOS A SANTO DOMINGO and the like, and hire a number of young people able to speak English with British and Dutch and French and Spanish accents. (They wouldn't need to actually know the last three languages, just to sound as if they were their native tongues and English—which they would have to speak to facilitate easy communication with the tourists—their second one.) Eager adventurers would see our advertisements in the travel sections of major newspapers in the northeast and other reliable places and besiege us with requests to pay fifteen hundred dollars for the privilege of being on one of our grab-bag tours.

Each Monday morning a new group would assemble at JFK to be greeted by a DU staffer who would get them together in the lobby for an initial briefing, tell tantalizing tales of previous excursions, and, somewhere along the line, drop a hint that, while perfectly safe, precautions are always necessary in case there is a flare-up of the unrest "that is, well, a chronic problem in the islands."

"Don't worry," they would be told, "DU has made every

arrangement for your protection. We drive you right from the airport to the hotel in our specially equipped buses. Within minutes you will be soaking up the sun and the atmosphere of some still-secret paradise. Within minutes you will be thrilling to the beat of different—native—drummers."

"Imagine, ladies and gentlemen," the spokesperson will say, "in three hours you may be in Haiti or Jamaica or Curaçao or . . . Let's get going!" and the group would be led onto the plane.

Once airborne, the venue would be hinted at by the kind of music piped through the cabin—a little calypso, reggae, salsa or . . . With the rhythms fading in the background, an announcement would be made by a properly accented "local rep," who "was flown up to New York just last night to accompany you back to his home island and to tell you about its wonders." That introduction would include a bit of island history, some talk about the flora and fauna (since it's the same all over the Caribbean, this part of the spiel would be used again and again), and a little information about the current political situation. Then a second hint would be made about possible demonstrations.

As the flight continued, a film would be shown about the island destination, and *appropriate* complimentary drinks would be served. Rum . . . or . . . tequila . . . or . . .

En route people would not be able to see much, except for the water below, but they would be reminded of where they were headed by the sound of the music, a constant background to their increasingly anticipatory conversations. "Day—O, dayayay—O . . ."

In the meantime, a ground crew, knowing which place the island is supposed to be this particular week, would have erected a proper sign by the end of the airstrip where they had parked the bus. Nearby a table would be set up marked IMMIGRATION (or EMIGRATION or something similarly appropriate); it would be manned by an official-looking person in a summery uniform of vaguely British, French, Dutch, or Latin-American design. (Note: There would be no real problem with local immigration authorities since, as noted, this would all be taking place on *American* soil.)

"Ladies and gentlemen [or "señores y señoras" or . . .], I do not wish to alarm you," another uniformed man—sporting a large mustache, the ends of which he would turn up when playing an Englishman and down when being more Latin—would say, "but just yesterday there was some minor trouble on the very road we take to your hotel. Please step into the bus at once, pull the shades, keep your heads fairly low down, and relax. We will get you there safe and sound. Your luggage will be brought in another vehicle."

On the way, people would not be able to see out of the windows, but they would know where they were, for appropriate music—once again, calypso, reggae, salsa, etc.—would blare from a speaker in the bus while the driver (again, with appropriate accent) would tell them how amazingly brave they are and what stories they will bring home to friends and grandchildren. After twenty minutes of riding hunkered down in their seats, the passengers would be informed that the danger zone was behind them and that they could now sit up, lift the shades, and enjoy their first view of "the tropical island of . . ." (whatever we call it).

What they will see, if the ground crew is on its toes, is another sign welcoming them to DU's HIDEAWAY HOTEL in ARUBA (or . . . or . . .). They would be driven up a short drive lined with palm trees and exotic plants to the main entrance of the hotel, where company representatives would present each person with a "local" gift and a baseball cap with the DU logo. They would be told that dinner will be served at 7:00 P.M. and that they should feel free to walk around the place, take a swim in the pool, or check out the beach, but, to be absolutely safe, to stay within the compound of the hotel. (Another bush-jacketed employee with an official-looking badge would be sent to stand by the gate to discourage the more adventuresome—and the power walkers—from leaving the premises.)

After a dinner of cuisine typical of . . . or . . . or . . . , there would be entertainment to match. "Come Mister Tally-Mon, tally me bananas."

In the morning an announcement would be made that, while everything is under control, everyone is asked to stay in or around the hotels on the island. "No problem, for there is plenty to do: swimming, tennis, even dance lessons in the samba, or the . . . or the . . ."

"And there is also shopping for beachwear and tropical

gear available in the hotel arcade." (Local authenticity is no problem here, for the stuff is all made in China or Indonesia or Mexico anyway.)

And so it would go for the next five days.

On the last night there would be a party.

There is something very moving and sentimental about drinks on the veranda of a hotel that overlooks the Caribbean. The guests, who would undoubtedly be wanting to save some concrete piece of their tropical adventure, will hold on to their swizzle sticks. It is essential that they be marked ARUBA, not SAN JUAN, not BARBADOS, and not ST. BARTS, for *these* folks, having been exposed to the culture, traditions, music, even the politics of their island paradise, will know the difference! We can't afford to confuse them.

The last morning the guests will reverse the journey they took to the hotel, arriving at the airport in the dark as it were, but very safe, very sound, and very proud of having endured the trip. They will have much to tell when they get home—and much to show. A tan, a new bathing suit with matching shirt, a necklace of coral beads perhaps, a cap that says DU, and a swizzle stick.

The next Monday, a new group will appear at JFK, eager to play potluck with our adventure tour company. They will be greeted by an official DU representative, who will give them an upbeat briefing, and a mild cautionary warning about the instability of the area, together with a reassurance that there is really nothing to worry about and an enthusiastic send-off as they board their plane for . . .

[twenty-six]

Colonists and Coneheads

STUDENTS OF SOCIAL stratification can find much colorful case-study material in the relationships among the groups of people who live in, summer in, or pass through resort towns along the coast of New England, places almost totally dependent for their livelihoods on the "outsiders" many of the locals claim they can't abide but reluctantly admit it would be hard to live without. I have been to many such places (and have a home in one of them) and have asked many old-timers to describe their areas.

They usually begin with a geography lesson.

"Well, it's on the Cape. Cape Cod. Down near the elbow. Ocean side."

"Chatham?" I ask.

"No, Harwich. Near Chatham."

Then they offer a bit of history, stressing how things have changed.

"Used to be, we were among the only folks that came to Harwich [or Bar Harbor, Menemsha, Truro, Little Compton, etc.]."

"Only folks?"

"Well, you know what I mean, summer people . . ."

At that point in the conversation, I go on sociological auto-pilot. I start probing about social organization, about notions of insiders and outsiders, about hierarchies. And most rise to the bait.

When pressed, without realizing what they are saying, they rank themselves by something akin to a caste system. While I may be wont to oversimplify, there does seem to be a pattern.

At the top are the Brahmins who—as anyone who reads

William Dean Howells, John P. Marquand, William Lloyd Warner, or *The Boston Globe* already knows—are the upper crust, revered by some and envied by most of the hoi polloi.

In fact, in most places, mainly fishing villages that have become resort towns, there are two sorts of Brahmins: "native" ones and colonists, also known as "the people from away." The native types claim exclusivity on the basis of having gotten there first (or, more accurately, second). They are the folks whose ancestors laid claim to what belonged to the *real* natives. They, poor like the Beans of Egypt, Maine and rich like the Beans of Freeport, Maine, and many in between, were once called settlers.

The modern-day Brahmins are the old-money gentry who landed a bit later—actually, quite a bit later. From Boston, Philadelphia, New York, and Washington, they are the ones whose forebears began to put these places on the social map in the late nineteenth and early twentieth centuries and who still think that the natives are there to do their bidding. They own the old estates, the family islands, the compounds. These days, when not wearing apple-green sweaters and cranberry-red slacks with tennis shoes, they affect a faded Ralph Lauren/Cole Haan look. (Real men, including land-rich locals, don't wear polo shirts, prewashed, prefaded jeans, tweed jackets, and Bean boots like those they call "sports." They wear matching khaki shirts and trousers and baseball caps.)

Then there are those whom the rich, poor, and middle-class locals—and some of the colonists—call "the newcomers." I would call them "entrenched outsiders." They are merchants, restaurant and gallery owners, professionals and retirees; sometimes they are artists or artisans. They all came from somewhere else to establish new homes in places where, not infrequently, they had been sent to camp as children or had vacationed with their families or taken holidays early in their careers.

The entrenched outsiders are the movers and the shakers, the people who lead campaigns to fix things that, in the eyes of many locals, "ain't yet broke." They are the anticipators and preservationists, ever trying to get ready for changes they think are inevitable and wrong. A strain on the water system. A decision to move the "transfer station" (a wonderful euphemism for the town dump) to a place farther out in the country, thereby threatening, as they see it, to despoil "the last bit of our virgin land." A plan to put up a modern condominium complex which would alter the cozy quaintness of *their* town. At the same time they are the cosmopolites who want to bring culture to the provinces—summer theater, dance, interesting speakers—activities they know will also serve those in the next category (who are a kind of distant kin), the true summer people.

Summer people are the ones who build the heavily glassed and well-decked and decked-out houses on the dunes or who gut and refit little Cape Cod cottages erected centuries ago by those who sought the hollows for shelter from the winter winds. Summer people (also called "nonresident taxpayers") make local realtors very happy and contractors very wealthy, and keep boatyard and hardware-store and garden-supply employees very busy. They pay ever-increasing taxes without too much grumbling, except about "the threat of those damn outsiders." They don't want encroachment on their preserves, either. (A friend of mine once defined a Vineyard ecologist as "a summer person who already has his three acres and wants to increase the zoning rule to five acres.")

Beneath the summer people who own their houses, and often spend most of July and August using them, are the renters. They are stratified in their own pecking order: those who come for a month, for two weeks, for one. The members of these distinct and distinctive subsets (recognized by the cars they drive: Volvos, Toyotas, and Chevys, respectively) stay in every conceivable type of dwelling: old refurbished capes; seaside shoeboxes with screened porches that invariably list to leeward; California-style ranch houses; and, sometimes, modern or colonial-style cedar-shingled homes of certain summer people willing, temporarily, to share their Shangri-las with land-poor folks for a cool $2,500–3,000 or more a week. (On Long Island the rents sometimes soar to $10,000.)

Taken together, the renters are the ones who, more than any others, support the fashionable boutiques, the art galleries, the antiques shops, and the better harborside restaurants.

Locals have nothing but contemptuous terms for the next

class of vacationers, those who come on bus tours to see Cape Cod or Cape Ann or Cape Arundel or to visit historic seaports like Portsmouth, New Hampshire, and Camden, Maine. In Camden they are called "coneheads," for, since the trips are prepackaged and prepaid, the visitors are assumed to be tightfisted, often shopping only for ice cream.

At the bottom of everyone's lists are the day-trippers down from Boston, who are readily identified by the souvenirs they buy and the tee shirts they wear. Some are strictly advertisements, town names linked to something that makes them special: "Camden, Maine. Home of the Schooner Fleet"; "Kennebunkport. Summer Home of the Presidents 41 and 43"; "Provincetown. Where the land meets the sea." Some are humorous: "Province-town. Where boy meets boy"; "I got scrod in Searsport"; "MY PARENTS WENT TO HYANNIS AND ALL I GOT WAS THIS LOUSY SHIRT." The latter reflects a sentiment shared by chambers of commerce from Mystic to Machias, whose members also wish they had bought more.

In most resort areas during the summer months, the year-rounders have to augment their labor force with armies of college students hired to work behind the counters of the arts-and-crafts shops and clothing stores, to pump gas, to wait on tables in all but the most provincial of the eateries (the ones manned by relatives and other townies), and to do all kinds of jobs in the hotels. Increasingly they speak with foreign accents. Irish is the most common.

Thousands of émigrés from the Emerald Isle—some permanent, most temporary, some legal, many undocumented—flood the coastal towns. They are welcomed with open arms. Until September 11, 2001, even the immigration authorities seemed to look away. Still, employers are able to hire prescreened foreign university students directly from Ireland and many other countries, including those in the former Eastern bloc. They are often recruited through special programs that allow them to spend the summer in the States and fill the increasing demand for minimum-wage workers while providing employers with the assurance that, unlike their American counterparts, they won't up and quit for two weeks of vacation before going back to school in late

August. Most are employed in retail shops, restaurants, or hotels.

Further observation by this intrepid ethnographer reveals the obvious. The hotels have their rank order, too.

At the top are the aging, once-elegant, gigantic wooden structures still visited by long-loyal patrons. Even when in the middle of town, they are as isolated from the common folk as are the compounds of the colonists—whose owners, it should be noted, are often the only people the residents of the old hotels visit. Then there are those who frequent the well-restored inns, and those who stay in the spate of recently built lookalikes, whose main difference from the older hotels seems to be the character of the heating and plumbing. Beneath the inns are the modern hotels, sometimes built to blend in to the local scene but often seeming to have been designed to ignore it.

On the outskirts are motels of every size and shape. They cater mostly to transient populations, many coming by family car, others on bus tours. They stop for a night or two, then move on.

Some who come by car, and the few who come by motorcycle, still stay in cabins, the kind with cutesy names like "Bide-a-Wee," "Sweet Dreams," "'Tween the Tides," "Fore 'n' Aft" and "Idlease." They eat in diners or in the fast-food and pizza places—Wendy's, McDonald's, Burger King, Papa Gino's—that have sprouted like weeds along every resort-land highway, replacing the old gas station/diner combos ("Eat Here. Get Gas.").

The entrenched outsiders often urge the summer people to join them in trying to zone the cabins, and also the motor-home parks, out of existence. "They spoil the neighborhood," they say.

The natives rarely seem so concerned.

When summer ends, the pace of life in New England's coastal resort towns slackens dramatically—as it does in the Green and White Mountains and in the Berkshires, too. The homes of the summer people, the hotels, the inns and B and Bs, and the little cabins are boarded up; the boats are hauled out and stored; and those who stay on shift into their off-season rhythms. One thing that hardly changes is the hierarchy.

Despite the fact that several rungs on the ladder are missing, relationships among groups tend to continue along the well-established patterns. The locals, rich and poor, still maintain their ambivalent attitudes. When George Bush Sr. became president, a number of people in Kennebunkport worried that "this place will become another Hyannis—or a Plains, Georgia." Others couldn't wait to cash in on the celebrity of their most illustrious colonists.

The entrenched outsiders go about their businesses of doctoring and lawyering and writing and throwing pots. Many of the shopkeepers, except for the ones who run their own general stores and the ubiquitous, oxymoronically named "mini-marts" and "superettes," head south to West Palm Beach, Sarasota, and Charleston to run shops in places that are often southern versions of their summer locales. And the members of the native working class scrounge for jobs or turn to the unemployment office for yet another long winter season, during which, with the others, they will spend endless hours grousing about "the goddamn summer people"—while eagerly awaiting their return.

p a r t   f o u r

Chance Encounters and Curious Connections

[twenty-seven]

Arnold

HIS NAME WAS Arnold, although he liked to be called Arnie. We called him other things. They weren't very nice.

Arnold was a camper, a cabinmate, a *nebbish*, and a *kvetch*. He never wanted to do anything. Not anything constructive or, for that matter, anything destructive—like raiding the girls' cabin or sneaking out after hours. He liked to complain.

Although we had spent three summers together, I hadn't thought about him in ten years. Not once. Not until I bumped into him—quite literally—one night outside an off-campus bar.

"Excuse me," I said, then looked up at a rather tall version of somebody who was familiar. It took a few seconds to place him. It was Arnold. I said, "Hey, Arnold, I mean Arnie, remember me?"

He looked down, puzzled, then smiled a bit, "Yeah, you're Peter. Peter Rose. What'a'ya doin' here?"

"I'm a graduate student. And you?"

"Law school, second year."

"What a coincidence. After all these years, we're both here at Cornell." I invited him to come in and have a drink with me. He was quick to agree, and we walked in, brushed past a rowdy group of undergraduates, and sat down at a table in the back. He ordered a scotch and soda; I had a beer. We started to talk. Or, better said, he started to talk—and I listened.

Arnold caught me up on his life—from adolescence (and the camper days) through college in the Midwest and now law school at Cornell. He spoke of his parents and his friends, had another scotch—double this time—and the loves of his life. (He was "between affairs," he said, sounding more sad than suave.) As he talked and drank, he grew more and more morose. I began to see the boy coming out of the man at my table.

Being polite, with slightly slurred speech, he asked me about myself. I gave him a three-minute synopsis of my own life but sensed that he wasn't particularly interested. There was a long silence. I nursed my beer. He tossed back what remained in his glass and, getting up from his chair rather abruptly, said, "I gotta go." Then he hesitated and sat back down.

"Hey, remember Lyon Mountain? The time we were supposed to climb it? Er, the time I tried to climb it?"

Flashback. There were twelve of us thirteen- or fourteen-year-olds and two counselors—big, bulky Steve Spaulding and small but lithe "Springer" Levy, a guy who always seemed to walk on his toes. Both were medical students. They were our leaders, our heroes, and, when they wanted to have fun at our expense, our tormentors. We were totally in their thrall (even when they bugged us about cleaning the bunk or tortured us by stuffing our mouths with peanut butter when we were asleep, then waking us up). In any case, there we were, laden with gear—packs, sleeping bags, first-aid kits, the works—trudging up a mountain trail, our first big outing of the summer season. We had all been quite excited about this adventure. All, I suddenly remembered, but Arnold. He didn't want to go. He said he thought it was silly. "After all," I could hear him say, "who wants to climb a stupid old mountain anyway?"

Steve and Springer would have none of this. We were the twelve musketeers, "One for all and all for one," that sort of thing. And so, like the rest of us, Arnold had gotten his kit together and, though he held us all up, managed to get to the parking lot where we clambered aboard the old army-style truck with seats facing each other. Springer was in back with us. Steve drove, sitting alone in the cab with fourteen bag lunches.

We arrived at the trailhead half an hour later, unloaded, and shouldered our packs. Each one of us was handed a bag with sandwiches, cookies, and oranges, and then we began the trek.

Within twenty minutes one of the kids asked if we could start eating. "No," said Springer, "not until we get over the shoulder of the mountain." We trudged on, increasingly strung out along the trail. Not surprising to any of us, Arnold was in the rear.

After what seemed like hours and was probably only forty-five minutes, the first members of the group rounded a bend and saw clear sky. We had reached the shoulder. One by one, we shucked our rucksacks, flopped on the ground, and tore open the now-quite-wrinkled paper sacks. We ate our sandwiches with a kind of desperation, then opened our canteens (I can smell their tinnyness as I write) and gulped the water. We threw the oranges at a big log, trying to see who could hit a big spot in the middle of it. Then we really started horsing around. Steve asked us to calm down, then asked whether anybody had seen Arnold.

We hadn't even noticed he was missing.

"Nope," somebody said. "He's probably still on the path."

At this point in my mental reenactment, I realized I was being interrupted.

"Do you remember that time we climbed Lyon Mountain?"

I snapped out of my reverie and looked into the slightly bloated face of a grown-up version of the missing child. "Yeah, I do."

"Do you remember that I never got to the top? Do you remember when you guys were halfway there, on the saddle or shoulder or something, and were waiting for me?" (I didn't have the heart to say that in my recollection he hadn't even been missed.) "Do you remember one of those counselors—I've forgotten his name—"

"Steve Spaulding," I interjected.

"Yeah, Steve, Big Steve. He came down the trail looking for me. He found me by a tree. I didn't want to go on. He forced me to. He made me get up and, almost pushing me, made me start walking again. I asked him to take my pack. He refused and told me I had to carry it myself. I hated it. I hated him. But, finally, I reached the ridge. And you guys didn't even seem to care that I made it. In fact, as I remember, your only comment was, 'Well, here comes Pokey, Smokey's stupid cousin. Where ya been, Pokey?'"

Arnold's eyes were a bit red-rimmed; I thought he was going to cry. Instead he called the bartender over and ordered another scotch. No soda this time. All the while, I was having more flashbacks.

There we were on the ridge, sitting on a big flat rock, looking down, then up. We had a mile to go to get to the campsite where we were going to stay the night. We would be dropping our gear there, then continuing to the summit. As Arnold approached, prodded by Steve (exactly as he recalled), we had indeed snickered, winked at each other, and called him something—"Slow poke" is what came back to me, not "Pokey." (Maybe it was "Pokey.") After allowing him but a few minutes to rest and eat his lunch (most of which he threw into the woods, along with the wax paper and the bag), our squad leaders called for us to hit the trail. Some did it eagerly; some less so. Arnold didn't move.

"You know, after I had been sitting on that stupid rock for five minutes, everybody started to get up and go. I never had time to catch my breath. Nobody cared. That counselor, Steve, he grabbed me, pulled me up with his two huge hands, and told me to march. I mean, for Chrissake I wasn't in the fucking army. But I got up and marched. Twenty minutes later I quit. I stopped dead in my tracks, curled up against a huge boulder, and refused to budge. That time the other guy came over and told me that he didn't care how I was feeling, I had to move on, get to the campsite at least, and then, if I wanted, I could stay there while the rest of the guys climbed to the top. I must have agreed, 'cause I have a picture of me going on, dragging my pack and finally getting to the place where, again, everyone else was waiting."

I remember the scene very well. Again, we were waiting and waiting, and, finally, Arnold appeared. A sad sack if I ever saw one. He was dragging his pack, as he said. Moreover, his sleeping bag was oozing out of it, and whatever else he had with him was, too. When he reached the group, he just sat down and cried.

He was crying now. Not loudly, just a kind of gentle weeping and wheezing. He caught his breath and apologized. Then he cried again. I was getting very uncomfortable.

He sipped his drink and started to talk again.

"You know what? My whole fucking life is like that trip. I never made it up the mountain. I never finished anything. I probably never will. I should have listened to what's-his-name. Springer. I should have listened to Springer when he said I would regret it if I didn't climb the mountain. I do." He started to cry again, this time with wracking shoulders, "I do."

I decided it was time to get him home and suggested we leave. He wouldn't hear of it.

"Come on, Pete, stay here with me."

I ordered some coffee and persuaded him to have some, too.

Then I got an idea.

"Hey, Arnold—Arnie—after classes in the spring I'm going up to the Adirondacks to see some friends. Why don't you meet me there, and you and I can take a day off and climb that stupid mountain. We'll both go all the way to the top."

He looked up and said, "That's ridiculous." Then he added, almost wistfully, "But thanks for trying."

It was time to go. I drove him back to his apartment and went home.

Three days later I was surprised to hear from him.

"Peter, it's Arnie. Sorry about the other night. I don't know what got into me. But, er, I remember you said that you might be going back to the camp sometime in the spring and that we might try to climb the mountain. Were you serious?"

Frankly, I don't know if I was or wasn't but I said of course I was. And he said, "You're on. Let's do it."

And so, in May, after having seen one another only a few times in three months, we headed off to test my cockamamie scheme.

We stayed for a night at my friends' place, then drove to a town near the old camp and not far from the mountain, taking a double room at a third-rate motel with a corny name, "The Lyon's Den." At a nearby diner we planned our campaign for the next day. That night we checked our gear: good boots with extra socks, small daypacks, canteens (they were now made of plastic but still smelled foul), a scout knife, and a first-aid kit. And then, about half past nine, we went to a convenience store for "provisions." White bread. Peanut butter. Jelly. Oranges, too. Back at the motel we made sandwiches and, without saying much, got ready for bed. Just before I fell asleep, Arnold asked if I thought this was all rather stupid. Although I was beginning to think so, I said, "No. It'll be fun."

We got up early, had a quick breakfast, and drove to the trailhead next to a parking lot much more civilized than I remembered it to be. By eight o'clock we were on our way. By half past eight we were at the place where we had first wanted to stop. Both of us were moving along quite steadily. Arnold showed no signs of fatigue—or remorse. We kept going. Within another half hour we were on the shoulder. We stopped for a few minutes, sipped some water, had a few bites of our peanut-butter-and-jelly sandwiches, and pushed on.

We passed the campsite without even pausing and began to ascend the steep part of the mountain, the part Arnold had never reached. It wasn't anywhere near as precipitous as I remembered; it wasn't even difficult—just steady one-foot-in-front-of-the-other climbing for a little more than twenty minutes. We were sweating, and we stopped to rest a few times, but both of us were undaunted. Arnold smiled, rather shyly, and moved on. At one point he took the lead.

At half past eleven or so we came to the part where the trail reenters the woods and goes along a sort of inclining balcony of big rocks that spirals upward around the main peak. Arnold was breathing hard (I was, too), but he wasn't about to let anything stand in the way of his victory. Finally, shortly after noon, we "summitted"—that's what the Everest climbers always say—and I thought, "This is Arnold's summit." But it wasn't.

As soon as we reached the top, whatever elation he felt was very short lived. His face, so flushed from exertion—and excitement—a moment before, was now drained of color. He had that same depressed expression I had seen that night in the barroom.

I asked him what was wrong. He had difficulty speaking. Then, pointing in various directions, he said, "Look there. And there. And there. All I can see are more mountains."

We walked back down—all six miles—in utter silence.

[twenty-eight]

Leopold and Me

WHEN I WAS a boy, if someone said "crime of the century," three words, run together as one, would pop into almost everyone's head: *Leopold-and-Loeb.* "Trial of the century." *Leopold-and-Loeb.* "Millionaire murderers." *Leopold-and-Loeb.*

For me, Leopold-and-Loeb meant something more. Although their senseless act of cold-blooded murder had occurred in 1924, nine years before I was born, the "crime of the century" had a very personal meaning. Their victim, Bobby Franks, was, I was told, a distant cousin. That revelation was a source of both deep-seated loathing and insatiable curiosity. As I grew up, I became fascinated by the story of Leopold and Loeb.

In time, I read a good deal about how the two very rich young geniuses, Nathan Leopold and Richard Loeb, students of law and philosophy, especially the philosophy of Nietzsche, thinking they were supermen, planned "a perfect crime," then actually carried out their perverse scheme. I read about how, failing to find the one they were after on the fateful day, they selected as their target another young boy they knew; how they bludgeoned him to death and then dumped his body in a swampy area some distance from the Chicago neighborhood where they lived; how they were quickly discovered when the police got the names of the manufacturer and prescriber of Leopold's glasses, accidentally dropped at the place where they disposed of the body; and how the great lawyer Clarence Darrow came to defend them, eschewing an insanity plea for another, one that would convince the jury to give them "life plus ninety-nine years."

I read Darrow's arguments in a collection of his most famous cases, *Attorney for the Damned*, edited by Arthur Weinberg. I read

Meyer Levin's novel *Compulsion* and Levin's "brief" that later appeared in *The Saturday Evening Post*, called "Why Leopold Should Be Freed." Still later I read two autobiographical works written by and presented to me by their author, Nathan Leopold.

Through an odd quirk of fate, he and I met in the early 1960s. At the time he was only partly free. He lived and worked in Puerto Rico, where he had been paroled after spending more than thirty-six years in prison in Illinois. (Loeb, held in another prison, had died in the 1930s, stabbed to death in a prison shower room.)

Rumors to the contrary, Leopold had not converted to the Brethren Church (though it was for them that he worked in a hill station near Mayaguez). His wife, whom he had wed with the permission of the parole board, was a florist, the widow of a local doctor. She was first described to me by a mutual friend as "a nice Jewish lady from Baltimore who came to Puerto Rico as a tourist and stayed." She and Leopold had met at a social at the San Juan synagogue.

After several years of working as a medical technician for the Brethren, Leopold had been allowed to move to San Juan, where he attended the university, received a master's degree in medical social work, and obtained a job in the social science division of the department of health. It was there that I first laid eyes on him.

Our meeting was awkward. At least for me.

I had gone to San Juan to serve as a consultant on several projects being run out of the social science office. On my first day, I breezed into the office, said hello to my friend, former professor from Cornell, and now boss Ed Suchman, and was asked if I'd like to meet the staff. I said I'd like that very much. We walked down the hall, opened the door, and there he was, sitting right in front of me. I had no idea he had been paroled, that he was in Puerto Rico, that he worked for the commonwealth. But I recognized him immediately. (Meyer Levin's article had been accompanied by a large picture of him, and he looked just the same: a sixtyish-year-old average-size man without any distinctive features save for piercing eyes behind thick glasses.) My heart skipped a beat, and I moved forward, hearing Ed Suchman say, "Peter, this is Nate Leopold."

Hesitantly (I now admit) I reached out to accept his

proffered hand. (Reminiscing about this strange encounter as I write, I think I was about as enthusiastic as Itzhak Rabin was in shaking hands with Arafat—and for a not-too-different reason. It was stained with blood. The blood of my people!)

"Pleased to meet you, Dr. Rose," the monster said.

We moved on through the office. I looked back over my shoulder a few times. "It really is him," I remember telling myself.

Two days later, after a series of meetings in the health department and at the University of Puerto Rico, I returned to the office and learned that I had been assigned an assistant. It was Leopold.

I had little choice. I was hardly in a position to object.

We began working together, designing a survey relating to safety among cane cutters. In his spare time, he helped me with another study, on the then-current state of opinions about Americans, i.e., "mainlanders." The latter was a part of a larger project being conducted by a Puerto Rican psychiatrist who was convinced that anti-Americanism among Puerto Rican males was due to a "castration complex." I had laughed when I first heard this but, in the end, came to agree with him. We learned that many men felt emasculated by the disruptive effects of employment opportunities for women in the government-subsidized underwear factories run by Peter Pan and Maidenform and other companies, where wives could find steadier work than could their cane-cutting, seasonally employed husbands.

A student of intergroup relations and of marginality, as well, I was intrigued by the challenge of Fernandez-Marina's hypothesis and also by his and others' attitudes toward certain minorities, especially Cubans and Jews (these, I learned, were most often to be found around the plaza in Old San Juan and were often one and the same folks). I decided I would like to do some research on my own on the Jews of Puerto Rico. It would be the beginning of what I saw as a larger project on the Jews of the Caribbean. I needed a point of entry. Leopold, overhearing me talk about this to someone in the office, volunteered to speak to his wife, who, he said, "knows every Jew on the island."

That was, if not the beginning of a beautiful friendship, then at least the beginning of a relationship where the norm of reciprocity functioned quite well. Leopold helped me, and, in a more modest way, I helped him. In the process, we got to know each other—though it wasn't until months later that he learned of my earlier connection to him and his crime.

With support from the Anti-Defamation League and a small foundation, I was able to return to Puerto Rico on several occasions after my formal relationship with the social science office had ended. My purpose for going back was to interview a number of members of the island's far-flung Jewish community. (For those with an interest in what I found, I can only report that, unlike the situation on almost every other major island in the Caribbean, Puerto Rico's Jews were all relative newcomers: almost all were first- or second-generation immigrants who got there by way of New York. Many moved down in the late 1940s with clothing-industry companies that were attracted to the commonwealth by a new economic plan with great tax advantages. There were also some Jewish professionals, including two German-born refugee doctors; a number of small businessmen, mostly Cuban exiles; and a few Jewish academicians, military personnel, and astronomers—based at one of the universities or one of the observatories—with similar backgrounds. There were no direct descendants of old Sephardim, such as one finds in Curaçao, Barbados, or St. Thomas, to be found there.)

It turned out that getting to know Leopold was more interesting than getting to know those I was there to study. While he always deferred to me, the Ph.D.-bearing social scientist, there were strains as well. He was, after all, very smart (as he was always portrayed) and well read, a master of many languages, a scientist and a technician. He was also rather vain and very opinionated, and he harbored many prejudices. Sometimes I argued with him. But mostly I listened, trying to figure out what made him tick.

He and I traveled the length and breadth of the island, often staying overnight in small hotels. (Because he was known to many from various news stories that had appeared when he first arrived on the island, he never used his name when we traveled. Instead, he would introduce himself—and also register in hotels—as "N. L. Forman," using his mother's maiden name as his own last name.)

Together we would visit my "subjects" at their factories, in their offices, sometimes in their homes. I would conduct the interviews about their backgrounds, how they happened to come to Puerto Rico, and the nature of their interactions with locals, with other Jews, and with other minorities. Leopold would sit next to me but rarely participate in the colloquies.

Only after about ten or twelve of these interviews did I realize that, with Leopold in the room, it was hard for the interviewee to concentrate on what I was asking. Like me that first day, they kept glancing at the small man beside me. (After the fact, I realized that they were asking themselves, "Is Mr. Forman really Nathan Leopold? He sure looks like that guy who was written up in the paper.")

Once reality hit, I stopped taking him with me into the homes and offices where I conducted my interviews. But we still traveled together and rode, usually in his car, from town to town, often late at night.

One night, driving on a narrow, winding road in the rugged mountains, Nathan turned to me and asked me where I was from.

"Northampton, Massachusetts," I replied.

"I know that. I mean, where is your family from? New York? Chicago?"

I knew we had reached a critical juncture in our relationship. I was also a bit frightened. Here I was, sitting next to a man who had committed "the crime of the century," cold-bloodedly murdering an innocent young boy who had been my father's cousin—albeit several times removed.

I answered his question. "Not from New York City, but from upstate New York, Rochester." Then I added, "Some of the family lived in Montreal and some in . . . Chicago."

"Chicago? Say, maybe I knew them."

It was now or never. "I think you did. The name was Franks."

Silence. Silence for almost an hour. He didn't say a word. I didn't either. We both stared ahead at the curvy road.

At about 10 P.M. we stopped for gas. "Want some coffee?" he said.

I said I would. The ice had been broken.

The next day, with the last in that series of interviews completed, we stopped for lunch and a swim at a beach in Arecibo before returning to San Juan. As we sat on the sand, Leopold began to talk about his days in prison. I listened. Once in a while I would ask a question. I wondered if he would bring up the crime itself. He didn't. Not that day or ever, though he was to tell me some time later, when we spoke of *Compulsion*, the major book about it—and about the trial and his incarceration—that he was especially offended by the author's implication that he and Loeb were homosexual lovers. I thought to myself, "He seems more upset about being accused of being gay than about being convicted of the most serious of capital crimes, premeditated murder, for which he was convicted and served nearly forty years in prison." I wanted to question him about the matter but then thought better of it.

Two days after our return from that last trip, Leopold dropped a book off at my hotel. It was *Life Plus Ninety-nine Years*. Named for the sentence handed down by the judge, it was his own story of the trial and of his life in prison. I still have it. Sometimes I pull it off the shelf and flip it open. Inside the cover he had written, "We sure had a swell swim in Arecibo."

The inscription matches the language of the book. Like much else I discovered about him—his interests in prison reform, recidivism, and medical research, and his strong opinions on matters of race, poverty, and criminality—it reads like a time warp of 1920s and 1930s portraiture and argot. (This also characterizes his less interesting second volume, *Grab for a Halo*, the story of his life after prison.)

Leopold and I continued to see each other on and off whenever I returned to Puerto Rico. We would often go on walks, often, he said, to see more birds. He was always a bird watcher. (Anyone who knows the story of the crime knows that the swamp where the body of Bobby Franks was dumped was Leopold's favorite bird sanctuary in the Chicago area.)

While he was on parole, Leopold wrote and published *The Birds of Puerto Rico and the Virgin Islands*. While he assumed the birds were the same in both places, he had never been able to confirm it. He had never been to the Virgin Islands because, by court order, he was not permitted to leave the island of Puerto Rico. (This held even when his beloved brother passed away and he asked permission to go to Chicago for the funeral.)

One day when I happened to be in San Juan, Leopold called to tell me that he had just received a cable from Illinois governor Otto Kerner releasing him from parole. After more than three decades in prison and at least six more years under a kind of house arrest in Puerto Rico, he was free. For a pregnant twenty or thirty seconds I hung on the phone, thinking of poor Bobby Franks while telling myself that Leopold surely had done penance for his crime. Then I said, "Nate, what shall we do to celebrate?"

He said, "I'd give anything to get off this island."

I said, "You're on. We'll check out the birds in St. Thomas." And, as soon as we'd hung up, I made reservations—one under my name, one for "N. L. Forman"—for two round-trip, one-day tickets to Charlotte Amalie.

We flew over. We took a taxi into town, walked around, and then went birding. We had an amazing day.

The next day, with the press having learned what we already knew, Nathan Leopold was again news. Again there was a review of "the crime of the century," replete with the full cast of characters: Leopold-and-Loeb, Bobby Franks, Clarence Darrow, Meyer Levin, and now Otto Kerner, too. I saw the early papers but, having left on the afternoon plane for New York, never saw any mention of his reaction.

On one occasion a few months later, back in Puerto Rico, I visited him and his wife in their apartment in Santurce. I hadn't been there before. While there I was struck by two photographs, each next to a vase with a fresh flower. I can still see them. The first was on the coffee table in the living room. The face was unmistakable. I picked it up, and, before I could say anything, Leopold said, "Clarence Darrow, the man who saved my life."

The second picture was in the master bedroom, through which I had to pass to go to the bathroom. It was on a dresser. I noticed it as I walked back through the room. It was a blown-up snapshot of a well-dressed young man of, say, nineteen or twenty. At first I thought it was Leopold himself but, on closer inspection, I realized it was somebody else. I was pretty sure I knew who. Looking into the room as I squinted at the picture, Nathan confirmed it.

"Dickie Loeb," he said, "the guy who ruined my life." He paused, then added, "Still, I gotta tell you something. You know what, he was really a swell guy, the best friend I ever had."

I never saw Leopold again.

[twenty-nine]

Mr. David

I MET MR. DAVID shortly after arriving in Northampton over forty years ago. I needed some repairs on a tweed jacket purchased six years before in a post-Christmas sale at a very "Ivy" men's store in Ithaca, New York, where I was then a graduate student. The jacket, worn and patched with leather at the elbows, was, along with the pipe I smoked, a youthful statement about the academic career on which I was embarking. It was also falling apart from the inside out.

I asked a friend where I might get the jacket repaired. He said there was only one decent tailor in town, Mr. David. And so I went to see him.

His tiny shop on Masonic Street had an aura of familiarity about it. I could feel it in the air. The place smelled of steam and ironing. It was strewn with pieces of material and spools of thread. It was dark, too, save for a spot of light emanating from a gooseneck lamp over a big sewing machine behind which sat a little old man.

"May I help you?" he asked. The accent also rang a bell.

"Yes," I said. "I'd like you to put a new lining in this jacket."

He took it, lowered his glasses from the top of his forehead almost to the end of his nose, inspected the whole thing very carefully, shook his head, and said, "Mister, it wouldn't pay. It would cost you thirty dollars easy. Do yourself a favor. Get a new jacket."

"But I like this one. It's, well, something special."

He looked up at me, smiled, and said, "What are you, a teacher?"

"Yes," I said.

He sighed. "All right, all right. Leave it. I'll see what I can do."

A week late I returned.

"Is my jacket ready?" I asked.

"Yes," Mr. David said. "It's all fixed. Gimme, uh, two dollars."

Surprised by how little he was charging, I said, "Only two dollars?"

"Yes, just two dollars."

I paid him and took the jacket. I looked it over and noted that, instead of replacing the lining, he had mended every rip and tear. I was impressed—and very grateful for his kindness. I didn't know what to say. I stood there for a few moments looking at him.

He spoke again. "So . . . you're a teacher. A good profession. The best. I know a lot of young people like you. Professors, too."

No longer able to contain my emotions, I said, "And I know people like you. You remind me of my grandfather."

Mr. David looked up at me, tilted his head, and rather quietly asked, "Was he a tailor?"

"Yes," I answered.

"Jewish?"

"Yes."

Now grinning, he asked, "From Poland?"

"He was."

"Tell me, son," Mr. David leaned closer, "was he a Socialist?"

"Of course," I replied.

Mr. David beamed. So did I. We shook hands and laughed, and, promising to come by soon, I bade him goodbye.

As I walked back to the campus, I decided I would visit him the following week. It was not to be. Two days after I picked up my jacket, I learned that he had died.

When I read the news in the local paper, I was very sad. Mr. David (I never learned his whole name until I read the obituary) was a link between my old world and my new one.

[thirty]

The Waiting Game

IT IS SAID that misery loves company. I'm not sure, but I do know that it triggers a bonding of sufferers, an interdependence that makes it somehow easier to bear the helplessness of being unable to do anything for those we want so much to succor. I found that out not long ago when I spent almost two weeks sitting night and day in the waiting room of the cardiac unit of the Yale New Haven Hospital.

Although I am a social scientist, I wasn't there to do research on small-group behavior or on how individuals cope with crises. I was there because my mother-in-law had been admitted with an acute heart condition. My wife was allowed to be with her much of the time. I, on the other hand, was pretty much confined to one of the special lounges set up for visitors. For me it was an exercise in anxiety, boredom, tension, frustration, and, I must admit, sociological fascination.

When we arrived, a working-class Italian American couple, an elderly Jewish woman, and two Grant Wood–types from the Midwest were in the waiting room. All were staring either at the floor or at the wall-mounted television set, its blaring sound competing against incessant Motown Muzak amplified through a ceiling speaker.

In less than an hour the Jewish woman broke the ice. Her question seemed odd, but I was to learn that it was a standard opener.

"You waiting for somebody?"

Tense and worried and in no mood to talk, I was tempted to say, "No," and let it go at that. I didn't. I said, "Yes, my mother-in-law." And before she could ask the next question, I answered it: "Heart. She's going to have angioplasty."

"Oh, angioplasty," said the woman, obviously familiar with the medical term I had heard for the first time just twenty-four hours before. "I know all about it. Sy, he's not my husband, just a good friend—well, more than a friend, we could have got married but, you know, he has children, I have children . . ." She blurted out the story of her life, and his, and told me about his nice son who lives in Florida and his not-so-nice daughter who lives nearby, and also about his "procedures."

I learned what the others already knew: that the woman had been sitting there for several days, every once in a while popping up to inquire about her "gentleman friend," sometimes going to sit by his bed.

During one of her absences later that night, the Italian husband leaned over and asked, "Your mother, huh?"

"No, mother-in-law."

It didn't really matter. He went on to say that with them it was his father. "Tough—I mean he was tough. Almost eighty. Massive heart attack two years ago . . . bypass surgery, triple, if you know what I mean. Then he was pretty good for a couple years. Worked in the garden. Drove his car. Then, bang, another attack and here he is. It's not good neither. They don't think he's gonna make it."

I said I was sorry and picked up my book. But he persisted. He wanted to talk, to tell me about "Papa."

In the middle of his story, two older white women, obviously sisters, came into the waiting area. Both were in their late sixties, one with dyed black hair, one whose hair was bleached blond. They had the same faces, the same stooped shoulders, the same polyester stretch pants and cheap tennis shoes, the same consumptive hack.

"Can you smoke in here?" the blond one asked me, ignoring the fact that someone else was speaking to me.

I acknowledged her with a nod and pointed to the big red NO SMOKING sign next to the television set. She shrugged and marched off with her sister, who had already taken out a half-empty pack of Camels and a Zippo.

While they were gone, the storyteller was called in to see his father and a new group came to join us. Actually it was one group and one single person: a black family of five and a young Spanish-speaking man. They were all "first-timers." I could tell because I noted that they were quite uncertain about the routines, even about using the intercom to check with the nurses in the cardiac-care and intensive-care units.

Before anyone else rose to their assistance, the woman from the Midwest, ever so quiet up to that time, got up, walked across the tiny room, and asked them the name of their patient. They looked a bit startled, then one of the younger ones, a daughter I assumed, said "Hattie Martin."

"Now, is she in CCU or ICU?"

"I don't rightly know."

"Never mind," said her helper. "Just press one of those buttons and say her name; they'll tell you whether she's there or not."

They learned that Hattie Martin was still in the "Lab," the place down on the second floor where angiograms were taken and angioplasty procedures were performed.

Just then two young doctors walked by, the ones my mother-in-law, who gave names to everyone, had taken to calling "Dr. Larry" and "Dr. Sunshine." He is a fellow; she is an intern. Most of those in the waiting area knew who they were. They were on the "Team." We all wondered if they were coming over to give somebody some news—hopefully some good news. We were all steeled to hear the worst. But in this case they just nodded and moved on down the hall, followed by the medical student who had been assigned to do a work-up of my mother-in-law the day before. (Learning of his passion for mountain climbing, she had called him "Dr. Bergsteiger.")

Though as yet unaware of the significance the white-coated figures had to all of us, the members of the black family sensed the tension in the atmosphere. Coupled with their own concerns about the fact that their patient was still "downstairs," it caused them to look even more upset.

The plain woman from the Midwest told them not to worry, that she and her husband had had to wait five hours and that their patient was now doing quite well. Then she resumed her previous pose, sitting straight and proper next to her speechless husband. In the five days I saw them together, I saw him open his mouth only once, but she was no longer reticent. She now seemed to want to talk, to participate in the often stilted conversations and cryptic commentaries. After taking her place next to her husband, it wasn't five minutes before she said, to no one in particular, or perhaps to all of us, "It's my husband's brother. He's from here, from Connecticut. Like George. I'm from Iowa. That's where we live now. Hardware business. Dan was stricken a few weeks ago. Only fifty-two. They said it's a good thing he had the attack. A warning . . ." And on and on. Medical history. Family biography. Views on the presidential candidates, especially regarding Medicare.

By midnight all but two members of the black family and my wife and I had left the hospital. My wife, who had been with her mother much of the time, thought we should stay a bit longer. The Joneses (we learned their names in a late-night discussion about the *Nightline* show we had watched together after switching away from Johnny Carson) left around 1 A.M. They looked very apprehensive after the wife, Ann, made a last visit to her mother, who was now with so many others' relatives in CCU. Before going, she said to me, "Things are stable now, but it doesn't look too good."

Our story was similar. We left for our hotel room at 2 A.M. Dr. Larry called us at 4:30. "Sorry to wake you, but she's having pains again. We're going to take her back to the lab."

"When?"

In a calm but firm voice he answered, "Now."

"We'll be right there," my wife told him. She hung up the phone. We dressed and rushed back to the hospital.

Twenty minutes after our arrival, the Joneses returned as well.

We nodded to one another with sad faces. "Did you get called back, too?" I asked.

"No," they said in chorus, "we just couldn't sleep."

Nobody said anything for the next two hours. Then, startling me out of my stupor, the husband—his name was Roosevelt—began to talk. He told me he was a minister; he said his wife was, too. He started to tell me about his childhood in Alabama. "My daddy was also a preacher and . . ." Just then an elderly black couple came in. They sat down quietly and listened as Roosevelt continued.

At 9 A.M. we were told things were going fairly well and that we could see our patient in a few minutes. While we were waiting to go in, a woman of about forty-five walked in. She punched the intercom button authoritatively and asked to see her father, Seymour Sinclair. I put the pieces together. She was the "ungrateful daughter" his friend had run on about the previous evening, the one who was described to me as "a very rich lady, well, not a lady, but very rich. Married to a doctor, too."

Later in the day a few of Norman Rockwell's models walked in. Six in all. A handsome gray-haired woman in a striped shirt and slacks; a middle-aged couple, he in a lightweight anorak and jeans, she similarly dressed; and three baseball-capped, freckle-faced redheads, Jim, Rickie, and Sam.

"I'm Mary O'Neill. May I see my husband?" the gray-haired woman asked into the speaker. The answer was "Yes, two visitors," and she and her son went in. The others sat with us.

Within about ten minutes, the younger mother struck up a conversation with the plain woman from Iowa who, with her still-silent husband, had come back an hour before. "Mary O'Neill," she told those of us sitting there, "was in this very waiting area only a week ago." Her husband, Kevin, had had angioplasty and had been moved to another area after twenty-four hours. Just when they were set to take him home, Mr. O'Neill had had recurrent pains and was taken back to the lab, then back to CCU. (His was a story I was to hear over and over and to become a part of when my mother-in-law's case followed a nearly identical course.)

The younger Mrs. O'Neill, who had accompanied her mother-in-law before, knew the ropes. She had initiated the conversation with the woman from Iowa with a "How's your patient?" query. She found out that things were not very good. Intentionally or not, she also managed to elicit an incredible amount of information about the family from the Midwest: work activities, recreational interests, family life, political attitudes, and economic forecasts. I sat there listening and taking mental notes. I smiled to myself. In half an hour they had touched on the topic of each of the first seven chapters of any basic sociology textbook!

All of this happened in a period of about twenty-four hours. The scenario was repeated day after day, as long as we were there. The players changed, although some were there almost as long as we, but the roles—as passive and seemingly helpless bystanders in the drama that centered on those they loved most—remained pretty much the same.

Old and young will come there to wait. None of them will know when they arrive whether their visits will be short or long, or whether their patients will live or die. White people and black people and Asians and Latinos will come to wait. Some will be very religious and welcome members of the clergy who are always hovering in the wings. Others will be offended by their sugarcoated sanctimony. Rich people and poor people will come to wait. Some will be elegantly dressed; some will be poorly clothed. And, despite the fact that some will be worldly and sophisticated and others quite provincial, most will be eager to talk. With rare exceptions, most will speak out sooner or later, revealing much about their patient—and much about themselves.

For most of those I saw in the waiting room at Yale it was a release to be able to open up with strangers. For me their talk offered an important distraction from my own concerns.

But what about me? Did I tell anyone about my mother-in-law or about my wife, her adopted daughter, or about our wonderful children? Oddly enough, I, who make a living talking and writing about people, said very little. Was it professional control? Perhaps. But it is also possible that others' words provided ample catharsis for me. I didn't feel the need to say anything, but I should report that my mother-in-law recovered nicely. But then, you see, she was a tough woman. Born in Czechoslovakia, raised in Vienna. Her husband was a physicist. In optics. They came to America in 1939 after the Anschluss. She was always active. Great walker. Mountain climber. Why, do you know that, right after her eightieth birthday, she hiked with us in Switzerland?

[thirty-one]

Remembering Varian Fry

AMONG MY EARLIEST recollections are the strange sounds of people living in our home in upstate New York. They were speaking German. They weren't relatives or friends, nor did they work for my parents. But there they were—Alma, Max, Walter, and a number of others.

By the time I was six or seven I had come to understand that our houseguests had fled for their lives from places called Germany and Austria. My father said they were "refugees." "People," he explained, "who have been forced to leave their homelands because they oppose a tyrant named Adolf Hitler or just because they are Jews, like us."

In time I was to learn that many such refugees had been assisted by individuals who risked their lives to help them escape and by others who arranged for their passage to America, signed affidavits so that they would not become "public charges," and provided temporary shelter while they struggled to start over in the new, alien environment. As I grew older, I became increasingly intrigued by the motivations of those willing to extend themselves to facilitate the escape and resettlement of such dispossessed people. That old interest in the dispossessed never waned, but it wasn't until the late 1970s that I began to turn my persisting curiosity into a more specific investigation focusing on the politics of rescue and the psychology of altruism. I paid particular attention to those who were links in rescue and resettlement chains, people I came to call "advocates," "agents," "gatekeepers," "guides," and "go-betweens."

Over the next two decades I spent a considerable amount of time visiting refugee agencies in this country and refugee camps overseas, getting a first-hand impression of those who were actually playing one or more of the different roles. Those I met ranged from the heads of huge international and nongovernmental organizations to representatives of a number of American refugee agencies to the foot soldiers working in refugee camps and resettlement programs. Some were professionals, but most were contract workers, often called by the telling oxymoron, "paid volunteers."

Early in my research I learned that most of the American refugee agencies had two distinctive traits: they were "church related" (the oldest being Hebrew Immigrant Aid Society; the largest, the U.S. Catholic Conference's Migration and Refugee Service) and they claimed to be strictly humanitarian organizations, formally eschewing all political agendas. There were a few exceptions—on both counts. One of these was (and still is) the International Rescue Committee (IRC), a private, nonprofit citizen's group that has always been nonsectarian in membership and quite outspoken in its ideological commitment to furthering democracy and opposing totalitarianism. Quite frankly, I found it the most interesting of the lot.

The IRC had been founded in 1942, through the melding of the International Relief Association, a voluntary agency started in 1933 at the urging of Albert Einstein and a cross section of European and Americans opponents to the rise of Nazism, and the Emergency Rescue Committee, established by a similar group of concerned citizens in 1940. When, in early discussions with those in the refugee field, I heard reference to the "ERC," the name rang a bell. I suddenly remembered my father, who was active in resettlement activities sponsored by the "Joint," the American Jewish Joint Distribution Committee, speaking of a new organization and an extraordinary venture it had engaged in just before the United States entered the war. The flashback, probably dating to 1942 or 1943, included a reference to an American writer named "Fly" or "Fry" who had gone to France with a list of prominent exiles to find and assist in getting out of Europe. My father had claimed that hundreds of refugees had been rescued, spirited out on a modern-day underground railway that ran from Marseilles over the Pyrenees into Spain and then to Lisbon, from where they would sail to America. Many of those who made it had been members of Neu Beginnen and other anti-Nazi groups; many others were prominent artists and intellectuals.

It would be forty years before I would learn the full story of the ERC's mission and the name of its principal agent—which turned out to be Fry, Varian Fry—again.

I first ran across a lengthy description of both in *Escape to Freedom: The Story of the International Rescue Committee* (1983) by Aaron Levenstein. In one of the chapters in his institutional history, Levenstein sketched out the nature of Fry's ERC operation, based in the Hotel Splendide in Marseilles, where, as far as the authorities were concerned, he was a representative of the World Committee of the YMCA, there to assess the relief needs of those in Vichy France and do charitable work among refugees.

Levenstein told how those initially on the list of persons to be rescued were selected by the members of an international advisory committee, which included the journalist Max Ascoli for the Italians, the Catholic philosopher Jacques Maritain for the French, the novelist Thomas Mann for the Germans, the statesman Jan Masaryk for the Czechs, and others. He noted that once Fry arrived on the scene, the original roster was expanded considerably. Part of Fry's success, he said, was due to the cooperation of certain key figures, not least Harry Bingham, an American vice-consul in Marseilles. Bingham turned out to be a notable exception to most other Americans in the foreign service at the time, one who worked his way around the U.S. Department of State's isolationism, strict neutrality, and sometimes quite blatant anti-Semitism. (Bingham, it would later be revealed, not only helped Fry, but also actually harbored several of the refugees in his villa on the outskirts of Marseilles.)

By all accounts, those saved by Fry's group were members of a stellar cohort indeed. Included in the ranks were Marc Chagall; Marcel Duchamp; Max Ernst; Jacques Lipchitz; Wanda Landowska; Lotte Leonard; Hannah Arendt; Andre Breton; Heinrich Mann (brother of Thomas) and Golo Mann (Thomas's son); Franz Werfel and his wife, Alma Mahler Gropius Werfel; Giuseppe and Amadeo Modigliani; Andre Masson; Walter Mehring; and Hans Sahl.

After reading Levenstein's brief summation, I sought other source material. The best was a book by Fry himself, *Surrender on Demand* (1945, reprinted in 1968 and 1997), which was later shortened in a special edition for high-school students under the title *Assignment Rescue* (1997). It was published with a new introduction by one of Fry's most colorful aides, Albert O. Hirschman, also known as "Beamish."

The shortened edition has a breathless "you-are-there" quality. The brief chapters are terse and picturesque, each with telegraphic title: "The Secret Mission," "Beamish, Franzi, and Lena," "We Deal with Gangsters," "Everything Goes Wrong," "The Door Swings Shut."

Reading the autobiographical accounts whetted my appetite for more of the personal side of the story.

Browsing in a used bookstore, I chanced upon a memoir by Mary Jayne Gold called *Crossroads Marseilles 1940* (1980). The author was already familiar to me, for I had been introduced to her by Fry himself. In *Surrender on Demand*, he described her as "a made-to-order charmer . . . young, blonde, and beautiful." Apparently, she was that and more: a wealthy, adventurous American socialite and social butterfly who was living a carefree life in Europe when, through another of Fry's principal assistants, a Smith College graduate named Miriam Davenport, she joined the team.

Gold's book is a pastiche of anecdotes and impressions of Fry and the intrepid staff at the "relief center," including Miriam Davenport, "Beamish" Hirschman, Bill Freier, Mary Jayne's special and aptly named friend "Killer," and the young refugee who was their office boy and gofer, Justus "Gussie" Rosenberg (now professor emeritus at Bard College). It also contains a number of snapshots of the proud, perplexed, and often demanding exiles who sought their assistance and many of the others with whom they had to do.

Nearly a decade after the publication of Levenstein's history of the International Rescue Committee and my discovery of Gold's memoir, another volume was added to my small but growing shelf of books and articles that made mention of Varian Fry's activities, as well as those of the Emergency Rescue Committee and its successor organization, the IRC. Unlike most of the others, Eric Thomas Chester's *Covert Network* (1995) was hardly a paean to the triumph of good over evil, or to the efforts of operatives with but a singular mission to save people from the clutches of Fascism.

Although he praises Fry and his group for their "dangerous and heroic" operation, Chester presents a very different assessment of its *raison d'etre* and the motivations behind the operation. He gives the impression that, instead of being an independent operative, as he is usually portrayed, Fry was working for the government instead of fighting it.

The fact is that—whatever his personal political proclivities (he did become increasingly anti-Communist in orientation after the war) or the later involvement of many supporters of the ERC and IRC with the Office of Strategic Services (OSS) and its successor, the CIA—when he was in France there is little question but that Fry was more often at loggerheads with American officials, especially those in the State Department, than in league with them. Certainly there was little sympathy in Foggy Bottom—or, for that matter, in the White House—for those who were working to get refugees out of Europe. Fry himself makes this very clear in *Surrender on Demand* and in "The Massacre of the Jews," an article he published in the *New Republic* in 1945.

In addition to a number of carefully crafted historical studies about the period, such as Michael R. Marrus and Robert O. Paxton's *Vichy France and the Jews* (1983) and David S. Wyman's *The Abandonment of the Jews* (1988), some of those Fry helped in those dark days (and some of those who helped him) also described the mission in Marseilles in very personal terms. Among the most useful are Lion Feuchtwanger's *The Devil in France* (1941), Walter Mehring's *No Road Back* (1944), Hans Sahl's *The Few and the Many* (1962), and the much more recently published book by Lisa Fittko, *Escape through the Pyrenees* (1992).

The basic story that most tell is that many of the refugees Fry was sent to assist had first sought safe haven in Paris. The time there had been short lived, as Paris soon fell to Hitler's juggernaut. On June 22, 1940, an armistice was signed and France was divided into occupied and unoccupied zones. Many of those in various expatriate communities took to the roads and railroads once again, seeking sanctuary, this time in various parts of the still-free south.

Soon the noose began to tighten in Vichy. Antiforeign and anti-Semitic scapegoating grew more intense, as did the activities of the Kundt Commission, a body made up of German diplomats, military officers, and secret police, whose assignment was to ferret out and force the "surrender on demand" and repatriation of German citizens as agreed to by the terms of the armistice. More and more exiles felt it imperative to move once again, this time out of Europe altogether. The "refugee telegraph" signaled that Marseilles was the gateway. Thousands poured into the city, finding accommodations in every conceivable sort of place, from fancy hotels and elegant villas to cheap *pensions*.

Late in the summer of 1940, more than a year before the United States declared war on Germany, Varian Fry, a thirty-two-year-old journal editor and activist in the campaign to support Franco's opponents in Spain and the cause of German democrats, flew on the *Yankee Clipper* to Lisbon and then traveled by train to Marseilles to establish the ERC's command post. He entered France with a list of two hundred prominent figures specially chosen to be helped to escape. It was a tall order, especially for one who had only been to Europe twice before and had rather limited French and German language skills and no prior experience in either data gathering or clandestine operations.

Although he developed into a master of negotiation who was able to manipulate many of the local parties and party members with a combination of charm, guile, and well-placed payoffs, after the United States entered the war, the American Pimpernel's luck began to run out. Under pressure from the Gestapo, the French police threatened to arrest him. Boldly, Fry asked the nature of the charge. He was told: "Parce que vous avez trop protégé des juifs et des anti-Nazis" (Because you have helped and protected Jews and anti-Nazis).

Although he managed to stay a while longer, Fry was finally arrested and deported. While the operation continued for several more months and nearly three hundred more refugees were assisted in escaping, the enterprise was closed down by the Gestapo on June 2, 1942.

As I read the same story over and over, I couldn't help but note how varied the portraits were of the man who for me—and I'm sure for others who knew only of his heroic accomplishments—had become a kind of icon. I thought seriously about continuing the quest to learn more about him: reviewing primary source material, field reports, cables, and letters, and then tracking down those who had known him as colleagues or clients, as well as some of his critics. I thought it would complement my more general research on the making of refugee policy, but then, realizing the enormity of such an undertaking, I decided to defer any action on the matter.

Sometime in the late 1980s, I was fortunate to meet and interview Harold Oram, one of the ERC's founders and a principal fund raiser and central player in the drama in Marseilles. (Oram was one of several people to whom Fry dedicated his book.) When I met him, Oram was quite elderly and frail and wracked with emphysema, but his memory was sharp and he was happy to whisper answers to all sorts of questions about his long, productive life as "a PR man for good causes," and especially about his activities in the late 1930s and early 1940s. He filled in many blanks about the early days of the Emergency Rescue Committee and then, much more specifically, about the undertaking led by the ERC's "Man in Marseilles," Varian Fry.

My last meeting with Harold Oram had begun with my asking him to describe the operation in France. He started by praising his old comrade and telling me how audacious the operation had been; about how Fry had been sent to Marseilles to carry out the secret and mainly illegal mission of rescuing the two hundred targeted "politicals, artists, and scholars, and ended by saving almost ten times as many refugees from capture, *refoulement*, incarceration, and, as we now know, almost certain death." Yet, even as he spoke, it was clear that he and Fry had had a rocky relationship. (I later learned that Oram had been considered the primary backup to replace Fry once his cover was blown but was held back, largely on Fry's own recommendation, because, as a Jew, Oram would have been even more vulnerable than he had been.)

With Oram's encouragement and that of several IRC staff members in New York, I once again began to think about trying to talk to others with first-hand recollections of Fry and to read his papers. While mulling this over, I learned that for years an English editor named Donald Carroll had been working on just such a study. His quest had begun sometime in the 1960s and then, like mine, had been abandoned, only to be begun again in the mid-1970s. For all his fits and starts, the far more determined Carroll had single-handedly tracked down and interviewed many of those who knew, worked with, and were rescued by Varian Fry. He had amassed a trove of information. Yet, aside from an informative essay, "Escape from Vichy," that appeared in *American Heritage* in 1983, Carroll had published very little. But his efforts did not go to waste.

At his request, Andy Marino, a young English writer, took over and, with dogged determination, completed the task. The result of Marino's effort, built upon Carroll's solid foundation, is a splendid new book, *A Quiet American: The Secret War of Varian Fry* (1999).

Fleshing out the bare bones of the well-known story, Marino tells much about Fry's background and his character. Most important, he details the ways Fry dealt with the multiple requirements of his singular mission in Marseilles and the problems he faced in dealing with the generally hostile American consulate; the local citizens and foreigners, including some very unsavory characters who, for a fee (the money coming from ERC backers in New York), were willing to prepare false papers, change money, and assist in maintaining the lifeline; and the few police and military authorities who allowed themselves to be coopted or bribed into giving an official imprimatur to clearly illegal activities. Marino adds much to our understanding of how Fry organized a true cross section of volunteers to assist him. There were Americans, British, French, Germans, Czechs, Italians, Poles; Socialists, scholars, socialites (like Mary Jayne Gold); politicians, pacifists, and soldiers; and some well-established writers and artists. In regard to such colleagues and others to whom ERC staffers often had to turn, Marino clearly states an important truth often ignored by others: "For every client who sailed [or managed to get over the Pyrenees], there was the invisible history of many man-hours of help from Fry and his staff who had to bully and cajole both the American consulate and the French authorities into granting the visas and papers."

A Quiet American is a compelling piece of narrative nonfiction that, like Fry's own account, reads like a spy novel set in a romantic and tough city of gangsters and opportunists, refugees and Nazis. One reviewer, Paul Hughes, described Marino's book as a "cross between *Casablanca* and *A Year in Provence*." I think it is much closer to the former than the latter. But even then there are caveats.

Varian Fry was a crucial middleman, but he was not a wheeler-dealer like Humphrey Bogart's Rick, that amoral and notorious character who became virtuous. Fry was a virtuous man who learned to wheel and deal to carry out his commission in France. Moreover, Fry's major achievement in life was not assisting one Victor Lazlo to get away from a Vichy-controlled area, but in facilitating the escape of hundreds and hundreds of Lazlos.

Other reviewers of Marino's book have compared Fry, the enigmatic hero, to another unlikely savior with a list, Oskar Schindler. In his epilogue, Marino himself comments on this parallel. "Schindler was a sensualist and an opportunist who stumbled upon a humanitarian duty he could not ignore. . . . Fry was a sensitive, even prissy individual, an aesthete and an epicure who was driven by idealistic motives to perform a humanitarian duty. Schindler's was the profiteering escapade that went awry once he discovered by chance that life was more important than money. Fry was on a deliberate mission."

Fry's personality and his reactions to others and to various causes are the important focal points in Marino's text. While Marino, like all who have written about him, tells the story of what Fry did and how he accomplished his mission, his analysis, like his protagonist, turns out to be much more nuanced. It is also a more detailed commentary on some of the illustrious exiles who moved through Marseilles and those who tried to help them than anything else currently in print.

Among other things, the closer look into the lives of many of the players in the Marseilles-based drama adds to a deeper understanding of a common phenomenon, the kind of apotheosis that takes place in the minds of some who hear the word "refugee" or see those ubiquitous pictures of beleaguered and bedraggled lost souls arriving in countries of asylum. In reality, as Marino shows so clearly, there are as few true saints in the exile community as in any other. Rather, there are strong refugees and weak ones, leaders and followers, complex personalities and rather simple ones, men and women who intuitively seem to know every trick in the trades of deception and prevarication and those who can't bring themselves to lie even when their lives depend upon it. Marino also makes clear something I have found in my own research: the same variations in character are also found among refugee workers.

Varian Fry himself may have been a savior, but he was no saint. He was a one-man band of multiple rhythms and temperaments, a tissue of contradictions. He was at once quite youthful and old beyond his years. He had a demeanor some described as "marked by gravitas," and yet he was known to take great pleasure in fine art, fine food, fine wine, and good company—including, on occasion, the company of prostitutes. He was a loner who needed people around him. He was cautious and impulsive, pensive and quick-tempered, humane and haughty—though never humble. He could be undiplomatic when it would have been better to keep his mouth shut and was filled with remorse whenever he realized his occasional indiscretions caused others to suffer. Like many of those on whom he relied and many of those he tried to save, he was a commanding presence who was also inwardly very insecure.

Shortly after being forced to leave Marseilles, Varian Fry wrote to his wife from Lisbon, saying, "I have learned to live with people, and to work with them. I have developed or discovered within me powers of resourcefulness, of imagination and of courage, which I never before knew I possessed. And I have fought a fight, against enormous odds, of which, in spite of final defeat, I think I can always be proud."

For one brief and shining period, Fry was truly a multiple role player: advocate, agent, gatekeeper, guide, *and* go-between. And he reveled in his ability to play them all.

Toward the end of his book, Marino quotes from another telling letter Fry wrote to his wife. It included this sentence: "One of the other American relief workers has called me 'the ideal type of social worker, intelligent, humane, and highly social.'"

Marino provides plenty of evidence to show that this self-assuredness was real, but that it was to prove to be quite ephemeral. Never again did Fry luxuriate in such self-satisfaction or such a sense of accomplishment. The brave, resourceful derring-do of his secret war against Hitler was never to be matched again.

Fry's deeds in France were hardly recognized until April 12, 1967, just five months before he died. At the urging of André Malraux, with whom he had worked in 1940, he was awarded the Croix de Chevalier of the Légion d'Honneur at the French consulate in New York City. Then, some thirty years after his death, he was honored once again when he was named one of the "Righteous among the Nations" at Yad Vashem, the Holocaust museum in Israel. There, at a tree-planting ceremony, Secretary of State Warren Christopher publicly apologized for the treatment Fry and the refugees had received by the Department of State during his days in Marseilles.

It is most likely that the general public in this country finally learned about this American hero when stories began to be written about an exhibition mounted at the new United States Holocaust Memorial Museum in Washington, D.C., in 1991. Like the abbreviated version of Fry's wartime memoir, it was called *Assignment: Rescue.* With an imaginative stage set, the entire presentation transported museum visitors back in time and onto the streets and into the coffee shops of Marseilles circa 1940. The exhibition, which included a photomontage of the likes of Beamish and Miriam Davenport and Harold Oram and many of their "clients"—and a number of critical documents—was remounted in 1997 at The Jewish Museum in New York.

In the spring of 2001, HBO/Showtime broadcast a feature film called *Varian's War.* The producers had clearly set out to tell the story of a homegrown hero still unknown to most Americans.

Unfortunately, what they created did not do justice to the man, his colleagues, or his cause.

Although Showtime's interpretation of *Varian's War* contains kernels of truth, the film is filled with errors of fact—about how the ERC and the mission got started, about Fry and his aides, about the selection process, about the roles of the French and German authorities. Despite the claim of its producers and publicists that theirs is the true story, those familiar with what actually happened have found the historical distortions inexcusable and wince at the caricaturing of the rescuers and asylum-seekers.

William Hurt as Fry, Matt Craven as Beamish, and Alan Arkin as Bill Freier, an artist-turned-forger to whom they often turned for fake documents, give quite credible performances, but the rest of the acting ranges from mediocre to awful. Most members of the cast never seem to present themselves as anything other than unidimensional Hollywooden characters. Here is a nasty Nazi. Here is an obsequious French policeman. Here is a prima-donnaish refugee *artiste*. Here is a fixer in the large mold of a Sydney Greenstreet godfather. (After being introduced to each of these tintypic characters I wanted to scream, "I get it. I get it.")

The only saving grace is that, with curiosity piqued as mine was by a story told to be by my father long ago, viewers of *Varian's War* may want to learn the true story, which, as I learned from the writings of Aaron Levenstein, Mary Jayne Gold, Andy Marino, and Fry; from the researches of the documentary filmmaker Pierre Sauvage; and from conversations with Harold Oram, two of Harry Bingham's sons, "Gussie" Rosenberg, and others who were there, the real story is far more interesting, exciting, and colorful than anything Hollywood could invent.

[thirty-two]

Passion and Politics

HOWARD FAST. NORMAN Corwin. Henry Wallace. Paul Robeson. A man called Newman. What these men have in common is that they were very much a part of Nathan Zuckerman's youth. Mine, too.

Zuckerman is, of course, Philip Roth's fictional character who, in many ways, is, well, Philip Roth. All three of us were born in 1933. We started life in the Depression, listened to Uncle Don read the funny papers, got our jokes from Jack Benny and our news from Lowell Thomas, thrilled to the songs of the Red Army and the Lincoln Brigade sung in deep bass by Paul Robeson, envied those old enough to fight the Germans and the Japanese in World War II, and came of age in the time of bobby-soxers, beats, and red-baiting.

Our ardent patriotism was to be tempered by what we were learning from our parents and their friends, many of them recently returned veterans, about anti-Semitism and other inequities, even within the army we so much wanted to be a part of. Norman Corwin's stirring broadcast "On a Note of Triumph," which had first swelled our hearts, soon proved a bit too sweet, too pure. He didn't speak of the GIs who railed against the presence of "niggers" and "kikes" in their ranks.

Our generation had missed the real struggles between the Stalinists and Trotskyists, and few of us ever called ourselves socialists, but we were politically engaged. Liberal pluralists, we wanted the country to live up to its ideals. We wanted to right historic wrongs. Some of us joined the NAACP; some supported World Federalism. We were FDR's children, but we leafleted for Henry Wallace in his ill-fated campaign for president against Truman, Dewey, and the Dixiecrats. We read Laura Hobson's

Gentleman's Agreement and the even more disturbing novel *Focus* by Arthur Miller, about a German American cipher named Newman who hated the fact that, owing to both his name and his physical appearance, he was constantly being mistaken for a Jew. We read many other books, too, including those by authors soon to be listed as "subversives." Among them was Howard Fast, who made Tom Paine, a real revolutionary, one of our icons. Sometimes we learned about such books from social studies and English teachers, individuals like Nathan Zuckerman's favorite, Mr. Ringold.

Roth describes Murray Ringold as having "masculine authority uncorrected by piety." He was the sort of man who might have done any number of things but chose his profession of teaching English because of his passion for what it represented and what he could do. "All he [Ringold] wanted all day long was to deal with young people he could influence, and his biggest kick in life he got from their response."

Murray Ringold, a Shakespeare specialist, was also an activist and a pragmatist. He was less concerned with abstract notions of world revolution than with organizing exploited teachers. Yet, with many others, the beloved teacher became a target and a victim, fired by the local school board for his alleged un-American activities. Murray Ringold was later exonerated and reinstated, but never recouped the losses he suffered while spending years in the wilderness selling vacuum cleaners. Through it all, he remained amazingly steadfast, an advocate for his craft, a believer in his mission and the political system, and still a major force in the lives of many former students like Nathan Zuckerman.

Fifty years after his graduation from high school, Zuckerman—who had moved far from Newark and become a successful writer and a celebrity—had a serendipitous meeting with his old teacher, now a very elderly elder-hosteler at a college nearby to which, as Roth explains in a lengthy aside, Zuckerman has retreated. ("My seclusion," Zuckerman says, "is not the story here. It is not a story in any way. I came here because I don't want a story any longer. I've had my story.")

Whatever the message those brief parenthetic remarks are supposed to convey (and I think they say a good deal), the reunion was an occasion of great joy, a chance to reminisce and for Murray to tell Zuckerman about his own life and that of his brother, Ira, a man Nathan once idolized as an exemplar of courage and romance.

Ira Ringold, younger, bigger, stronger, tougher, far more radical, and far more restless than his brother, was always a maverick. He left home early and was schooled through experience. He mined zinc in the hills of New Jersey, rode the rails, worked in the stockyards and on the docks, served in World War II. At home and overseas he witnessed and fought against the exploitation of immigrant workers and black soldiers.

Soon after the war, Ira, already enraged by the what he viewed as the injustices of capitalism and racism, became a protégé of his Leninist army buddy Johnny O'Day, a member of the Communist Party and a stage personifier of Abraham Lincoln. Ira's orotund rendition of "With malice toward none, with charity for all" and other famed phrases of the Great Emancipator lead him into a new career as "Iron Rinn," a radio actor on the network program "The Free and the Brave." Each week audiences across the country would listen as the "Iron Man" became Nathan Hale, Wild Bill Hickok, Jack London, and many other celebrated figures of speech. His success was to lead him into the bourgeois world that he decried.

In the six evenings they spent together, Murray Ringold told Zuckerman something of his own experiences in the intervening years and much more about the life of the rough-hewn, mixed-up utopian Ira, including the details of his wretched second marriage to a faux-genteel, gentile-wannabe princess, Eve Frame (née Chava Fromkin).

Frame, Murray related, was an actress of some note when she swept Ira off his feet. It was a rocky relationship from the start, much of its difficulty having to do with Eve's attempts to civilize her husband, to make him respectable. It ended in disaster; Eve sought revenge against Ira by exposing him, not just as a card-carrying Communist but as a secret agent of the Kremlin. His fate was sealed in a book written by Eve and her right-wing WASPish collaborator Bryden Grant, a *Journal-American* reporter, later to become a smooth-talking U.S. congressman. Their "J'accuse" was a pastiche of half-truths and vengeful inventions titled *I Married a Communist,* published in the watershed year 1952.

The breakup of the oddly matched couple and subsequent series of breakdowns are not surprises. Early on we learn that, during their courtship, Ira had given Eve a copy of Arthur Miller's *Focus.* In a tip-off to what is to come, Roth explains that "Murray compares Eve to Newman, the face that betrays." But we are to learn also that the Iron Man himself was not the paragon of rectitude, virtue, and innocence the young Zuckerman had found so appealing. He wasn't even the committed Communist the spiteful Eve sought to destroy. According to his aged brother, Ira was like so many others floundering around for a place in a rapidly changing society. "The truth is that Ira's passion was to be someone he didn't know how to be. He never discovered his life. . . . He looked for it everywhere. . . . He couldn't find it anywhere. Eve didn't marry a Communist; she married a man perpetually hungering after his life. That's what enraged him and confused him and that's what ruined him: he could never construct one that fit."

There are many threads here; many layers; many ways to interpret the story and its principal characters. Ira isn't Everyman, but he is a familiar type. So, it turns out, is Eve—at least, it is said, to her creator, Philip Roth.

Not a few reviewers have made the observation that Roth's representation of Eve is a not-too-carefully masked vendetta against his own ex-wife, the British actress Claire Bloom, a literary payback for what she had written about him in her much-discussed 1996 memoir, *Leaving a Doll's House.*

To be sure, there are a number of interesting parallels between Bloom and Frame: their Jewish origins, their love affairs, their several marriages to movie stars and flamboyant businessmen (Zuckerman calls Eve's second husband as a "rapacious capitalist," Bloom describes her own in similar terms), their acting careers. Even more pointed is the fictional presentation of a tortured triadic relationship between Ira, Eve, and Sylphid, her daughter from a previous marriage to the actor Carlton Pennington. With an ironic twist, the fictional dynamic in many ways mirrors what Bloom reports about Roth's strong rejection of Anne, her daughter from an earlier marriage—to Rod Steiger.

Readers of both books will note that there is surely more than a kernel of truth in the comparisons that have been made. It would not be the first time that Roth has modeled his characters on real people and used the pen to skewer his nemeses. Yet what is really more important, I think, is that the story he tells in *I Married a Communist* is a good, evocative one, not just about the people who, whatever the real roots of their personae, are so skillfully drawn, but about the formative years of a generation—Zuckerman's, Roth's, and mine.

[thirty-three]

Travels with John Updike and Henry Bech

JOHN UPDIKE AND I have met on two occasions, most recently when we shared a drink in Northampton, Massachusetts, at the premier of my Smith College colleague Ronald Perera's opera based on Updike's wickedly funny novel *S.* The other time was nearly thirty years ago. It was in Israel. We were both there on lecture tours arranged by the United States Information Agency, and one day we shared a podium.

I was there to discuss my research on American-style racial and ethnic pluralism in the aftermath of the Black Power Revolt; Updike was in Israel to talk about his own take on American society, a world populated mainly by middle-class WASPs. Our points of view were as different as our subjects, although, it turned out, we had more in common than one might have thought from what we were saying there.

Updike was well known in the country, despite the fact that much of his fiction was viewed by Israeli readers—as by many of their American cousins—as something quite removed from their everyday lives. For many Jews who read it and commented upon it, there was a rather common agreement that it was a kind of "ethnography of the other"—interesting, but in a voyeuristic sort of way. There was one exception, a controversial new book about a wiry-haired little man named Henry Bech, a Jewish writer seemingly related to Norman Mailer, Saul Bellow, Bernard Malamud, and Philip Roth. A playful spoof and wry send-up, *Bech: A Book* (1970) even begins with a Rothlike ploy where the fictional character writes a letter to his creator. Signed

"Henry Bech," it begins "Dear John, Well, if you must commit the artistic indecency of writing about a writer, better, I suppose, about me than about you."

From the start Bech is not only a composite of Mailer, Bellow, Malamud, and Roth, he is also Updike's Nathan Zuckerman. He is a writer with problems—problems with writing, problems with women, problems with celebrity and success, problems with failure.

Updike's stories about Henry Bech are not just works of parody and tomfoolery; they are filled with insight and empathy for certain sensibilities, and they are, to me, generally on the mark. Coming from the author of *The Poorhouse Fair, Couples, Marry Me, A Month of Sundays, Rabbit Run, Rabbit Redux, Rabbit Is Rich, Rabbit at Rest,* and a number of other books peopled by those who eat white bread and drink lots of bourbon and scotch, this may seem a surprising achievement.

For many "ethnics," Jewish and otherwise, Rabbit Angstrom's sort of WASPish *angst,* and that of most of Updike's characters, *is* often hard to appreciate, harder to feel. But Henry Bech is, as he might say, something-different altogether. Creating him was, I imagine, quite easy; making him believable for those most at home with the Jewish American belletristic genre was much more difficult.

It is not easy to be a credible outsider-within. Jewish writers are well aware of the pitfalls. Many admit that because "WASP cool" is not their thing, it is difficult to "do" WASPs, except in exaggerated caricature. Updike, by contrast, seems to have been able to cross over. This opinion is not mine alone. With some notable exceptions, it is—was—a view shared by many Jewish critics and by even more Jewish readers, including some of the members of that curious and well-read group of listeners at the auditorium in the American embassy in Tel Aviv.

Updike and I were up on the stage. Our audience was made up, mostly, of academics, writers, and politicians.

After our respective presentations, I was asked some sharply worded questions about what what my speech would mean to the historic relationships between blacks and Jews. I answered each directly and quickly. The majority of those in the audience were clearly restless. It was obvious that what most really wanted to ask—and say—had to do with Updike's novels, not the reflections of an itinerant sociologist.

Updike was peppered with questions, some—in good Israeli style—very direct: How had he, who was known mainly as the quintessential chronicler of white Anglo-Saxon Protestant Americans, decided to write about this Jewish guy, Henry Bech?

I don't remember Updike's responses exactly but do recall that he was a bit evasive, seeming to want to hear what they had to say rather than to say much himself. The author was at once respectful, thoughtful, and watchful—something like a fox, a literary fox. He was processing what he was hearing, filing it away. He didn't lick his chops but smiled rather benignly.

After the session ended, we had lunch with some of the more important members of the audience. Sitting next to me, the writer, who was on his first trip to Israel, told me about the itinerary that had been carefully planned for him and his wife. It was one that highlighted Christian sites. I was doing some processing of my own and thought to myself that our session, that luncheon, and his tour around the country were bound to appear in some new stories sometime soon.

My prescience was realized several years later in "The Holy Land," a story that was to appear first in *Playboy* magazine, then in *Bech Is Back* (1982).

In one lengthy scene in that hilarious yet poignant twice-told tale, Bech, having been picked up at the official city guesthouse, Mishkenot, by the Jesuit archaeologist Pere Gibergue, is shepherded from one sacred spot to another. "I should never have married a Christian," he laments as the party fights its way up the Via Dolorosa through a throng of pilgrims.

Bech's wife, by contrast, is enthralled by everything—The Way of the Cross, along which they walk, and all the places to which they are taken. She isn't parochial either. She is fascinated by the Jews, by Zionism. She loves Israel; she loves Israelis. Bech is far less comfortable. To her Israel is a dreamland, evoking the past, challenging the future; to him it is "a ghetto with farms." With an obvious nod to American Jews who have written sarcastically about their chauvinistic, smug, self-satisfied *landsleit* Bech says to his wife, "I know these people. I've spent my whole life trying to get away from them, trying to think bigger."

Yet, as much as he is put off by his fellow Jews and their own very special places, such as the Wailing Wall, Bech has an even more uncomfortable feeling about the Christian shrines. About to enter the Church of the Holy Sepulchre, Bech resists.

"Let's go," he says to Bea.

"Oh, Henry, why?"

"This frightens me."

The narrator, Updike, then explains: "It had that alchemic stink of medieval basements where vapors condensed as demons and pogroms and autos-da-fé. Torquemada, Hitler, the tsars—every despot major and minor who had tried to stunt and crush his race had inhaled these Christian vapors."

That brief chapter is the only one that deals with Israel and its people. But there is plenty more about going places, most of it far more humorous, if no less biting.

We learn early on that what has made Henry Bech the in-demand cultural icon he has become is a best-selling first book, *Travel Light,* a motorcycle odyssey set in the Midwest. The book, it turns out, was pure fantasy. Until he gained wide fame and a modest fortune from *Travel Light*'s stirring insights into American culture, Bech had never been west of the Hudson—or anywhere else. Then, suddenly, he became a guest of talk shows around the country, a featured speaker at small colleges with cooing co-eds, and a world traveler. Most of his foreign sojourning was arranged (like John Updike's—and like mine) by USIA; like me, he was almost invariably "handled" by a partnership of odd bedfellows: embassy personnel and local officials.

Bech's first major overseas adventure was to several Eastern bloc countries. The representatives of the Communist bureaucracies and the fawning of party members he encountered are closer in feel and figure to the personae who populate the English writer Malcolm Bradbury's *Rates of Exchange* and *Why Come to Slaka?* than to those of Mailer, Bellow, or Malamud, even of Roth. (While Bradbury's writers and lecturers, like their inventor, do their overseas gigs for the British Council, the English agency most like our USIA, their hosts are cut from the same cloth as Bech's.)

It is 1964. Bech flies to Moscow at State Department expense for a month of "cultural exchange." Updike tells us that, while there are problems, "Russia seems Jewish to him, and, of course, he seems Jewish to Russia." It is a good beginning.

Bech goes from Russia to Rumania, "a Latin land in a Slavic sea . . . where, during World War II, its anti-Semitism had been the most ferocious in Europe." Here, more than elsewhere, Updike notes Bech's sensitivity to his ascribed identity.

Hearing someone referred to as a "Jewess," Bech is knee-jerk defensive. "In my country . . . 'Jewess' is a kind of fighting word." Yet, Updike, knowing the likes of his character, repeatedly refers to Bech's ambivalent feelings about who he is. He has him write an unsuccessful novel, *Brother Pig*, and has it negatively reviewed by one Deborah Frueh, who "maligned it as 'a flight of Jewish self-hatred lived far from New York, in the haven of Seattle, amid New Age mantras and medicinal powders, between Boeing and Mount Rainier.'"(Seattle, I should note, is not too far from where the colorful guru of Updike's *S*, who turns out to be a nice Jewish boy from the Boston area, holed up in his New Age ashram.) Updike's Bech is also the author of a Jewish antidote to the deracinated *Brother Pig*, called *The Chosen*. (No relation to Potok's work of the same name.) It didn't sell either.

While sometimes way off target—as when he writes of the "cabalism among the peasant Jews of stagnant Slavic Europe" (Jews were often very poor but they were never peasants)—most of the time the author shows sensitivity to Bech's roots and to the meaning of Jewish tribalism, that special feeling of interdependence that even self-hating Jews have toward other Jews. "It may be loathing but it is not fear, nor the need to be guarded."

Again and again, Updike seems to ask, rhetorically, Who is this creature I have created? At one point he muses, "[He is a] Jew, a modern man, a writer, a bachelor, a loner, a loser."

There are a number of points in the recounting of Bech's

adventures in Soviet-era netherworld where I feel Updike is speaking directly to—or perhaps for—me, for his travel-based anecdotes often evoke a giddy sense of déjà vu.

Referring to his passing from one East European country and city to another, Updike says of Bech that his passport is "so stapled with visas it flutters when pulled out." I have several such expired passports in my desk drawer.

While my "official" travel in that region of the world, in that period, was limited to several trips to Poland, Bech's experiences in Moscow and Kiev, Yerevan and Alma Alta, Bucharest and Prague brought back my own encounters in venues arranged and facilitated by university officials and American cultural attachés in Europe, the Middle East, Africa, and Asia over the past three decades. On tours to speak in the mainland Chinese cities of Shanghai, Beijing, Xian, Nanjing, and Ghanzhou not too long after the "opening" to the PRC, the rhetoric, the humor, and the pathos I witnessed often matched that heard and seen by Henry Bech on his first big trip in Communist lands. Despite marked differences in skin tone and appearance, my audiences in China were similar to Bech's and so were many of the responses. Even in non-Communist parts of the Chinese world—in Taipei and Kaohsiung, Hong Kong, Singapore—I found a sameness of reaction (the propaganda was, of course, all about the scourge of communism rather than its glory) and a oneness with Bech.

Interspersed with his politically charged travelogues, Updike tells many other stories about Bech's life, marked by mimicry. For example, in "Bech Takes Pot Luck," the character is again more Mailer-Bellow-Malamud-Rothish, especially in the fact that he summers on an unnamed island that we might call "Martha's Vineyard," where, in fact, Saul Bellow has a home. The island of Updike's fiction is a place of old Yankees, some original settlers, and many summer people, not a few of whom, like many who spent July and August in Chilmark, Menemsha, and West Tisbury, or in the Cape Cod towns of Wellfleet, Truro, and Provincetown (Mailer's summer home), are liberal/left Jewish intellectuals, artists, writers, and, as Updike puts it, "old *New Masses* editors possessively squatting on seaside acreage bought for a song in the Depression." (He is wrong here. Most Vineyard and Lower Cape Jews got their places much, much later.)

Bech's love life is important, too. In "Bech Panics," and in many other chapters, we learn about his affairs with a number of women. In descriptions and asides there are painful but accurate reproductions of the snide kind of deprecating put-downs of certain types of women familiar to readers of some of America's best-known Jewish writers. Not that all the Jewish females are unappealing Marjorie Morningstars. There are attractive sycophants, editors, students, and housewives. There are Gentile ones, too. Among the latter are two sisters, sleek Norma and pudgy Bea. Bea, a divorcée with children, a dog, and a house in Ossining, eventually becomes the wife Bech will take with him to her "Holy Land." It is she who both domesticates and frees him. She builds a study for him in her (now their) mock-Tudor home where, finally, he completes his long-delayed book, *Think Big*, which, like *Travel Light*, becomes a best seller and for which, we learn in the last chapter of a third volume, *Bech at Bay* (1998), the writer wins the Nobel Prize for Literature.

Before I comment on the most recent book (and what I was convinced was the swan song of Updike's Zuckerman until I scanned *The New Yorker* of January 25, 1999, and found a new story, "His Oeuvre"), a few brief words about the middle volume, *Bech Is Back*. I read it again recently, and, as on my first reading, I was especially taken with accounts of Bech's travels. His public experiences in Bea's ancestral Scotland (which, in its bleak moroseness, Bech finds more appealing than "his" Israel) and in Venezuela, Korea, Ghana, Nigeria, Kenya, Tanzania, Canada, and Australia again seem to parallel my own, many of them in those very countries. Reading the anecdotes, I recalled having lectured in many of the same universities and cultural centers—and perhaps to the same audiences—as Updike/Bech. There is an uncanny familiarity to much of it, not least in the inevitable query often posed to me—and to Bech—when I had been in a new country for only a few hours: "I know the question is foolish, you have been here only a day, but what are your impressions so far?"

Updike follows discussion of this classic interrogative with a pointed jab by a memeber of a host society: "A day or a week . . . Henry Bech will go back and write a best-selling book about us. Everybody does." (N.B. He's wrong. I never wrote such a book, but, in point of fact, I'm thinking about it!)

At the end of *Bech Is Back*, having finally broken through his writer's block and gained new fame, our hero is ready for a new life. He leaves Bea and moves back to New York.

Sometime later he starts traveling again. A trip to Prague is described in an Updike novella, *Bech in Czech* (1986), which reappears in the United Kingdom in a Penguin Edition, *The Complete Henry Bech* (1992). Eight years later the story would become the first chapter in the last volume, *Bech at Bay* (1998), of the clearly incomplete saga. Here again, Bech—this time taken to the old cemetery in Prague's Jewish quarter and then to Kafka's grave in another one—wrestles with his Jewishness and with others' perceptions of it. And he reflects on his own country, its sins and its virtues. "America has its rough spots," he muses. "If the muggers don't get your wallet, the nursing home will—but it's still a country that never had a pogrom."

The rest of *Bech at Bay*, subtitled by Updike "A Quasi-Novel," is, like the first two books, a pastiche of loosely linked short stories. Three of the best are in the middle: "Bech Presides," "Bech Pleads Guilty," and "Bech Noir."

In the first of the stand-alone pieces, Bech has reached that advanced stage of authorship when his writing consists mostly, it seems, of contributions to festschrifts. The writer becomes the president of an honorary group of literati called The Forty and described as "a wistful imitation of the French Academy." The second is about the experience of being sued for libel in L.A. "Bech Noir" is a fanciful tale of intrigue with a new sidekick, Rachel Teagarten, "twenty-six, post-Jewish, frizzy big hair, figure on the short and solid side," known, like Batman's partner, as Robin.

Bech's escapades with his Robin is the most inventive of the lot. It is about literary criticism and sweet revenge, a piece that will appeal to all writers—Jewish and otherwise—who have ever received negative reviews. Ordinary readers may like it, too.

The account of mayhem and murder begins with the death under the wheels of the Sixth Avenue subway train of an English critic who, in the *New York Review of Books*, had called *Think Big* "prolix and *voulu*." (Bech had to look up *voulu;* I did, too. It means "willful.") Updike goes on to describe a plot to poison the old Seattle critic, Deborah Frueh, the one who, long ago, had accused Bech of being a self-hating Jew in her review of *Brother Pig*. More recently, she had dismissed *Think Big* as "inconsequential," an even greater insult.

The offended writer's weapon of choice is cyanide. To get it to Frueh and get her to take it, he writes a letter in a childish scrawl asking for her autograph, her signature to be returned in an enclosed envelope whose flap he has covered with the bitter venom. The letter is signed "Your real fan, Mary Jane Mason." It is the first of many such requests, for Bech keeps searching the obituaries but sees nothing of the demise of his nemesis. Finally, there it is—"eight inches of *Times* type: the death of Deborah Frueh." He is elated. But his joy is short-lived. It is time to move on. He next sets out to get Aldie Cannon, editor of the web paper *Cannon Fodder*, another critic who hadn't liked his novels. Bech drives him to suicide. And that ain't all . . .

Henry Bech, who once—at the end of *Bech: A Book*—prematurely "entered heaven" by gaining admission to the American Academy of Arts and Letters, wins the big one: The Nobel Prize for Literature. In the final chapter, we learn that, like other winners, he is the butt of envy and much caviling by his less-successful (at least in garnering prizes), often more serious peers. In a mock *New York Times* op-ed piece, one disgruntled writer fumes, "If the time for an American winner had at last come round again, then a deliberate affront must be read in this bypassing of solid contenders like Mailer, Roth, and Ozick, not to mention Pynchon and DeLillo, in favor of this passé exponent of fancy penmanship, whose skimpy oeuvre fails even to achieve J. D. Salinger's majorest total abstention from publication."

The writer is, of course, John Updike.

He never got the prize either.

[thirty-four]

Milton Scholar

HOW MANY JEWISH men do you know named Seymour, Sanford, Stanford, Howard, Harold, Henry, Irving, Morris, Mortimer, Morton, Martin, or Milton? I know hundreds, maybe thousands. The vast majority are between the ages of 50 and 80, many of them second-generation Americans also possessed of "typical" last names: Cohen and Levy and Goldstein and Shapiro. Indeed, for years I thought that Howard and Harold, and especially Irving and Milton, were as Jewish as Cohen and Levy. Then, one day, lightning struck. These are not Jewish at all, they are English, English surnames, as in John Howard, John Irving, and John Milton.

I felt as if I'd discovered something significant about the semiotics of acculturation and decided to share my epiphany in proper academic form. I started writing a learned paper about it.

While it was still in the draft stages, I had to leave it to attend a meeting of the Eastern Sociological Society. There I chanced upon Stan Lyman, an old friend, fellow iconoclast, and author of a number of intriguing articles and books, including two favorites, *The Seven Deadly Sins*, on the sociology of evil, and *A Sociology of the Absurd.* Like me, he is a skeptic about certain scientific pretensions of the discipline we share. And, again like me, he has never abandoned his curiosity about the fads and foibles of human life and on group and intergroup relations, especially in this country.

I thought he would especially appreciate what I had "discovered," not only because he, too, was intrigued by language and labels and liked to play with words and titles, but because he, the son of Russian-Jewish immigrants, had one of those names. Stanford.

Lyman's reaction to my thesis was underwhelming, to say the least. In fact, he said, "That's ridiculous. You are so wrong!"

On the defensive, I said, "But Stan, you are a perfect example of what I'm talking about. I mean, Stanford Lyman, come on, man. What kind of a Jewish name is that?"

"Look," he said, "my name is Stanford and my three brothers . . ."

Before he could say more, I interrupted and finished his sentence: "are Melvin, Marvin, and Myron, or Arnold, Merwin, and Sheldon, or Byron, Bruce, and . . ." This time he cut me off.

"Wrong. Wrong. Wrong. You're not even on the right track."

Frustrated and exasperated, I said, "O.K., wise guy. They're Harvard, Princeton, and Yale."

"You got it."

First I thought he was kidding. Then I saw that he was serious. His immigrant parents had decided that nothing could be more American than naming their boys for nearby Stanford (they lived in San Francisco) and a few other, more distant, institutions. This was an even better form of "naches fun die kinder" (that pointed Yiddish expression for the pleasure one gets from the accomplishments of one's offspring) than giving them faux British first names.

I later learned that, like my friend Stanford, a distinguished Berkeley-trained chaired professor of sociology at Florida Atlantic University, the other Lyman boys "grew" into names which, I learned, were indeed for real. One of them, Princeton, became a career foreign-service officer, holding a variety of important diplomatic posts, including several ambassadorships. He was, for a time, coordinator for refugee affairs in the Department of State, where I had the opportunity to work with him on several occasions.

Yet, I must say that, despite my comeuppance by the Lymans (whose brothers, had there been more boys, might have been called Emory, Reed, Rice, and Whitman) and the fact that I have actually run into a passel of Cornells (Cornell Levine, Cornell

Rosenberg, Cornell Weinstein) and Dukes (Duke Shapiro and Duke Lapidus) and at least one other Yale (Goldstein), I remain convinced that these are exceptions and that I am right about the vast majority of Jewish Stanfords and Sanfords, Mortimers and Miltons. In fact, other—even more astute—observers of the American scene have corroborated my great find.

Not long after my deflating encounter with Stanford Lyman I came across an essay in an old copy of *Commentary*. There it was: my whole thesis in one sentence. "In America, it makes a great deal of difference if your first or last name is Milton." The writer was Milton Himmelfarb.

Much more recently, in his novel *American Pastoral*, Philip Roth carried my, and Himmelfarb's, revelation regarding this appellative expression of symbolic assimilation one step further. Describing one of his key characters, Seymour "Swede" Levov, Roth writes, "Actually [he was] only another of our neighborhood Seymours whose forebears had been Solomons and Sauls and who would themselves beget Stephens who would in turn beget Shawns . . ."

I never did finish my paper.

[thirty-five]

What's in a Name?

I OFTEN THINK of my late friend and Smith College colleague, professor of English Ronald Macdonald, who, whenever asked how he felt about having a famous name, replied, "How would you feel if your parents gave you a fine Scots name and you ended up a hamburger clown?"

My name is neither fine nor Scottish, but it is also famous, at least it was for a time, when another fellow (also known as "Charlie Hustle") made Pete Rose one of the best-known monikers in the USA.

Contrary to others' expectations, I never got very excited hearing or reading about Pete Rose when he was up, nor did I cringe when he was down. I never thought much about it, more likely than not because I was never really Pete Rose at all but Peter Rose (except to my sister-in-law and to used car salesmen and telemarketers, who always call me Pete). But others thought about it, not least among them my students, who first papered my door with headlines touting my namesake's sensational statistics as a batter and a base-runner and an all-round player and then, after his fall from grace, decorated the same door with clippings that said PETE ROSE SUSPENDED and PETE ROSE GOT WHAT HE DESERVED and PETE ROSE BRINGS SHAME UPON HIS GAME.

One other group, whose members, unlike my witty students, didn't know the difference, used to send me letters asking for my autographed picture.

Dear Pete,

My name is Johnny Jones. I live in Greeley,

Colorado, and go to school. I am in the fifth grade. You are my favorite guy. I would like you to send me a photograph with your name.

Your friend,
John Jones

Dear Pete Rose,

I think you are terific. I amire you and hope to ba basball player to. Please send me your picature.

Bill Shantz

Dear Pete,

Hi. I like the way you play baseball. I collect cards and I have many of you. I would like to have a card with your autograph. Please send it to me.

Sincerely,
Sam Georgio

There were many more just like these, *all mailed to me.* It took me a long time to figure out the reason for this—and the misunderstanding. It seems that, while I was listed along with thousands of others in *Who's Who in America*, the "real" Pete Rose was not. But the children, writing formal letters for school projects—encouraged by clever teachers who urged them to "write to someone famous"—were told they could find the addresses in that roster of (dubious) fame. And so, without reading beyond the first line, they would address their requests to "Pete I. Rose, 66 Paradise Road, Northampton, MA 01060," or to my office.

Just before the revelation of illegal gambling, including betting on baseball games themselves, Pete Rose got his 4,256th base hit. The sports press went wild; the fans ate it up. Among them was a woman in Las Vegas who was taking a college course called "Success, American Style." She, too, wrote to me. But after opening with a long single-sentence paragraph explaining that she was now a student at UNLV but used to live in Dayton where her husband was in the air force and where they were Cincinnati fans and especially fans of mine [read Pete Rose] and how they had been there the day I had broken the record and wanted to write about it, she asked me to send her four to six pages about how I became a baseball player and . . .

I did not respond, but I kept the letter, as I have kept many of the others.

I should tell you that, in the early days, I did respond to every request. Because I was traveling abroad a great deal in the 1970s and 1980s, I kept a stack of small passport photos in my desk drawer. I discovered they came in handy for other purposes, too. So, when Johnny Jones or Billy Shantz or another member of the would-be knothole gang would write to me and ask for an autographed picture, I would sign one of the little snapshots and send it to the requester with the following text.

> Dear Johnny,
>
> I was delighted to receive your letter and your request.
>
> It isn't often people ask me for my autograph or my picture. But you have asked for both. They are enclosed.
>
> I'm sure you will be surprised to see that I don't look the way you thought Pete Rose would look. That is because I am somebody else.
>
> If you want to write to the baseball player, he can be reached by contacting the manager of the Cincinnati Reds, who will see that he gets your letter.
>
> I'm sure Pete Rose will be pleased to hear from you. I know I was.
>
> Your friend,
>
> The Other Pete Rose

part five

Coda

[coda]

With Few Reservations

IT WAS A blustery December day, the end of the first year of the third millennium. I was sitting in the living room of the home in which Hedy and I have lived for more than thirty-five years. It is a house owned by Smith College, a perk of sorts. We were discussing the fact that on my retirement we must move. It was something we had always known we would have to do but had put off thinking about. Now the time was drawing nigh.

Should we go to Connecticut to be near our daughter? To California to be with our son and his family? Should we move—lock, stock, and barrel—to our island retreat on Cape Cod? Should we move to a condo in Boston or stay in Northampton?

Over the next few months, our ruminations about where to go started us reminiscing once again about where we had been—and about who we are. We talked about many of the things discussed in the previous essays, which Hedy had read in draft form, sometimes again and again, offering her comments and criticisms about subjects she knows almost as much about as I. (At this writing we have been together fifty years, having met when she was seventeen and I was nineteen.)

As if making two imaginary lists, we started talking about bad times and good ones. We kept coming up with snapshots of memories. They poured out like a stream of consciousness. Sometimes the memories seemed spontaneous; sometimes they were triggered by a conversation or something seen on television or read in the newspaper.

I told Hedy about an article about a family of recently arrived Bosnian refugees and their mixed emotions: the excitement tempered by apprehension, the joy of making it and the pangs over what they have left behind. It reminded her of her own voyage to this country in 1947 in the hold of a Greek ship filled with French war orphans—and two from the Netherlands: she, eleven, and her sister Betsy, nineteen.

The girls had been taken from Amsterdam to Marseilles by a Dutch representative of "The Joint," the American Jewish Joint Distribution Committee, named Roosevelt. Hedy commented that she always thought the escort had to be a relative of the president. "Maybe it was an omen," she mused. Then, growing serious, she recounted the hardship of the trip, her crouplike illness, which led to a medieval "cupping" by the ship's doctor to rid her of infection, the spoiled food, and the anxiety for one who was very loyal to her Queen and to the House of Orange about leaving the Netherlands to live in a new land.

Although I had heard the story hundreds of times, I urged her to continue. She did, relating, once again, her first impressions of America. She mentioned the extraordinary sight of the Statue of Liberty, the busy New York harbor, the handkerchiefs handed out to children at Ellis Island ("I will never forget it—total strangers giving us gifts"), the neon Mobil horse down at the Battery, and bananas.

She said she hadn't seen bananas since before the war, and that one of the first things she did after her aunt Anna Schwarz (the woman who would become her new mother) picked them up was to ask her to buy some bananas. "She did. A whole bunch. And I ate them all and then got sick from stuffing myself," she said, smiling broadly. Then her expression changed as she retold the story of how her Uncle Alfred (who became her new father) had tried to persuade his sister, Rosa, Hedy and Betsy's mother, and her Dutch husband, Jacques Cohen, to leave Holland as he had fled from Vienna, and why they had refused. ("Those crazy things happen in Austria," her mother had said, "but not here. Not in the Netherlands.")

Her grandparents, her father, and his four brothers and their entire families were deported "to the East" and perished in the Holocaust. Her mother died while they were in hiding.

Watching Hedy's face as she recounted the story, I was

reminded of an incident thirty years earlier when I was a visiting professor at Flinders University in South Australia.

We were on a beach near our temporary home in Adelaide, sitting with the Norwegian scholar and poet Sigmund Skard and talking about the war that had occurred twelve thousand miles and, seemingly, as many light-years away. Our children, Lies and Dan, ages ten and eight, were playing in the sand.

Sigmund, the son-in-law of the Norwegian foreign minister who fled to England with the king when the Nazis occupied their country, told us of his own harrowing escape. He, his wife Åse, and two sets of twins went to Sweden, crossed the USSR on the Trans-Siberian railroad to Vladivostok, and then went by boat to Yokohama, where they managed to get aboard the last ship to sail to America. Hedy briefly told him something about her own experience, quite literally living the life of Anne Frank hidden in an Amsterdam cellar. He listened carefully, only occasionally asking a question, while watching the two happy, spirited children make sand castles and run into the water.

A year later we received a warmly inscribed book of poetry written by our friend Sigmund. Thumbing through it and trying to translate Norwegian into English via German cognates, Hedy ran across a very special poem. The English translation of the title is "Jewish Children in Adelaide." In it Sigmund contrasted the carefree behavior of Lies and Dan as they romped in the surf with what their mother had related to him.

Remembering the beach on the Southern Ocean made me think how many of our own good times have been spent on the edge of some body of water. In our early days together, days off meant canoeing on an Adirondack lake; later it would be sailing and kayaking and rafting in Maine and Massachusetts, in the Caribbean and out West.

There was that day on the roiling Colorado River. It was almost the end of a ten-day rafting trip through the Grand Canyon. Fourteen-year-old Dan was sitting as far forward as was allowed by the boatmen. Like the rest of us, he was wearing bathing trunks, a life jacket, and sneakers to fend off the rocks should we be dumped. He was hanging on to the lines, bracing himself—as we all were—to run "the awesome Lava Falls rapids," a "class V," according to aficionados' measures. He was clearly in seventh heaven.

I mention my reverie to Hedy, and she says that she thinks that trip was the second biggest thrill of Dan's life before leaving home. The biggest was the day he got into Harvard (I can still hear the whoop of excitement when he opened the letter).

Dan graduated in from Harvard in 1984. Lies, who went to Oberlin and then to Smith, got her B.A. the year before.

I swell with pride remembering how lucky I was to have participated in both of their graduations. Lies's was particularly meaningful because my mother and mother-in-law, with whom she had very special relationships, were both able to attend. (It so happened that Sigmund Skard and his psychologist wife, Åse, who was receiving an honorary degree, were there, too.)

While the occasion was personally very special, for me to be in the Smith ceremony was hardly unusual. I did it every year. Being a part of the one at Harvard was an unanticipated fringe benefit of my status there that year.

Even though I was a visiting professor the year Dan was a senior, I had assumed I would be sitting next to Hedy in the audience on graduation day, along with all the other family members. But, a week or so before the big event, my old friend David Riesman walked into my office in the sociology department and asked me if I was going to march in the academic procession.

"No," I remember saying. "I'm not on the faculty."

"Nonsense," said David, "you are this year, and you should march."

And I did. And, just as had happened in Northampton the year before, as I walked between the phalanxes of graduating seniors bedecked, in my mortar board and bright-red Cornell robe (this time flanked by two men I greatly admired, Riesman and Harvey Cox), I was again called from the sidelines. "Hey, dad." This time it was Dan, standing with other seniors from Dunster House. I stepped out of line and hugged him as I had when his sister had called to me in the Smith ceremony the year before. (For the record I note that, while Åse Skard had been made a Norwegian knight before Smith granted her its highest honor, at Harvard royalty truly reigned supreme. When we got to the platform, climbed the steps, and took our seats, we listened to all the speeches and then watched as two kings received honorary degrees from President Derek Bok: Juan Carlos of Spain and Benny Goodman, the King of Swing.)

Thoughts about the *rites de passage* of our kids lead to other reminiscences.

We are in Baltimore where I have my first full-time teaching job, at Goucher College. It is 1960. Hedy calls to me from the kitchen. "It's time."

A nervous young husband doesn't quite know what to say. I pick up the prepacked bag, and we walk to the car for the drive to the Johns Hopkins Hospital. The doctor is there when we arrive. Hedy is taken to the labor room. The contractions are growing stronger, more frequent. The doctor asks me if I'd like to stay with her. I say I would. I sit with Hedy. The doctor checks in periodically. Finally, it is time. "Want to come along?" he asks.

"But," I say, "I thought it wasn't allowed."

"No. It's fine." Then he adds, "You know, I think that if you're there at the laying of the keel, you ought to be there at the launching."

I was there. It was one of the most memorable moments of my life.

I was still thinking about the events at "The Hopkins" forty years before when Lies called the next day. She wanted to know how her mother was doing. Hedy was in the midst of a ten-month treatment protocol for an aggressive form of breast cancer. Lies was anxious, but she knows her mother is a fighter. I know it, too. But I was worried. She needed me, and yet I didn't know how to help. And I needed her. We are partners, soul mates, yin and yang. Since 1953.

I am returning east by car from my first trip to California, trying to make it across the country at breakneck speed in four days. I am trying to get back to camp for the first day of the

"Institute" we always ran for all our staff members. I am on the schedule to discuss the rules of the waterfront—explain the way we teach swimming and canoeing and sailing. (Having grown up in the business, I have already played nearly every role: hike master, cabin counselor, assistant program coordinator. This year I am the waterfront director.)

Dog tired from the long drive, I pull into camp about nine o'clock at night, a day later than I had planned. I enter the Big House through the back door and walk through the kitchen and into the large dining room where all the tables have been stacked up, and some forty counselors, specialists, and other staff members are folk dancing. Before going upstairs to see my mother, who has just had an operation, I scope the scene. One person, a bit younger than most of the others, catches my eye. She is very pretty, with long braids and a ruddy complexion. She is clearly enjoying herself.

I run upstairs and, according to my mother's recollection many years later, ask her two questions: "How are you feeling?" and "Who is that young girl with the red face and pigtails?" She answers both, the latter by saying something about the fact that her name is Hedy and she is Dutch.

I go back downstairs and join the dancing, angling my way over to where the "Dutch girl" is standing. I ask her to dance. She looks puzzled, most likely because she has no idea who I am or where I have come from. But she agrees. We dance, and I ask her another question: "Would you like to go to go out later in the evening? There's this great roadhouse across the lake called the Owlyout . . ."

"I'm sorry," she says, "someone has already asked me."

I ask her about the next night. She is startled but says, "O.K."

We have been together ever since.

After dinner one evening, Hedy and I started discussing another special memory, this one bitter/sweet. It is about how we learned of the birth of our first grandson.

Hedy was in her office at Wesleyan University in Middletown, Connecticut, working late. I was in my office at Smith doing the same thing. My phone rang and I picked it up. It was a friend with terrible news. A colleague's son, a very thoughtful young man I had enjoyed talking to about his experiences in college just two days before, had just committed suicide. I called Hedy to tell her what had happened. The conversation was brief. What was there to say? I hung up and drove over to the home of the shocked and grieving family.

Hours later I returned to our house, emotionally drained and eager to talk to Hedy again. About to reach for the phone, I noticed that the brand-new answering machine was blinking. I thought of ignoring it but didn't. I lifted up the receiver. The message was from Dan, then a graduate student in San Diego.

"Tried to reach you guys but nobody answered. Wanted to tell you that you're grandparents. Your grandson, Jordan, was born a few hours ago. Susan is O.K. Me, too. We'll call again in the morning."

Tragic death. New life. All on one November evening a few days after Thanksgiving, 1989.

Thinking about Jordy's birth reminds us of his father's.

It was May 1962, and, although she was nine months pregnant and about to give birth at any moment, Hedy had urged me to attend a lecture by a man I much admired, Richard Lee, then New Haven's mayor. About ten minutes into his talk, a young colleague came into the auditorium, stood in the middle of the aisle looking around, and then made a beeline for me. When he was standing about ten feet away, he said, in a stage whisper I can still hear, "Peter. You'd better get home. Somebody just got a message from your wife. She needs you. She's having a baby or something."

It wasn't a something.

I rushed home and took her to Cooley Dickinson, the local hospital. Because it was a quiet night, instead of going to the smallish labor room, she was led to a much bigger one near the back stairway. In the midst of her contractions, somebody quietly entered the room. Only half seeing him, I assumed it was her obstetrician. When I turned, I saw no doctor but my friend and department chairman Ely Chinoy. He said he heard that

Hedy was about to give birth and decided that *I* needed some fortification. He handed me an old-fashioned hip flask filled with Scotch, said hello to Hedy, and took his leave. Hedy was clearly surprised and not particularly pleased by this intrusion, but didn't say a word about it until many years later. In fact, Ely's merry prank turned out to be one of our most cherished memories of a man we both came to love and admire and, too soon, to mourn. He died in a car accident on April 15, 1975.

Ever since his death, I have never been able to celebrate my birthday on September fifth without thinking of Ely and calling his wife, Helen, one of our closest friends. Shortly after I came to Smith, I learned that he and I had been born on the same date, though eleven years apart. For the fifteen years we knew each other, we had always joined forces on that special day.

Thinking about Ely, who was in many ways a sort of older brother I never had, I am startled to realize that he has been gone for more than twenty-five years—and I have been at Smith for forty-two.

"Hello, Professor Rose, this is Charles Hunt Page," said the stentorian voice on the other end of the phone. Thinking it was a friend imitating the well-known sociologist, who was editor of the major journal in the field, the *American Sociological Review,* I started to make a smart comeback. Before I did, the voice said "I'd like to talk to you about a job at Smith College." I decided that maybe this was the real Charles Page and listened to him. By the time the conversation had finished, I had agreed to consider leaving Goucher and become a candidate for a position at Smith. The rest, as they say, is history, our history.

It seems like yesterday that we came to Northampton. It seems like yesterday that Hedy and I were married.

It was March 1956. Hedy was in her second year of college at the University of Rochester; I was in my second year of graduate school at Cornell. Once we were married, she transferred to Cornell, and we settled into a more normal married life in Ithaca, New York.

After Hedy graduated and I finished my dissertation, we moved to Baltimore, where I had taken the job at Goucher instead of accepting one at Dartmouth. It had been a difficult decision. Some of my friends thought that I, a part-time professional skier who had always hoped to find a position at a place like Dartmouth or Middlebury or the University of Colorado, was crazy. Looking back, I think it was the first time I really understood Frost's "Stopping by Woods on a Snowy Evening." In addition to being a skiing enthusiast (nay, fanatic), I was already deeply involved in the growing civil rights movement, and my duty won out over my desire. I opted to go to the troubled city of Baltimore, then undergoing painful upheaval over the issue of desegregation, instead of to Hanover, New Hampshire.

At Goucher, as part of a three-person department of economics, sociology, and anthropology, I taught both sociology and anthropology and did "applied research" on race relations at the Council of Social Agencies. Hedy, who had majored in American Studies and also obtained teaching certification at Cornell, taught, too, first in the public system, then in a small preschool she organized. It was the beginning of our teaching careers, hers much more catholic than mine. By the time she stopped teaching full time, she had taught at every level, from that preschool in Baltimore to high school and college—at Smith, Hampshire, the University of Massachusetts at Amherst, and Wesleyan University, located seventy-five miles away from our home in Northhampton.

The years at Wesleyan were, for both of us, a period of adjustment. Hedy was there for nine years, directing graduate and undergraduate programs in education. Her responsibilities meant that she had to be on campus five days a week and, because she often taught at night, she usually stayed in Middletown from Monday to Friday. And she was expected to be there for much of the summer, as well. Over those years we both learned something of what it was to be apart for long stretches. It was more difficult for me to adjust to than it was for Hedy. For her it was a liberating experience, which was fair enough, as, for years, I had been the one who went off on my own to moonlight in many colleges and universities, to lecture, and to conduct research while she stayed at home in Northampton.

We both learned to live with the weekdays-apart/weekends-together schedule. Hardest of all were the early summer months, especially after we built our dream house on Lieutenant Island. I would go out there alone to write while she continued to run her program.

A few weeks ago we were driving to that home in Wellfleet on Cape Cod. We started to talk about our first trips to the Cape.

I had been there many years before, visiting one of my closest friends in my freshman year at Syracuse, Warren Witherstein, a native of Provincetown. It was in the late summer of 1951. It was a fabulous trip: we visited funky bars and great restaurants, rode up and down the beach in a souped-up dune buggy, and sailed a friend's sloop way out in the bay. I fell in love with the Cape and decided then and there that I would be back the next year.

I didn't go back for more than fifteen. I couldn't bring myself to do it. The fond memories could not erase the thoughts of Warren's premature death.

A restless soul, he dropped out of college in the middle of our sophomore year. It was the time of the Korean War. Warren was trained as a navy pilot, taught to fly his fighter plane from the decks of carriers. One day he didn't make it back. "Lost at sea," the navy reported. His mother wrote to tell me the news. I still have her letter.

My eventual return to the Cape began rather serendipitously in the faculty club at Smith in 1969.

I was having lunch with Smith's chaplain, Richard Unsworth. He was asking me what Hedy and I were going to be doing that summer. From previous conversations he knew that, after selling our camp, I had taught at the University of Colorado the year before and had thought of returning to the Rockies.

"How about Cape Cod?" he asked me.

"Why Cape Cod?"

He explained that he was looking for someone to rent his house in Eastham because he had just agreed to go to Africa for a major portion of the summer.

I asked him to tell me about his place and the area. He began to paint an intriguing picture of a cottage within the newly established National Seashore. It was situated on the edge of the Nauset Marsh, "across which," Dick told me, "you can see the great beach and the little shack Henry Beston described in the classic book *The Outermost House*."

That night I talked it over with Hedy and the kids, and we decided it might be fun to try a very different kind of vacation. I called Dick the next day to tell him of our decision. We asked for two weeks.

The Unsworths invited us over for a drink to seal the deal. During the evening, Joy Unsworth said that she knew we were going to love it, but we should understand that this was going to be an expensive commitment we were undertaking.

I blanched and blurted out, "But Dick said it would only be a hundred dollars a week!"

"Oh," she said, "I don't mean the cost of the rental. I mean when you try to buy a home."

I remember laughing and saying, "No chance of that. We're mountain people."

After two weeks in Eastham, we extended our visit another week in order to look for property! A year later we bought a tiny house, actually an architect's studio, in South Wellfleet. A perfect rectangle, it was appropriately called "Shoebox." We have been on the Cape every summer since then, the past decade living in the new house we built on a knoll on an island not far from the Shoebox.

The new house also has a name. We laugh about how we chose it.

We never could have built the place without some modest successes with my books, especially several textbooks I had written and anthologies I had edited in the 1970s and 1980s. So, in a mock tribute to those with the perspicacity to publish my work, I had proposed that we call the knoll "McGraw Hill," the house "Random House," and the main room "Prentice Hall." Hedy thought naming the property, the house, and a room for my publishers was pretty funny but more than a bit crass. In the end we decided on a good, old Dutch name, Nooitgedagt. Hedy translates it as "Never thought," but I prefer a much more American variation: "Who'd a thunk it!"

Had my mother known any Dutch, she might have said

"Nooitgedagt!" when, more than sixty years ago, I caught my first big fish. I can see it as if it happened yesterday.

We were visiting family friends, the Holsteins, at a rented house on Fourth Lake in the Adirondacks. That night there was to be a fish fry, the fish to be caught by "Uncle Phil."

Philip Jr., my best friend, and I begged to be allowed to go fishing with his father. "Uncle Phil" was a big sportsman. He told us we were too small to go out in the boat and couldn't possibly handle the equipment—casting rods, automatic reels, gaffs, etc. He said that when we were older he would take us.

Dejected, we watched Uncle Phil gather up his gear, get into the sleek Cris-Craft driven by a local fishing guide, and take off from the dock.

My mother, sensing our disappointment, said that we would go fishing anyway. She jerry-rigged two poles and lines and put on hooks and sinkers she found in the boathouse. We went back on the lawn and turned over a few rocks, and found some big, fat worms. Then, like Tom Sawyer and Huck Finn, we took off our socks and shoes, rolled up our pants, shouldered our poles and went back to the dock and dropped in our lines.

Two minutes later I got a solid hit. I was startled. I must have sensed that the fish was huge, for I was almost pulled into the lake. Knowing nothing about what I was supposed to do, I wrestled with it as it flailed around. I was worried it would get off the hook. In desperation, I yanked back, and out of the water popped a huge bass. I backed up and, inelegantly, pulled it up on the dock. Somehow I got the hook out and put it in a burlap bag.

Calming down, I continued fishing, but my beginner's luck had run out. Still, it turned out that I was much more successful than Uncle Phil, who came in an hour later, empty-handed.

At dinner, while all the adults had to eat store-bought fish, Philip and I tucked into my three-pound smallmouth. We offered to share a bit with his dad. He smiled wanly and said, "No thanks."

I should note that Philip and his younger brother, Jonathan—cofounders of the very innocent Robin Club I described in the first story in this book—were members of my only juvenile gang. Indeed, the three of us once took air rifles down the streets of their very upper-class neighborhood and popped out eleven streetlights in a row.

We were about to do more when, turning the corner to continue our mayhem, we found ourselves face to face with a very big policeman. How he found out we didn't know, but there he was, waiting for us next to his prowl car. We were caught. Red-handed. Our weapons in our hands.

The huge sergeant glared at us, took the BB guns away, and put us in the car. We sat in the back seat and hung our heads. We were scared stiff.

Instead of hauling us to the station house downtown, the officer drove us to the Holsteins' house, three blocks away. The boys' parents were away, and mine were at their place, house-sitting and taking care of them and of me, the only child of a man who, it happened, was at the time the head of the state's Crime Prevention Bureau!

My father was shocked when the big cop told him what we had been up to.

He thanked the officer for bringing us home and, the minute the policeman left, read us the riot act. I have never seen my father so angry. Yet, years later I realized how really lucky we were.

The revelation came when I was studying in the Maxwell School of Citizenship at Syracuse. I learned that Nate Goldman, a favorite professor, had written his doctoral dissertation on "Differential Selection of Juveniles for Court Appearance." The dull-sounding title said it all. Had we been three poor kids living in the inner city and done the same deed, perhaps even a less serious one—like shooting out just a few lights—we would have been taken in, booked, arraigned, and perhaps convicted of a minor crime, thereby establishing a record and a reputation.

Nate Goldman's first big research project, conducted in the late 1940s, had taken him to inner-city neighborhoods. My own, conducted in the late 1950s as part of my own doctoral project, involved going to tiny hamlets to study isolated minorities in general and small-town Jews in particular. A combined exercise in observing and interviewing "isolated minorities," it began with the necessity to devise a number of research techniques, modifications of what I had been taught in my first year of grad school at Cornell.

Given the fact that there was no such thing as a roster of small-town Jews, I concocted a scheme I called "snowballing" to find them. To get as accurate a picture as possible, I needed to talk to as many people as I could. I contacted all those I knew who fit my criteria (by identifying themselves as Jews and living in villages of fewer than ten thousand residents in rural New York, Vermont, and northern Pennsylvania counties) and asked them to give me additional names. Within a month I had quintupled the Jewish part of my "database." Pretty soon I found the same names and addresses being cited. I was sure I was exhausting the universe of small-town Jews. I stopped seeking names and prepared to go into the field to meet forty individuals chosen at random from those in my pool.

I called those I wanted to visit and made appointments. Primarily interested in talking to the heads of household (a euphemism, in those pre-consciousness-raised days, for "the *men* in charge"), I tried to see them either early in the morning or early in the afternoon at their places of business or offices (I had learned that most were either dealers of some sort or doctors). I then went back to one of my dreary motel rooms to write up my notes, stopping for lunch and dinner at the local greasy-spoon restaurant. After but a week or two of this schedule, I changed my tactics. I decided I would interview only late in the afternoon.

The interviews went amazingly well, and, almost inevitably, our conversations extended well beyond the promised hour.

One day I was talking to a store owner—I'll call him "Abe Cohen." We were in an office piled with boxes, ledgers, and family photos. The room was over a veritable emporium of soft goods and hardware in the middle of the main street of the village. From his chaotic perch, the proprietor was filling me with graphic images of how he had come to the village thirty years before with two trunks filled with ready-to-wear dresses in the back of old Ford truck; how he rented a small store and put up his first sign and waited for customers, who were quite wary of this stranger; how he eventually found acceptance; how the little shop turned into a miniversion of the sort of department store familiar to city folks; how . . . We were interrupted by the ringing of the phone. Mr. Cohen answered it.

"My wife," Mr. Cohen mouthed, pointing to the mouthpiece.

"Yes, it's that fellow from Cornell."

Pause.

"I don't know, we're still talking."

Pause.

"I'll ask him." Mr. Cohen turned to me, "My wife wonders if you'd care to join us for dinner. We could continue our conversation—and you can meet the family."

I objected (but not too strongly). "Oh, but on such short notice. No, I couldn't to that."

Ten minutes later I was following Mr. Cohen home. There I learned that, in this case, moving the meetings to late in the day had led to two interviews: one informal, the second more so. At the Cohen's dinner table I heard from his wife and two children contradictions about reactions to the presence of Jews in the small towns. I also learned the real meaning of the famous sociological concept "latent function." The ploy served me well. From the Abe Cohen household in West Podunk to Irving Zelinsky's abode in East Nothing, I would manage to realize the goal of every ethnographer: almost going native (in this instance partaking of the cuisine of those who claim they have the best of both worlds). Typical menus: borscht and brook trout; *kreplach*, *knadle*, and fried chicken; local spuds with brisket. (And, I should note, whatever I ate in those homes was considerably better than the cheap diner food that had marked the beginning of the project—and the table conversations prove invaluable to my research.)

I tell Hedy and a dinner guest who grew up in one of "my" towns about how often I have thought of that first research project. The guest asks me if I can remember how I came to focus on the study of small-town Jews and their neighbors?

As I think about it, I hear voices, see faces.

"Hey, Rosie," says one of my classmates at Chateaugay High School. (We are at the baseball diamond early in the season.) "Let's see your good *Jewish* arm."

"Is it true you don't celebrate Christmas?" asks another.

"Hi, David," says the immigration officer as I drive my father's Pontiac station wagon back into the States from Canada. "How're things at the store?"

I look at him rather puzzled. He blushes and waves me through.

The border is four miles from Chateaugay, and the officer lives in town. It is a small place where, presumably, everybody knows everybody. He, however, seems to have difficulty telling the Jews apart. Both of them! Unlike me, David, the only other Jewish teenager in town, is tall and blond—and he drives a Buick. His parents own the only dry-goods store in town. Mine are social workers.

Aside from moves back and forth from central New York to the North Country, where I first learned about the concept on which I would write a master's thesis, "the exemption mechanism" (otherwise known as the "some-of-my-best-friends are . . ." syndrome), and later a doctoral dissertation called "Strangers in Their Midst," and occasional family trips, I didn't travel much when I was a child. And Hedy's only big adventures—aside from coming to America—were tours to Chicago and Buffalo with her high-school chorus and a trip to Wyoming for a national Girl Scout encampment.

Our kids grew up in a different world. They were faculty brats, living with anxious words like "tenure" and happy ones like "sabbatical." They traveled the globe with us, living in England and Japan and Australia and visiting many other countries in Europe and Asia. Both are well educated, with advanced degrees. But neither is an academic, nor wants to be one. Perhaps they had enough of it in a home where both parents were college teachers.

Thinking about all this reminded me of a very special trip we took in September of 1978.

We loaded a borrowed station wagon with what seemed like

all of Lies's earthly possessions—clothes, posters, books, plants, stereo, etc.—and took her to Oberlin, Ohio, where she was to start her first year of college. We spent part of the day unloading the wagon and helping her get her room in order. Late in the day it was time to go. We looked at her rather wistfully, told her to enjoy herself, to take advantage of all the school has to offer, and to feel free to call us at any time. She waved and we left.

A little more than a decade later, it was Lies's turn to take *me* to college. I was to spend two years visiting at Harvard. Because of Hedy's teaching schedule, she had to stay in Middletown. I would be alone, and so I opted to live in a tutor's suite in Lowell House. I was a bit apprehensive about this new venture and worried about how I would fit in.

Lies said she would help me get settled. I filled the back of my station wagon with some of my most important possessions—clothes, books, posters, plants, stereo, etc.—and we headed for Cambridge. Lies and I unloaded the wagon and brought the stuff into my rooms. She helped me unpack some of it, then, seeing the time, said she had to get back. I handed her the keys and walked out with her. She started to step into the car, then hesitated. She got out, hugged me again, and told me to enjoy myself, to take advantage of everything the place has to offer, and to feel free to call her any time. She drove off, and I stood in the entrance waving to her.

Lies never sought to become a professor, but she did become an almost perpetual student—studying various times at Cornell, Oberlin, Smith, Harvard, Visual Arts, the New School, and NYU—and eventually a teacher. Art and art history. Her passion for both and her language ability (mainly in Italian and French) led her to travel widely herself. Between college and graduate school and before settling down to teach, she spent three years in Rome, perfecting her Italian and living like some of the Romans—the poorer ones! For more than half the time there she lived in a working-class neighborhood, immersing herself in the culture and accumulating art and artifacts and other stuff along the way. She left for Italy with one big suitcase; she came home with nine. Her penchants for going places and for collecting have never left her.

Dan is very different. Unlike his sister—and his father—he is not a collector; nor is he a person chronically ill with travel sickness like the two of us. He may have had touches of the disease when younger, but I'm convinced he was cured by a "San Diego or Bust" trip from Cambridge, Massachusetts, to La Jolla, California, back in the late summer of 1984. He was heading for graduate school and a new life in the Far West. It is a miracle that he got there driving an old Volvo wagon that was so underpowered that I think roller skaters could have passed him going over the Continental Divide. Repeated breakdowns thwarted his journey, rising costs of repairs thinned his billfold, and uncertainties about his decision to go West to graduate school gnawed at his heartstrings. Still, he made it.

Over the next eight years he completed a doctorate in cognitive and computer science at UCSD and met and married Susan Gruber, one of the graduate students he taught while working as an instructor in the computer science department at the university. With their first child, Jordy, they later moved to Silicon Valley where, for a number of years, he worked for Apple Computers.

Robert, Dan and Susan's second son, was born in Cupertino in 1992.

A few years ago while we were visiting them in California, I was walking with Jordy and Rob and asked each what he liked to do best. Jordy said, "Reading and computers and biking and computers and swimming and computers." Robert talked about dinosaurs and fish and drawing—and about drawing dinosaurs and fish. I started laughing to myself, reminded of that old joke in which an elderly Jewish lady is walking with her grandchildren and meets a friend.

"Your grandchildren?" he asks.

"Of course."

"How old are they?"

"Well, the doctor is four and the lawyer is six."

Had he asked me, at the time I would have said, "The paleontologist is four, and the computer scientist is seven."

Just the other day, Hedy and I resumed recollecting. This time the talk turned to how truly fortunate I have been to have been able to see so much of the world, to have taught in so many interesting places, to have had not one but three Fulbright grants, along with various fellowships, that have allowed me to spend time in Bellagio and Bogliasco in Italy, at Oxford in England, and at the Hoover Institution at Stanford (where, like the refugees I study, I, an old-fashioned liberal, sometimes felt like someone washed up on a foreign shore). At some point in the conversation, Hedy asked what, to me, was the best time of all. A tough question. I said, "Let me think about it."

All the next week I played back the tapes of memory. Each "clip" suggested another era, incident, or place. A number of things came into my head. Hiking with my father. The crazy bar mitzvah when I got the horse. The night Hedy and I met. My first book contract. The ordeal of writing the book. Its publication. Waiting for the first reviews. Getting tenure. Going abroad for the first time. Seeing the cellar in Amsterdam where Hedy and Betsy were hidden. Seeing the Jungfrau, the Temple of the Golden Pavilion, the Klongs of Bangkok, Ephesus, Jerusalem, Table Mountain at Capetown, and the Grand Canyon—from the bottom up. Being a participant in both of our kids' college graduations. Getting lost in the Pentagon. Getting ousted from a pub for demonstrating against racial discrimination in Leicester. Watching Hedy get hooded when she got her doctorate. Speaking at the first commencement of University College Utrecht in the Netherlands, a new institution I helped to establish in a venerable old university. Writing my fiftieth review for the *Christian Science Monitor*. Being asked to become the first senior fellow at Smith's remarkable Kahn Liberal Arts Institute. Staying in touch with so many people I had taught in Sociology 213—known to generations as "Peterrosesminorities"—and in other courses on race, immigration, refugee policy, and the broader study of American society and culture who claimed that I had had an impact on their lives. Welcoming back scores of members of Smith's unique "Foreign Legion" to a very special reunion celebrating the fortieth year of the American Studies Diploma Program for foreign graduate students and my thirtieth as its director. It was hard to decide which was best. And so I kept musing. Then, suddenly, in my mind's eye I saw the decorations in a place called the Gamut on the Smith College campus. In my head I could hear live jazz.

It was a very special evening, a party Hedy arranged for a watershed birthday. (The invitation, which I didn't see until that evening, had a picture of a little boy, me, dressed exactly as I am today —in tee shirt, shorts, and Bass moccasins, and a caption saying "NOW WE ARE SIX . . . TY FIVE.") Many of those who matter most to me were there: Lies and Dan and Susan and the boys; scores of colleagues and former students; Dick and Joy Unsworth; Helen Chinoy; Charles Lieber, my first editor; and other special friends. There were speeches and toasts and a special poem by Ron Perera, the composer mentioned in the beginning of my essay on John Updike; there was a short but ever so sweet "Happy Birthday, Grandpa" from each of my grandsons. Hedy spoke, as did Dan and Lies. It was almost too much.

The last speaker was our daughter-in-law, Susan. She took the mike, paused, looked at me, and said, "One usually has a good deal to say in the choice of a husband, but not in the selection of a father-in-law, but I lucked out." Now that was high praise indeed.

It was a night to remember.

The next day I went to a local shop called Peaceworks and picked out a delicately fashioned silver Hopi pin for Hedy. It was a stylized bear.

I gave it to her that night. Enclosed in the box with the pin was a simple poem I had written. It was a thank-you for so many years of for*bear*ance, and for a fabulous party.

As Hedy unwrapped the package, I thought to myself: "We have many more miles to go, but for me it's already been quite a trip, an incredible journey traveling through time and space, around the world with a great partner and very few reservations."